"Harvey Diamond gives every woman a powerful tool for the restoration of her physical health. He speaks from a point of view so many of us now want: with an awareness of nature, consciousness and their role in healing. I deeply welcome this book into my own life."

Marianne Williamson,
Author, *A Return to Love,*
A Woman's Worth, Illuminata

"In my practice specializing in women's health, I have often wished for a book that would dispel the current hysteria and melodrama around cancer. A book that would clearly and succinctly describe the changes necessary to prevent heart disease and cancer. A book that was engaging and easy to understand. A book that was free of preaching and dogmatic statements. A book that proposed simple changes that anyone could make no matter what the size of their pocket book, or how difficult their circumstance.

"Harvey Diamond's book will inspire and support women to change their health and the health of their loved ones. It is a book that will support the highest vision of women's health."

Carolyn DeMarco, M.D.,
Author, *Take Charge of Your Body*

"This is the breast cancer book we've been looking for. Harvey de-mystifies modern medicine's incurable disease, and puts you in charge."

Dr. Marcus Laux, N.D.,
Editor, *Naturally Well*

This extremely well-researched book sends a welcome message of hope to millions of potential victims."

Edward A. Taub, M.D.,
Author, *The Wellness R$_x$*

You
CAN
Prevent
Breast Cancer

BY:

Harvey Diamond
Author, FIT FOR LIFE

You CAN Prevent Breast Cancer

1/97

© *Harvey Diamond*

Published by:
ProMotion Publishing
3368 F Governor Drive
Suite 144
San Diego, CA 92122

1(800) 231-1776

ISBN 0-9636328-1-7

Printed in the United States of America

**THIS BOOK IS WRITTEN IN PRAISE
OF OUR GLORIOUS
AND LOVING GOD**

TABLE OF CONTENTS

PART TWO
THE CARE PROGRAM

Foreword

When I first saw the manuscript for *You CAN Prevent Breast Cancer*, an initial reaction was "How in Heaven's name can a diet guru like Harvey Diamond write a serious book about breast cancer?" After all, here's a subject that has occupied some of medicine's finest minds and researchers for a century.

But this book represents something far more important than just a review of breast cancer and its management. Harvey Diamond here made the important transition from treatment to *prevention*. He has been a vanguard for the real revolution in medicine that is slowly, painfully, and inexorably taking place. To those with open minds and the vision to see some of the future in an age of accelerating knowledge and rapid communication of knowledge the great movement to people taking increasing responsibility for their own health was inevitable. In *FIT FOR LIFE* and now in *You CAN Prevent Breast Cancer*, Harvey Diamond moves from past to future. Away from the all-knowing physician to the new age of health care based on personal knowledge that keeps up with new research. For a lay person to write a definitive book on breast cancer wouldn't have happened just a few years ago. But this is no ordinary book, nor is Harvey Diamond just another health enthusiast. He has here amassed a phenomenal array of information, documentation and help for all women who don't want to be haunted with their worst fear—that of disfiguring and potentially fatal breast cancer.

So what do we as physicians know about the cause of breast cancer? Precious little. No one knows for sure what causes breast cancer. And while lung cancer and heart disease each cause more fatalities in women than does breast cancer, the incidence of breast cancer has been on the rise for decades. And again, we don't know why.

A few "risk factors" have been identified. The most significant ones are:

(1)   being over age 50. You will be much more likely to get breast cancer as you get older.
(2)   being born in North America or Northern Europe.
(3)   having a mother and sister with a history of breast cancer.
(4)   if you are over age 30 with your first pregnancy.
(5)   having benign fibroadenomas of the breasts.

These "risk factors" mean merely that these women should do periodic self-examination, and have a mammogram every one or two years. Yet the American Cancer Society states that 75% of breast cancer cases occur in women with no known high-risk factors, and only 5% of breast cancer cases are in the hereditary category. Regular use of alcohol can increase the risk of breast cancer, as can excess use of diagnostic X-rays. 80% of "suspicious lesions" found on mammography are benign, and 5-10% of cancers are missed by mammography. What this all says is that we don't know where most breast cancer comes from and that mammography is not the perfect diagnostic tool though it's the best we have at present. And because mammography is so inexact, numerous unnecessary breast biopsies are done. It's a pretty imperfect system, but still our only means for early detection of breast cancer.

But back to Harvey Diamond and this book. After reading his manuscript carefully, it became obvious that this was not meant to be a medical textbook on breast cancer. Medical texts deal exclusively with diagnosis and current treatment, while Harvey covers a much broader landscape. He alludes to diagnosis and current forms of treatment, but his real message is how to *prevent* breast cancer.

My surgical textbooks are objective, analytical, filled with studies, charts and graphs and are completely unexciting to read. This book is alive with people, with ideas and with common sense. It springs to life and beats with a heart of its own. Harvey talks about personal friends, patients, inspiring cancer recoveries, mammography, mastectomy, radical surgery, heredity, nutrition, attitude, vegetarianism, laughter, chemotherapy, radiation therapy, atherosclerosis, the lymphatic system's important role, walking, rebound exercise and much more.

But don't get the impression it's a helter-skelter, hodgepodge of disconnected information. It's not! Rather it's an exciting tour through a complex subject—one where Harvey Diamond has penetrated much of the mystery with his Natural Hygiene understanding and a prevention program that I believe puts together the best information available anywhere.

Harvey Diamond first takes us doctors to task for the approaches of the past (and often still present) for diagnosing and managing breast cancer. He then correctly points out that researchers today do not know what causes breast cancer, that there is a worrisome increase in frequency of breast cancer, and that breast cancer remains the greatest fear that besets women during their lifetime.

Then he presents his view of what does cause cancer and builds, finally, a simple, effective program to address these causes. But this isn't just anybody's theory or a guess. His program to keep your health, and your breasts, is based on a growing body of sound scientific evidence starting to pour from the world's best research laboratories. Harvey presents all this with a common sense that only the author of the largest selling diet-health book of all time (*FIT FOR LIFE*— around ten million copies in twenty-nine languages) could do. This book is fun reading, inspiring and will change how you live, eat, play and think about cancer. And I know of no popular or medical scientific text on breast cancer that brings together the wealth of wisdom you will find on these pages. Every women in this world should read it—and reread it. My bet is it will be cherished by all who do. It is a book of a tragic and terrible disease and about tears for those who have suffered with it. But above all it is a book with answers, a book therefore of real hope. It will help end your fears about cancer of the breast.

Hope here springs first from Harvey's genuine concern for women and the plight they face with breast cancer. He addresses this subject with passion and with an abundance of carefully put together facts and studies gleaned from television specials, magazines, newspapers, medical journals and books. He has also drawn from twenty-five years of his own study of diet and health, of disease prevention, of Yoga and Eastern medicine—all subjects about which he is knowledgeable. His book is a treasure trove of exciting health information, a program to promote and restore robust health, to really prevent breast cancer (and most other cancers as well)! Harvey's program allows readers that all-important sense of personal security felt when they take back responsibility for their own health. Once again every woman can feel a new joy and hope knowing that good health, free of breast cancer, is an attainable, achievable goal. This is a book to read, savor and reread.

During my years of surgical practice, I've cared for thousands of people with cancer. During my general surgery training, I participated in many radical mastectomies for breast cancer, fortunately an operation no longer recommended. I saw the disfigurement, the swelling and weakness of the arm, the difficult surgical task of recreating a substitute breast or what most women did, simply wear a bra padded to replace the missing breast. These experiences were unpleasant and the operated women I knew had lost more than a breast. And all too often the cancer would recur and the hopelessness of a broken spirit would be added to their disfigured body. As they wasted away with each clinic visit it was emotionally painful to share in each woman's despair.

I knew I had nothing more to offer medically, except morphine-type drugs when the pain became too much. I would occasionally visit these patients in their homes to show that I cared, but the sense of helplessness was depressing to me. The fortunate ones had loving families and supportive religious beliefs that saw them through. In my zeal, I remember the strong feelings that somehow, someway, we in medicine had to find a way to stop this awful disease that destroyed the lives of so many women— many still young with children to care for. It was heart-breaking to feel the pain and to know there was nothing I or medical science could do. Occasionally, a desperate patient would turn to some quack remedy or illegal foreign clinic, but I have never seen a cure from such approaches. What makes me excited about Harvey Diamond's program is that I genuinely believe that it will work and that *prevention* is where the real hope is in the struggle against breast cancer.

My physician colleagues may not agree with every idea in this book. But the extensive bibliography of recent anticancer research presented in this book is eloquent testimony to a new hope for cancer prevention never before known. Harvey Diamond has done a service to patients as well as physicians by moving us to the most promising hope of our times that cancer really can be prevented.

It still makes sense to diagnose breast cancer as early as possible and this has given impetus to annual mammography. But studies suggest we may be overusing this X-ray procedure. It now appears that women under age fifty unless they are at high risk (e.g. strong family history of breast cancer) should probably not have mammography. And even in the age fifty to seventy-five group some European centers are now recommending a mammography only every two or three years.

But discussion of early detection really misses the point of Harvey Diamond's excellent book. The American Cancer Society predicts that 182,000 new cases of breast cancer occur each year in the U.S. and that 46,000 women die from it each year. Harvey Diamond's strong appeal is for all women to make a major shift in focus from "waiting to see if I get breast cancer," to simply *preventing* it in the first place.

The real question is whether there is any way to really prevent breast cancer. Harvey responds with a resounding, yes! He then brings impressive evidence to support such a claim and outlines a common sense program based on the latest anticancer research.

So, is there absolute scientific proof that the program in this book will positively prevent breast cancer? No, of course not. Life is seldom that simple. My guess is it would take five million dollars and watching twenty thousand women over twenty years to "prove" such a thing. I recall the controversy for forty years on whether cigarette smoking produced lung cancer! And even today the struggle continues to try and get cigarette smoke out of public gathering places! Fourteen million Americans died from diseases of cigarette smoking in those forty years. Harvey Diamond's plea is that we not wait for the estimated 3.6 million new cases of breast cancer to occur in the next twenty years, but to do something now. Plus, when scientific evidence and epidemiological studies start to point strongly to major life-style changes that do prevent cancer— items that Harvey fully outlines in this book—one must conclude that the odds are high that this program will work. At the very least, women who follow Harvey's program will have more energy, stay slimmer and feel better. After examining this book and its bibliography, my experience with human disease tells me Harvey is right on course and that this program will prevent not only breast cancer, but a wide variety of other cancers and degenerative diseases.

While physicians are still focused on treating breast cancer already present, Harvey Diamond moves the discussion to taking charge of your own life so you can prevent breast cancer. By the second time I had read the manuscript for this book, I was even more convinced that this book, like *FIT FOR LIFE* before it, will become a modern health classic.

Yes, it should be read by every woman in America. In an age where there are too many books out there on any subject, this one is in a class by itself. Harvey Diamond, and his years of preparing it, make the difference. It is a treasure-house of great health ideas that will turn cancer worry and fear into real hope for the millions who will read it. My wife loves this book. So will you.

Kenneth M. Kroll, M.D., Fellow,
International College of Surgeons

Kenneth M. Kroll received his Bachelor of Science degree from Rutgers University, his medical degree from Harvard and finished surgical specialty training at Stanford Medical Center. He is a board-certified surgeon and a Fellow of the International College of Surgeons. He is a member of the AMA, the AUA and the American Academy of Anti-Aging Medicine. Dr. Kroll is Vice-President of Science and Chief Medical Officer for a California-based company and resides with his wife, Diane, in Carmel, CA.

PART ONE

HEALTH IS YOUR BIRTHRIGHT

Chapter One

WHAT'S GOING ON?

In the midst of a conversation with a casual acquaintance, the woman with whom I was talking asked me if I was working on another book. Since I was knee-deep in my research of this book at the time, I said, "You bet," and proceeded to give her an enthusiastic overview, starting with the name of the book which seemed to capture every woman's attention. At that time, whenever I had occasion to describe the nature of the book to a woman, I jumped at the opportunity to do so. After all, I'm a man writing a book about breast cancer, a subject of tremendous concern to women. Any and every woman's feedback on the goal I wished to achieve in its writing was openly welcomed and greatly appreciated.

I told her this would be like no other book on the subject of breast cancer. It wasn't going to be one more recap of a bad situation getting progressively worse that posed lots of questions and no answers, one more treatise that left women feeling like helpless victims waiting for the axe to fall with no hope beyond that of "early detection." I told her I was convinced that women were being made to unnecessarily worry, anguish, live in fear and suffer immeasurable pain. It simply did not have to be the case. The only reason it was, was because the true nature of lumps in the breast was not understood. The measures women could take to prevent them, or quickly remove them if they developed were virtually unknown to them. Women had been whipped into such a frenzy of fear that the mere mention of the term "breast cancer" filled them

1

with horror and dread, and invariably resulted in them prematurely and unnecessarily "going under the knife." This fear was so intense that women were increasingly having both of their breasts removed **before** any sign whatsoever of cancer or even a lump![1-5]

I told her that this book would liberate all women from this cycle of fear and pain and put them in complete control of their bodies and their lives so that they could live without worry and with the confidence that they would not become one of the ever-growing statistics. I wanted her to know that women had a choice in the matter, that they were not hapless victims with no influence over whether they developed breast cancer or not.

On the contrary, there were absolute, concrete actions they could take to **dramatically** reduce their chances of ever developing breast cancer and, equally important, steps they could take to remove lumps from the breast without ever undergoing any surgery whatsoever. Steps that prove themselves relatively quickly, so that any and all other forms of treatment would still be available to them if need be. But they should know that their first line of defense could eliminate the problem before it became a problem, with no surgery, radiation or drug therapy.

Whenever I would give this quick description of the book to a woman, I always looked forward to their initial reaction and feedback so as to confirm to myself the level of interest women had on this subject. Invariably, I would hear comments like, "Wow! Tell me more!" or "What a timely subject," or "Hurry up and write it, I can't wait to read it." Comments from those who had already had some experience with breast cancer were different: "Too bad you didn't write it three years ago," or "I wish I could have heard that I had choices before my surgery, I thought it was a mastectomy or death."

But when I looked at this woman, I realized I was to get no such comment. In fact, as I spoke, her face became

2

flushed and her eyes filled with tears. It didn't take a psychic to see that either someone very close to her or she, herself, had been to the mat with breast cancer.

I have wanted to write this book for over fifteen years. It's been bubbling and churning inside of me screaming to come out. In all of that time, as I gathered information and experience on the subject, I knew deep in my heart of hearts I could never rest or ever feel fulfilled until I wrote it. If there was ever even the slightest, most infinitesimal doubt in my mind that I should write it, for whatever the reason may be, those doubts were forever obliterated as I listened to the story this woman told me about her personal experience with breast cancer.

There are not words in the English language I could use to describe the horror and the hell this person had lived through for six years and was still dealing with. I have seen plenty and I have heard plenty but sitting and looking into her face as I listened to her describe her ordeal was almost more than I could handle. Here was a very pretty, vivacious woman in her late thirties telling me what would have sounded like science fiction to most people. By the time she was finished, I was beside myself. I felt infuriated, angry, outraged. I thought I would explode. I wanted to scream or smash something, just somehow vent the unbridled rage I felt for the injustice of what this woman had been put through.

I couldn't possibly give you the detailed, long version of her story because, number one, it would take too long, and number two, I don't want to so gross you out right here in the beginning that you put the book down. Even the short version, which I must share with you, will "strain the friendship."

Starting in 1987, she has had no less than seven surgical procedures. The first was a double mastectomy (one of which was a radical) and removal of lymph nodes from both sides including her arms. The second operation was to insert expanders under the skin of her chest to sufficiently stretch the skin so as to accommodate implants which were to be put in. Every ten days or so, for months, she would have to go in and have a saline solution injected into the expanders to keep them full, as the solution would constantly seep out of the expanders into her system. Operation number three was to have silicone implants put in. Operation number four was to replace one of the implants because it punctured. Operation number five was to replace the other implant because it, too, punctured. Operation number six was to replace both silicone implants with saline implants because the first one that was replaced, punctured again! Operation number seven was to make and attach nipples to her chest out of flesh from her buttocks.

She insisted on having numerous photos taken of her body at every stage of her treatment, from the very beginning when she had her breasts intact, to the end when she had nothing but scars and implants. As I looked at these photos and the large, brutal scars that are a permanent part of her body, I became physically ill. If you could see these pictures you would think this woman a saint that she can still smile so readily.

Although she was heavily pressured to submit to chemotherapy and radiation she refused because she was already in so much pain that she couldn't imagine surviving any more. Especially the degree and intensity of pain that accompanies chemotherapy. For years she had so many shots in her thighs for pain that both legs were constantly black and blue and ached all the time.

She had no health insurance and had to pay for everything herself. She owned her own business which she lost, along with her house and her car. She could not get credit and for seven years, through all the pain and operations, she still had to work in order to pay for everything. For seven years all money she earned went toward paying for her next operation. By merely reading the words on these pages you could never fully grasp the unrelenting physical and emotional pain and suffering this woman has had to somehow endure.

Not only has her body been ripped apart and torn away, but also everything she had worked so hard for and built up for herself has also been destroyed. And **she** had to pay for the entire ordeal out of her own pocket. It was more money than she had and she is still paying, still in pain and working on herself every day to move beyond the anger, put the entire ordeal behind her and move on.

The reason her story so infuriated **me** and is the basis for the introduction of this book is because all of the torment that she went through all happened because of one tiny lump in one breast that was no larger than the size of a single pea!

Now, right now, you may be thinking something along the line of, "Hey, cancer is cancer, no matter what size it was it had to be dealt with." Dealt with, yes. But in a far more sane and sensible way. Not the go-for-broke, all out assault that is overkill in the extreme and which, unfortunately, has become standard medical treatment.

By the end of this book you will see that the appearance of a lump in your breast, whether the size of a **pea** or a **walnut**, is no reason to run out like a scalded cat to have your body mutilated and disfigured and then bombarded with the most deadly and harmful substances known: radiation and chemotherapy. Especially in light of the fact that members of the medical profession, the experts in the field, openly admit that they don't even know what breast cancer is. They don't know what causes it, they don't know how to cure it and they don't know how to prevent it. So to compensate for this total lack of knowledge, the cancer is attacked with a vengeance, in the hope that an all out assault against the body will somehow exorcise the cancer without killing the patient. This overly aggressive treatment can be likened to demolishing an entire city because there is a criminal hiding in it somewhere.

This is precisely what happened to the woman whose story I have related here. After discovering the lump, which was not painful, not even tender, she had a biopsy. She was told that there were cancer cells found and that she should immediately have her breast removed and all the surrounding tissues and muscle as well. Everything, right down to the bone. "Just to be sure." That is a radical mastectomy.

She was still trying to deal with the shock of learning that she had cancer when her physician recommended that while she was having her right breast removed, she should just go ahead and have her left breast removed as well. The reasoning was that, if cancer appears in one breast, there is a certain likelihood that it **could** appear in the other one as well. "Why take a chance of going through this again? Let's just get rid of both of them in one fell swoop and then you'll never have to worry about breast cancer again. And, oh yes, while we're at it, we'll remove all your lymph nodes from your chest and both your arms as a **precautionary** measure."

She was devastated. She went from feeling fine one day, no pain, no discomfort, to finding out the next day that the whole upper part of her body was going to be torn asunder leaving her with no breasts and the prospect of considerable further surgery to reconstruct what was taken away. "Are you sure that's the best course of action?" she asked. "Can I get a second opinion?"

Three other doctors from the **same hospital** gave their concurring opinion and between the four physicians, she was, according to her, "frightened to death of what **might** happen to her and made to feel like a fool if she did not submit to the surgery." This all happened so fast, that she was hardly given time to even think it over. At this most

6

vulnerable time in her life she was being literally bullied into this course of action.

With no one to turn to, and no one to give her another point of view, she gave in and allowed this ultra-extensive, disfiguring surgery to take place. After telling her of my experiences of helping women with breast cancer and of others who successfully overcame their breast cancer without surgery, her words were, "My God, why couldn't I have known you then?" I told her that, for whatever the reasons—and we may never know what those reasons are—she had to go through this in her life. Although it may be of very little consolation to her now, I was going to see to it that millions of women have the opportunity to avoid a similar fate.

There are choices women have outside of surgery, chemotherapy and radiation and they are not even being told of them. This book is going to change all that. If a woman learns of the choices she has and still opts to go the traditional medical route, so be it. At least she had the chance to hear that there were other options open to her. But to not even be given the opportunity to **hear** of her choices while being pressured, bulldozed and terrorized into surgery as though it was the only viable course of action, is outrageous and entirely unacceptable. It would be one thing if the incidence of, and death rate from, breast cancer were steadily decreasing, but the exact opposite is true. It has been getting worse and worse for over **one hundred years!** In light of this and the fact that those in charge don't even know what causes breast cancer, let alone what to do about it, I would think another course of action, other than the one that has failed so miserably to date, would be welcomed with open arms—**and minds!**

I told you that I have wanted to write this book for over fifteen years. There are three reasons why I did not do so until now. First, I wanted to have more experience with cancer in general and breast cancer specifically. Only time could bring that—which it has. Second, I wanted to have a major success in some area of the health field that would stand as testimony of the fact that I could present a subject in such a way that it would appeal to millions of people. *FIT FOR LIFE* has succeeded in doing that. And third, I wanted to be fifty years old. Silly, perhaps, but I've always felt that by virtue of living for half a century one automatically earns the right to at least be listened to. I turned fifty in February, 1995.

In 1979 I had my first encounter with breast cancer. Because of that experience, I knew that I would someday write a book on the subject. I had been studying in the field of Natural Hygiene with great intensity for nine years and the publication of *FIT FOR LIFE* was still six years off. I was as convinced then as I am today, that anyone who understood and practiced the principles of Natural Hygiene, even moderately, could ensure for her or himself a long, disease-free existence.

In 1971 I was particularly gung-ho because I had re-captured my own health and been able to see, firsthand, hundreds of people do the same by following the simple principles of Natural Hygiene I outlined for them in one-on-one counseling sessions. At that time, I loved talking to anyone who would listen about health and my enthusi-asm for the subject definitely bordered on fanaticism. I welcomed any challenge from people to show them how they could heal even the most seemingly catastrophic prob-lems. I had seen so many examples of people overcoming serious health problems that my excitement for the sub-ject alone was all a lot of people needed to make the simple changes I suggested.

I had, and still have, the utmost confidence that be-cause the human body is self-repairing and self-healing, it can, given the right environment for healing, overcome any ailment so long as it has not gone to the point of irre-versibility due to irreparable damage.

This was precisely my frame of mind when I received a phone call that day in 1979 from a woman friend of mine whom I had spoken to on several occasions about the beautiful and remarkable healing capabilities of the human body.

I must have made an impression on her because she was calling me from the hospital where she had just been given the results of a mammography she had taken. It was obvious from her voice that she was in a highly agitated state of mind. The mammography had detected a rather large lump in her breast. Compared to the pea-sized lump that was the rationale for the carnage performed on the woman earlier described, this one was huge, being about the size of a quarter. Her voice was so shaky and she was so upset I could hardly understand her.

Part of the problem was that her physician was **there** at the phone with her literally berating her for being so foolish as to call "some nutritional friend" for advice when **he** just finished telling her that she **must** make arrangements **at that moment** for the removal of her breast or she would die!

Now, try to picture this. She goes to her doctor to find out what, if anything, was found on her mammography and he shows her a huge lump and then proceeds to scare the juices out of her by telling her that without an **immediate** mastectomy she would die. No biopsy, no tests, no anything. He doesn't even know if cancer was present or not. It was "let's cut now and talk later." He didn't say that she **may** die or that with a lump that size the chances are that there's cancer and she could die. No. He says to her, no mastectomy and you're dead!

So she tells him she knows someone who knows a lot about nutrition and she wants to call him first and he erupts at her. "How could you do something so stupid when your life is at stake? This is not time for nutrition, this is time for surgery. You had better do what I say and stop messing around." He was standing next to her at the phone

harassing her while she was trying to tell me what was going on. It was a real scene, believe me.

Finally, I said to her that if she had a lump in her breast big as she described, it had been growing for some ten to fifteen years at **least**. No matter what she decided to do, she certainly could take twenty-four to forty-eight hours to go home, reflect, talk to friends and make a rational decision without her doctor yelling in her face that either she listens to him or **dies!** I suggested that she hang up the phone, tell her doctor she will call him in the next day or two and come directly to my office so that I could tell her of an option she would never hear from her doctor.

Within an hour, we were sitting and talking. When she walked into my office she looked horrible. Her face was ashen and there was fear in her eyes that was so obvious you could have sliced it up and served it on a platter. Her voice was shaky, and as soon as she started to talk, tears and sobs poured out of her. I naturally assumed it was because she had found out she possibly had cancer, and may face surgery or chemotherapy, or both, and she was scared.

As it turns out, it wasn't so much the cancer and treatment that had her so upset. It was her fear of being cut with a knife. Now, I'm not just talking about the normal fear or apprehension one might have about being operated on. No, she had such a paralyzing fear of being cut that **anything** would be preferable to submitting to surgery.

I proceeded to tell her that Natural Hygiene, my field of study, had an entirely different way of looking at lumps in the breast than did the medical profession. I explained the lymph system to her (which is invariably involved with lumps in the breast) and told her that she could take the hygienic approach to getting rid of the lump and in four or five weeks would have absolute evidence as to whether or not she was being successful. At that time, she would definitely see whether her lump was the same size, larger or smaller. I assured her it would be smaller. Since in her mind she would literally rather do nothing than undergo surgery, she was willing to try **anything** that did not include being cut. I told her that since her situation would be an invaluable test case for me, I would tell her exactly what to do and supervise her all along the way.

The first thing I did was to fill her with positiveness about her body and its ability to heal itself. Her doctor's message that she was going to die was not exactly the best jumping off place. I explained to her that success depended upon certain dietetic maneuvering that would allow her lymph system to repair and heal itself. She promised me that she was extremely disciplined and would follow my advice to the letter without the slightest variation.

When she left my office she was smiling and filled with hope. I spoke with her practically every day and told her exactly what to do. She followed my suggestions implicitly. Within the first ten days she was certain that the lump had decreased somewhat in size and it was no longer tender to the touch. In three or four weeks her lump went from the size of a quarter to the size of a dime. In another three or four weeks, it was gone. **GONE!** She had another mammography and there was not a trace to be found.

It seems almost pointless to tell you how overjoyed this woman was. You couldn't make her stop smiling with a gun. As far as she was concerned, she had been given her life back. One of the very first things she did was to call her doctor with the good news and to get a copy of the original mammogram so I could have the two, one showing the lump, the other showing nothing.

Now, most people, including perhaps yourself, most assuredly this woman, would naturally assume that her doctor, upon learning of her nonsurgical removal of this large lump from her breast, would walk barefoot over hot coals and broken glass to find out what she did so he could share it with his other patients and with his colleagues in the medical profession. You would think he would want to trumpet the good news from the highest mountain. He would not even take a phone call from her. **He was angry at her for ignoring his advice!** His secretary told her that it would be best if she were to find another physician. And no, she could not have a copy of the original mammogram.

I lost contact with my friend and did not see her again until some seven years later when we ran into each other quite by accident. She was still smiling, and she looked great. In the two months I had worked with her, she had lost about thirty pounds and she had obviously kept it off. More importantly, no more lumps in her breasts. In terms of what my mission in life is and what goals I wish to accomplish in educating people as to how they can insure their own good health, she told me the greatest thing I could ever have hoped to hear.

She said that she no longer felt like her own body was a stranger to her or that the workings of her inner body was something that was out of her realm of understanding. She felt in charge and in control of her health. Whenever she put on weight she didn't want or started to feel unwell, she knew exactly what to do to turn it around. She thanked me profusely for what I had done for her, not realizing that what her words had done for me was equally as great.

There are literally millions of women in this country living in fear, biding their time waiting for "the axe to fall." They're afraid of their bodies, afraid that their bodies will turn against them. Afraid of cancer. Afraid to get a mammogram for fear of what it may reveal. I know women who for a week or more before they're scheduled for a mammography are nervous wrecks. By the time they have the mammography and are waiting for the results, it's everything they can do to not to keel over from fright. If it's negative, the sigh of relief is as though they have just had a death sentence commuted. But that fear sits in the back of their minds building until the next mammography or, God forbid, a lump that might appear in one of their breasts. That is no way to live. It is something that must change. It can change, and if I have anything to do with it, it **will** change.

This book has been written to empower you, to free you, to put you in charge so that you can live your life with the confidence of knowing you are not going to become a medical statistic. Worry and fear can be cast aside and become a thing of the past. And I am not telling you this just for effect or to give you false hope. **YOU CAN PREVENT BREAST CANCER!!**

I want you to be very clear on something. Just because the people you have been turning to for answers don't have any, does not mean that there are no answers or that because **they** don't have any, no one does. There **are** answers and there are plenty of women all over the world who have discovered this for themselves. It is not a closed club, you can join their ranks. The only thing preventing you from learning how to live a life free of breast cancer, or the fear of developing breast cancer, is a lack of information. My sincerest wish is for this book to change that for you.

There are basically three categories that women fall into as relates to breast cancer. The first is far and away the biggest group and they are my **primary** audience. This group is comprised of all the women who have yet to have any problem whatsoever with lumps in their breasts and they want to do whatever possible to keep it that way. You are being told from every quarter that early detection is the key factor in breast cancer. Hogwash! Prevention is the key factor in breast cancer. Early detection is defeatist and negative. Buying into the idea that early detection is the most important aspect of breast cancer is admitting and accepting that there is nothing you can do except wait until **after** you have cancer. Then your fate lies in the hope that you will require the very least amount of disfiguring surgery, and the least amount of brutalizing chemotherapy and/or radiation. Prevent the problem from occurring in the first place and there is nothing to detect. That is why this book is first and foremost a book on *prevention*.

The second group are those women who have already been through it with breast cancer, have lost one or both breasts, had lymph nodes removed, endured chemotherapy and/or radiation, gone through reconstructive surgery, and the very last thing on earth they want to find out is that it's back and they have to go through it all over again.

The third group are women who have just found a lump in their breast or have been told that a mammography has detected a mass, a tumor, a lump, something "suspicious" that has to be investigated further. Women at this point are faced with, probably, the most important decision of their lives. They must decide what course of action to take.

Most of the advice and suggestions in this book are directed toward the first two groups of women; those who have had no problem and those who have been through some form of treatment. Their goal is prevention. You who are in the third group have a more immediate need, and I will address your options later on in the book as well. My aim will be to show you how you can rid yourself of the lump in the least invasive way possible so that you can go on to utilize the information in the rest of the book and prevent the lump from ever returning.

Regardless of which of the groups described above you fall into, one thing I can absolutely assure you of is the fact that you **will** be confronted with information in this book that will challenge your present beliefs and way of thinking on the entire subject of breast cancer. Let me tell you that for there to be a significant change in the present incidence of breast cancer **and** a lessening of suffering and decline in deaths from breast cancer, a fundamental change in thinking **and actions** must occur. There is an old saying, short but right on target: "If there is no change, then there is no change."

Change is a most interesting phenomenon in life. On the one hand, we all want change. We need it, we cherish it, we demand it. Imagine a world without changes like electricity, air flight, telephones, computers, televisions, automobiles. Without regular and significant change, life would become unbearably boring. On the other hand, the new information that heralds in these changes we crave are, all too frequently, met with negativity and resistance. Nowhere is this more prevalent than in the area of the sciences.

History is rife with examples to prove this strange irony: from Galileo being vilified for pointing out that the sun, not the earth, was the center of our universe, to Dr. Ignaz Semmelweis being hounded out of his chosen profession for suggesting that doctors wash their hands before surgery.

• From a time when the medical experts of the day warning that washing the entire body more than once a week was harmful, to suggesting that patients spend time in stables where they could inhale the fumes from animal dung to help heal tuberculosis.

• From refusing water to fever patients as it would be hurtful, to suggesting that fresh air would be injurious to the bedridden.

• From the admonition to eat only well cooked food, nothing fresh, as it would be detrimental, to suggesting that bananas, being such a potent drug, should only be available by prescription.

• And the granddaddy of them all, the idea that blood should be drained from the sick to make them well. All of these "established, proven methods" were eventually thrown on the junk heap of history, but not before the new information that brought about their change was obstinately, sometimes violently, resisted.

Much of today's barbaric treatment of women who develop lumps in their breasts needs desperately to be thrown on that same junk heap. And you can be certain that there will be resistance to this change as well. But it doesn't matter, because this is a change that is inevitable. When you consider that the only change in breast cancer over the last one hundred years is that the problem has become progressively worse, this is a situation that is screaming out for change. The one and only surefire way to rescue women from what is coming to be known as "the other epidemic" is to stop focusing on early detection and treatment and start focusing on prevention.

I understand what a massive undertaking this is. It will disrupt the status quo. That is never easy. But, we simply can't sit idly by and allow this situation to continue as it has for **another** hundred years! There are too many lives at stake. It is going to call for another way of thinking about your body, how it works, what supports its health, and what undermines it. Respect and admiration for your body has to replace your fear of it. A brand new awareness of how magnificently capable your body is in insuring its own well-being is essential. A new understanding is needed of what cancer actually is and the role you can play to avoid it. All of these things are essential to become free of the fear of breast cancer and all these things will be made clear to you as you read the pages of this book.

Over the years, we have all been systematically conditioned to believe that these issues are far too complicated for us to grasp and are best left to the specialists in the field, so we have abdicated all responsibility to them. It may surprise you to learn that it is not nearly as compli-cated as you might think, and you are far more capable of understanding what breast cancer is and how to prevent it than you may realize.

Before getting on with it, there are questions that are surely to come up for many of those who are reading this that I need to address. These questions are: "With all due respect, you are not a doctor or a cancer specialist. You are the author of a successful diet book. So what qualifies you to give advice on this subject? Why should I believe what you have to say on this?"

It's quite true that *FIT FOR LIFE* focuses on weight loss, but be clear that it is not merely a book on weight loss, it is a book about health and how to achieve it. In a state of health one is not overweight, so the book describes how weight can be lost when overall health is achieved. Health is always the goal.

When I embarked on my studies a quarter of a century ago, I did not take up the study of weight loss, I took up the study of health: how to acquire it and how to maintain it. I could have studied in the field of medicine, osteopathy, homeopathy, chiropractic or any other specialty, but I chose to study in the field of Natural Hygiene because it is the one that made the most amount of sense to **me**.

Hygiene looks at the body and the pursuit of health differently than the other specialties mentioned. This is not to imply that adherence to one discipline negates the others. All have their place and are appropriate under cer-tain conditions. No one approach to health care has all the answers or is the best choice in all situations or under all circumstances. Those who would tell you differently are looking out for their own interests over yours. As it hap-pens, Hygiene is the approach that helped recapture my health while losing fifty pounds that I've managed to keep off. With such positive results in my life, I just naturally made it my field of expertise.

Compared to other branches of the health services available to Americans, Natural Hygiene is relatively unknown. But don't let that fool you. It has a 160-year written history and is phenomenally successful in dealing with a very wide range of health problems. This fact is quickly born out by anyone who adheres to its simple, logical, common-sense principles.

In the early 1980's, after I had been studying on my own for about eleven years, I discovered that there was a highly comprehensive, all-inclusive course on Natural Hygiene being offered by The American College of Life Science in Austin, Texas. I completed this course and was awarded a Ph.D. in Health Science in 1983. So that there is no misunderstanding, the College had no campus, was strictly a correspondence course and was not accredited. The course did, however, contain a wealth of information which was instrumental in solidifying my understanding of Natural Hygiene.

In my estimation, the significance of this kind of traditional "book learnin'" is equalled in importance by experience and observation of which I have over twenty-five years' worth. Incidentally, the course I studied has been translated into German, Spanish, Italian and, most notably, French, and was adopted as part of the curriculum of the Department of Medicine, University of Paris. The course is taught as Naturotherapy to the Department's medical students. The course is still available today from the College in Austin which has been renamed, Life Science Institute, Inc.

In all honesty, what I have studied or not studied is irrelevant. The only thing of relevance and importance is, can the information in this book help you prevent breast cancer? Where the information comes from and who imparts the information means nothing. The only thing that matters is, does it work? I'm not asking you to believe me and blindly follow my recommendations. It must make sense to **you**. You have to feel excited and confident about it. What I have written is written in a totally nontechnical way. It is simplified and in layman's terms. I feel that too many women have been convinced that the subject of breast cancer is far too complicated, mysterious and bewildering for them to grasp and understand, and they therefore **must** seek the advice and services of highly paid specialists. This is extremely convenient for those making their living selling the advice and services.

I know the probability is good that you have an interest in or at least a concern, at some level, about breast cancer. What woman wouldn't? Here is what I ask of you, dear reader: a fair hearing. As hard as it may be to do, try to read what is here with no preconceived or predetermined ideas about what breast cancer is and what can be done about it. You have been blessed from birth with common-sense, logic and basic instincts to help you and to guide you. You are far more capable of discerning what is best for you than you have perhaps been led to believe.

There is a tendency in the scientific community to reject anything out-of-hand that is not in line with traditional thinking. I'm not suggesting that what I am offering up be accepted without question just because it falls under the category of new information. I think that new information should be scrutinized to the fullest extent to prove whether it is viable or not. It is rejection without investigation for no reason other than the fact that the new information is in opposition to prevailing thought that is preposterous and prevents valuable life saving information from reaching the very people who could benefit from it the most.

I am telling you that breast cancer does not have to be the killer that it is; that the number of women dying from it can be dramatically diminished; that the majority of surgical procedures, including mastectomies, can be eliminated; that the number of diagnoses of breast cancer can be drastically reduced; that there are steps you can take to protect yourself and prevent lumps from developing or turning cancerous if they do; that you can live your life free of the fear that you may become a breast cancer casualty.

All of this is possible for you and all I want is a fair shot at proving it to you. Read what I have to say and see if it doesn't make sense to **you**. If it doesn't, then don't use it. But if it does, if it rings true to you, if it makes sense, if you can honestly say, "It seems reasonable enough. I can at least try it to see if it can increase my chances of protection," then I assure you, you won't be disappointed.

I do not wish to minimize or make light of, in any way, the severity of the breast cancer situation as it exists today. But you are only getting part of the story. There is another whole side of it that has yet to come to light. All you're being told about is the deadliness of breast cancer, it's pervasiveness and the dreadful statistics that are daily being racked up. The fear! Women weren't put on earth to have to live in fear of **their own bodies!** That is a totally unnatural and unnecessary situation that **can** be changed.

Once again, I'm not asking you to take my word for anything. There is no proof in the world better than personal verification. If you will incorporate into your lifestyle the principles presented in this book, you will not jeopardize or compromise your health one iota. If anything, you will feel better, have more energy, lose weight (if necessary) and be more confident about your overall well-being. You can **prove** this for yourself. It won't matter who says what about it. Either it will prove itself to you or it won't. All the experts in the world could praise a program or treatment up one side and down the other and it may not work. Or they could ridicule a program or treatment and describe it as useless and it could be just the answer for some individuals. It happens all the time.

If you can, with absolutely no risk to yourself, try something that may prove to be a Godsend to you, and there is **no downside**, why would you **not** try it?

One of the primary reasons why *FIT FOR LIFE* enjoys the enormous popularity that it does is because I challenged people to try the suggestions in the book for only ten days to see for themselves if they worked for them. They took me up on it and *FIT FOR LIFE* has become one of the most popular diet and health books in history. Having been translated into twenty-nine languages, it has millions of adherents all over the world who have discovered the glory of uninterrupted health. I want to invite you to join them. Here is an opportunity for you to go on a journey of discovery; of yourself and of your life here.

A life that can be devoid of the fear and apprehension associated with breast cancer. It is, after all, **your birthright!** As you read what follows, I'm sure you'll encounter certain passages that will challenge your present belief systems. That's O.K. All I'm hoping for is that after you have read the book in its **entirety**, you'll be sufficiently intrigued and curious to at least give it a try to see if it fulfills the promises I'm making about it. All I need is for you to give it a chance.

I knew that if people took up the challenge in *FIT FOR LIFE* and simply followed the recommendations as they were presented, they would lose weight and feel better. Well, that has come to pass beyond my most hopeful expectations. I am just as certain now that if you will take the challenge here and follow the recommendations in **this** book, your reward will be to live your life with something so valuable no amount of money could buy it: peace of mind.

Chapter Two

KEEPING ABREAST

A sk the next ten women whose paths you cross what their greatest personal fear is as concerns their health and well-being. Don't be surprised if all ten, without hesitation, say breast cancer, which for most women, is **the** health issue of the 90's; so much so that it is being referred to as "the other epidemic." If you were to add together all deaths from breast cancer, all deaths from all other forms of cancer, all deaths from AIDS, diabetes and, in fact, all causes of death of women by disease, they would not even come close to equalling the number of deaths from cardiovascular disease alone. But it is breast cancer that women live in terror of and dread the most. Why? That's not a hard one to figure out. All you have to do is compare the treatment and aftermath of treatment associated with heart disease to that of cancer. It's like the difference between getting a mosquito bite and being mauled by a grizzly bear.

If your doctor should report to you that your cholesterol level is much too high and there is far too much fatty plaque in your arteries, that's not good news because it puts you at high risk of having a heart attack. Hearing such a diagnosis would certainly alarm you, but the fear or dread you might experience from such a diagnosis is like a stroll on the beach compared to what the words "you have cancer" evoke.

After all, the treatment to ward off the heart attack is pretty straightforward. Stop pumping so much fat and cholesterol through your arteries, cut down on your salt, fried foods, cigarettes and alcohol consumption and get some moderate amount of aerobic exercise on a regular basis. That's basically it. Not so with cancer.

For most people, the word cancer conjures up the worst of all possibilities. Not only is there the disease itself, which is viewed as this merciless horror that relentlessly eats away at the body, but there is also the treatment which can be as agonizing as the disease itself. Between the painful, disfiguring surgery, the radiation that can burn holes in your skin and chemotherapy which is the most excruciatingly painful treatment ever devised for any disease, the overall effect of being told you have cancer is on par with being told you have to pay a visit to hell and duel the devil with burning pitch forks. That's for cancer in general. A diagnosis of breast cancer for a woman is worse yet because it has all the negatives associated with cancer and its treatment plus the **added** ordeal of having one or both breasts removed. For some women, this can be the most devastating part of having breast cancer.

We're not talking about the removal of some nondescript organ here. Remove a gall bladder, a spleen, an appendix, or a man's prostate and, yes, it's physically painful and having surgery, any surgery, is unnerving. But with rest and recuperation, the scar from the operation heals and life goes on pretty much as it did before. Remove a woman's breast and there's another whole set of variables that come into play. The psychological and emotional scars can last long after the physical ones have healed. The removal of a breast goes to the very heart of a woman's image of herself.

Let's face it. Certainly in this country and a good portion of the rest of the world, there is a fixation on women's breasts. Anyone not aware of that must be visiting from another planet. The female form, of which the breasts are a most significant feature, has been celebrated in art, music and poetry throughout history. A woman's breasts are deeply and profoundly associated with her femininity, her sexuality, her body image, her feeling of self-esteem and beauty. I have had women tell me that they felt afraid that their husbands might not think they were pretty or attractive after the loss of their breasts. They no longer feel whole and attractive. This is enormously disconcerting to a woman in a way I am certain no man could possibly comprehend.

One woman I know was so apprehensive that she said she could hardly look her own husband in the eye, let alone get undressed in front of him. Fortunately her husband was sufficiently enlightened to recognize that he was in love with **who** his wife was, not what her body looked like and everything turned out fine for them. But what of single women who have had one or both breasts removed and want to marry and have children?

I was watching a program on CNN[6] about several women who had survived breast cancer and its treatment, and one woman's story couldn't help but bring tears to my eyes. She was single, in her late thirties and had both breasts removed. She was discussing her state of mind as relates to dating. Her situation was in the forefront of her mind at all times.

She wants to go out with men and eventually wants to marry. She has no breasts and she has no hair as a result of chemotherapy treatments. She felt as though her femininity had been taken from her. She said that worse than not having breasts was the fact that she had no hair on her head and always had to deal with whatever wig she was wearing. She not only felt conspicuous about that, but constantly anguished over when to tell the person she was dating exactly what her situation was.

Instead of thoughts about what a nice evening she would have being with a new friend and enjoying herself, her thoughts were about whether or not he would be understanding and kind and would her wig stay in its place. It was impossible to watch this woman and see the sadness in her eyes and not be deeply moved.

It is no small wonder why so many women are living in fear of breast cancer. It was such stories as this that filled me with the fire to finish this book as soon as I possibly could to help ward off such tragedies in other women's lives.

It would probably be the greatest understatement ever uttered to say that women, all women, would do practically anything to avoid ever having to deal with breast cancer, its treatment and aftermath. There is one way and one way only to insure that: prevention! It goes without saying that if women knew how to prevent breast cancer, they would do whatever they had to do. But, so far, that information has not been forthcoming. It's a complicated subject, no doubt about that, so women rely on the advice of those people who have been designated as "experts" in the field.

One of the most important steps in overcoming a problem, any problem, is to know that there **is** a problem. In that regard, I think a brief overview of the present situation as regards breast cancer and what the experts are offering up, is in order. Considering that women are looking to the experts for answers and direction, it may come as a cold, hard shot of reality that you don't want to hear to learn that the experts themselves are in just as much of a quandary over breast cancer as you. They're stumped! They **want** to get a handle on it, of course, and they **are** trying, but as of right now, they are virtually incapable of supplying you with the answers you so desperately need and want. Of course, this will never be openly admitted because such an admission would cause unbridled panic amongst the populous. But facts are facts and the truth of what I am saying is absolute and easily proven, as you shall shortly see.

One most disturbing fact is that for the last thirty years, **at least**, the problem of breast cancer has done nothing but get worse. Not only here in the United States but throughout countries rich and poor, industrial and rural, breast cancer incidence is on the rise.[7] Breast cancer is the most common form of cancer in women.[8] Approximately 185,000 women are diagnosed with breast cancer in the United States every year.

Of those, approximately 46,000 die.[9] Every twelve minutes, day and night, without stop, another woman dies. During the writing of this book, that fact started to prey relentlessly on my mind. When I went to a movie to relax, what I thought about was the fact that while I was in the theater watching a movie for two hours, ten women died. It got to the point where I started measuring what I did, not by how long it took, but by how many women died of breast cancer while I was doing it. I guess you could say I became obsessed with finishing the project. I was so convinced that the book would save lives that I actually started to feel guilty whenever I was doing anything other than writing.

Since 1950, the incidence of breast cancer has increased 60%, making it one of the fastest growing killer diseases in the nation.[10] Since 1960, the number of American women who have died from breast cancer is more than twice the number of all Americans killed in World War I, World War II, the Korean War, the Vietnam War and the Gulf War. Half of these women died in the ten years from 1983 to 1993,[11] which shows the death rate to be **increasing** as time goes by. In 1962, one in twenty women got breast cancer.[12] In 1982, the number was one in eleven.[13] In 1993, the number was one in eight[14] and by the year 2000 it is projected to be one in seven.[15]

On ABC's Nightline,[16] Cindy Pearson, Program Director for the National Women's Health Network, was asked, "Is there a breast cancer epidemic in this country?"

Her reply: "What else would you call a condition that has increased in incidence every year for the last forty years with no explanation and no effective cure? I think there's nothing else to call it but an epidemic."

You will notice that a lot of the material I use to make my points comes from common, everyday sources. Not that I don't also use scientific journals. I do. But quite frankly, the vast majority of the population does not read these journals which are written in difficult to understand, scientific jargon. I much prefer to use the very sources that you are most apt to be familiar with: television, radio, newspapers and magazines. Also, when it comes to scientific studies that are published in the journals, it is well known that any premise whatsoever can be "scientifically proven." Depending on who is funding the studies and what outcome is desired, even two opposite views can be proven.

The most classic example of science **proving** both sides of an issue is to be found in the *New England Journal of Medicine*,[17] easily one of the most prestigious and well respected of all American medical journals. In one issue, there are two articles on the subject of heart attacks in women. One article "proves" that by giving female hormones to post menopausal women you can **substantially protect them against heart attacks**. The second article, equally well substantiated, "proves" that by giving hormones to post menopausal women you **substantially increase their chances of having a heart attack**. Now mind you, these two contradictory studies weren't in the same journal on different dates, two years apart or something. They were in the **very same issue!**

What I like to do is use the very media that you see or read everyday, to point out what is being told to you by the people who are immersed in this subject of breast cancer and are talking directly to you. How often do you sit down and read scientific journals? Probably never for most of the people reading this. No, the average woman on the street will read newspapers or magazines several times a week and never have the opportunity of even **seeing** a scientific journal.

I see it as my role to point out to you what you may be missing in the very articles you're reading, or programs you're watching or listening to. You see, you may come across an article on breast cancer and read it and be lulled into thinking that more is being done or more progress is being made than is actually the case.

With great regularity I'll read an article in the newspaper which is quite long, two thousand words or more, and it will be filled with what **may** happen, or what **might** take place, or what is **perhaps** the case, or what outcome is **hoped** for, or what avenues of study **look** promising, or that researchers are encouraged by **prospects** that can and should be pursued further, or that the answer is just around the corner, and on and on and on. Buried deep underneath all of the wished for progress are perhaps one or two sentences that reveal the true state of affairs in terms of actual progress being realized.

The thing is, most people never notice these few sentences which are not highlighted or embellished upon. They're basically lost amidst the fluff. People just don't have the trained eye to seek out and find these buried jewels which give us a more honest and accurate evaluation of the overall situation. When they **are** scrutinized more closely, a definite, unmistakable pattern emerges. I have been playing this hide-and-seek game for twenty-five years. Those few sentences of worth jump out at me now like loud, florescent neon lights that are flashing away in rapid fire.

It is essential I weed through and extract some of these statements and present them to you so that you can see them in the clear light of day without all the distractions that customarily accompany them and only serve to divert your attention away from the really important stuff. And nowhere can this strategy be used more effectively than in the area of showing you just how baffled the experts really are when it comes to the subject of breast cancer.

Following, are some of the most revealing and telling statements made by the people in the best possible position to know the real status of the headway being made in the battle against breast cancer.

"There are two things we don't know about breast cancer. We don't know the cause and we don't know the cure."

Nancy Brinker, *Chairwoman of the President's Special Commission on Breast Cancer*[18]

"Nobody knows what causes breast cancer, nobody knows how to prevent it, and nobody knows how to cure it."

Linda Ellerbee, *Narrating an ABC Special On Breast Cancer*[19]

"Despite decades of research, there are still gaping holes in our knowledge of breast cancer. No one knows for sure who is at risk, how to prevent it, or what causes it."

Host on a PBS Special on Breast Cancer[20]

"We don't know what causes it...there's no way to prevent it."

Jane Pauley, *Narrating a PBS Special on Breast Cancer*[21]

"No one knows how to prevent it, and the mortality rate from breast cancer has not improved for decades. Researchers say it is also disconcerting that the rates have remained so high."

Column in the *New York Times*, *10/20/93.*[22]

"So many questions, one answer: We don't know. Breast cancer, never have so many been given so much conflicting advice and so few definitive solutions."

Cokie Roberts, *ABC Nightline.*[23]

"Throughout countries rich and poor, industrial and rural, breast cancer incidence is on the rise. No one knows what's fueling that increase."

Science News, July 3, 1993.[24]

"This continual rise in breast cancer is unexplained. We have some hints at what's causing it, but we don't know the whole story and we also don't know how to stop it or how to cure it when it occurs."

Cindy Pearson, *Program Director for the National Women's Health Network, ABC Nightline.*[25]

"We really don't know what causes breast cancer. We don't really even have a clue what causes breast cancer."

Doctor Susan Love, *breast surgeon, Author of one of the most authoritative guides on breast care, past Assistant Clinical Professor at Harvard Medical School, Director of U.C.L.A.'s Breast Center.*[26]

"Women are very frightened by breast cancer and there is nothing they can do to prevent it."

Maryann Napoli, *Associate Director of the Center For Medical Consumers in New York.*[27]

"If we knew how to prevent breast cancer, believe me we would have done it. We don't know how."

John Laszlo, MD, *Senior Vice President for Research, American Cancer Society.*[28]

"We don't know the natural history of this disease. We don't know whether treatment is necessary and we don't know if it works."

Dr. H. Gilbert Welsh, *Senior Research Associate of the Department of Veterans Affairs.*[29]

"It's horribly frustrating because I tend to like to look at prevention. If we knew what caused it, we could figure out how to prevent it, but we don't know yet."

> Dr. Janet Osuch, *Breast Cancer Specialist at Michigan State University.*[29A]

"Scientists do not understand much about the causes of breast cancer. So while they can detect and treat breast cancer, they do not know how to prevent it."

> Robert Bazell, *NBC News Science Correspondent*[29B]

Of all these quotes you have just read, do you see the most notable message? Did you notice that in every one of these quotes it was stated in no uncertain terms that "we don't know," or "no one knows"? Be very clear on something; these statements were not made casually. The evidence of their accuracy is so overwhelming, that to say anything else would be foolhardy. They are merely stating the obvious. Be assured, they would much prefer **not** to admit such things but they had no choice.

It is so extremely important that you take these comments seriously and place the full measure of importance on them that they deserve. That is the only way you will be moved to take the actions necessary to protect yourself.

I know that a great number of women reading this, perhaps including you, are going to be deeply stunned to learn that so little **is** actually known about breast cancer and all that you have read or heard that gave you the impression that more was known and more headway was being made has only been what the researchers think **may** be the case, or what they **hoped** would be the case. After all, you have to be told **something**. Imagine your reaction if you asked experts in the field a pertinent question on breast cancer and all they could do was turn their palms up, scrunch up their shoulders and say, "Sorry, but I just don't know." So instead, they tell you what they think **may** be the answer. What you're getting is conjecture and speculation, nothing concrete. Over time people tend to see what **may** be as what **is**, and they are lulled into complacency.

Let's look at the three most important issues in question.

1) **They don't know the cause**. Without question, there **are** risk factors, but what are they? You're probably familiar with the most often mentioned ones: The hormone estrogen, early menstruation, late menopause, pregnancy late in life, having no children, birth control pills, heredity and environment (which includes a lot of factors including pesticides), other chemicals, **and** diet. Remember, these are **guesses**. None have been absolutely proven. They may all play a role or none may play a role. They may only be contributing factors...or not. Jane Pauley, on a nationally broadcast program on breast cancer, states that, "Most women who get breast cancer do not fit into any high risk category. There's no way to predict who will get it."[30]

Dr. Susan Love states that, "80% of the women who are diagnosed with breast cancer have no risk factors whatsoever, except being a woman."[31] Based on that, one could say that the only absolute risk factor is, being a woman.

It's interesting that, for whatever reason, most women seem to think that the biggest risk factor of all is having a family member who has had breast cancer. Equally interesting is the fact that only 5% of breast cancer cases can be linked to a family history of the disease.[32] That figure is more a coincidence of the law of averages than it is a major risk factor.

Also, a recent study has found that when a woman moves to a new country, her risk of dying of breast cancer will rise or fall to match the death rate of women in the newly adopted country. This points to environmental factors, such as diet, as having more impact than family history. The study contradicts current notions that most of a woman's risk of breast cancer is set by puberty or early adulthood. Dr. Noel S. Weiss, professor of epidemiology at the University of Washington School of Public Health in Seattle, says, "The importance of this study is that it reinforces our notion that your risk of breast cancer isn't something you're born with."[32A]

2) **They don't know the cure**. Although the bulk of research dollars are spent on the, so far, fruitless search for a cure, there is no magic bullet for breast cancer that is administered and the disease goes away, or we would surely know about it. Yet we hear of the "cure rate" of breast cancer patients. If a woman is still alive five years after her cancer is first treated, she falls into the category of "the cured." To put it mildly, it is a great big, humongous stretch of the word. Surviving five years is hardly a cure. Especially when you consider that **twenty** years after diagnosis, 88% of those women who have died, did so of breast cancer.[33] In other words, eighty-eight out of a hundred died of what they were "cured."

The five-year survival number you hear about is a completely and totally arbitrary one. It is a "line drawn in the sand" with no meaning whatsoever other than that the patient has managed to survive five years after diagnosis. It hardly means cure.

You know what I'm reminded of every time I hear mention of the five-year survival? I saw a movie once, I forget which one, but some tribal warriors captured some enemy and made them run through a gauntlet of men who beat them with punches, kicks, clubs and other assorted weapons of destruction. The prisoners were told if they could make it to the end of the gauntlet they could live. Some **did** make it, although they were crippled for life. But, I guess it was better than being killed.

Women who are diagnosed with breast cancer have to not only deal with the progression of the disease itself, but they also have to withstand the treatment, which, as we know, can be horrific. If they submit to surgery, radiation and chemotherapy, referred to by Andrea Martin, Executive Director of the Breast Cancer Fund, as, "The slash, burn and poison routine of cancer treatment," it **will** take its toll. At the end of the five years, a woman could be disfigured, bald, psychologically crushed, emotionally bankrupt, in constant pain and on drugs to quell the pain and be declared "cured." I don't think so.

3) **They don't know how to prevent it**. Of the three, this is the one that is most self-evident. If there were any means in place by which to prevent breast cancer, the problem would not be getting worse every passing year. The irony is that prevention, which without question is the most important aspect of breast cancer, is given scant, if any, attention whatsoever. Yes, scads of lip service are given to the subject of prevention, but that's it. The vast majority of money spent on breast cancer research, which is many **billions** of dollars a year, is spent on after-the-fact research, such as early detection and treatment.

The National Cancer Institute receives approximately 1.8 billion dollars a year in federal money for research, and a paltry 5% is spent on prevention.[34] And only 5% (1/4 of a percent of the total) of that already pitifully small amount is spent on breast cancer.[34.1] That's not just peanuts, that's barely peanut **skins!** Why?

Why, when no one, and I mean **no one** could possibly cast doubt on the fact that prevention is the key to ending, or at least to diminishing the pain and suffering of breast cancer, is so little attention actually paid to it? It is a troubling question, and the answer, at least in part, is not one that is very pleasant to think about. I know it's going to sound cynical and coldhearted, but a big part of the reason has to do with money. There's simply more money involved in chasing cures and selling drugs than there is in teaching life-style changes to prevent disease. Ouch!

I know how much it must disturb you to hear that, but to deny that money is a factor is foolish. Let me be as clear as I possibly can be here about something. I'm not suggesting or even remotely hinting that there are people sitting around saying things like, "The heck with prevention, there's no money in it. Let's concentrate on what will make the most bucks." No way. But when we talk about the money generated by the health care industry in the United States, we're talking about the biggest money making machine there is.

Most people think that we spend more money in the United States on national defense than on anything else. We do spend a lot: **three hundred billion dollars** a year. But multiply that by **three** and you still don't equal what is spent on health care, which clocks in at a mind boggling one **trillion** dollars a year. That's one thousand billion! This is going to sound heartless as hell, but who stands to lose the most amount of money if cancer is prevented? The cancer establishment!

Consider the words of Dr. Samuel Epstein, Professor of Occupation and Environmental Medicine at the School of Public Health, University of Chicago Medical Center: "The cancer establishment, the National Cancer Institute, the American Cancer Society, and the pharmaceutical companies associated with them are virtually indifferent or hostile to problems of cancer prevention."[35] Can you think of any legitimate reason why a pharmaceutical company, or anyone for that matter, should be "hostile" toward cancer prevention? I can't either.

So...having acknowledged, admitted and accepted that the cause, cure and prevention of breast cancer has eluded them, the experts have found themselves in the position of having to offer up **something**. They can ill afford to look perplexed and give us the old "Gee, I don't now what to tell ya'." And what they have pinned all their hopes on, **and yours**, is what is referred to as "early detection." With nowhere else to turn, all energy is being directed toward early detection.

As part of President Clinton's attempt to provide health care for one and all, the government asked outside experts to devise a strategy to deal with the growing incidence and death from breast cancer. In an address at the opening session of a conference on breast cancer at the National Institutes of Health, Donna E. Shalala, Health and Human Services Secretary, stated that, "The plan must address why the incidence of breast cancer is steadily rising, and what action we must take to detect breast cancer earlier."[36]

Dr. Timothy Johnson, ABC News Medical Director, says, in discussing what women's options are, that "The only thing they can do right now is to try to detect it early through self exam, physician exam and mammography."[37] (Note the word "**only**.")

Dr. Susan Love was asked by a woman what she could do to lower her risk of breast cancer and Dr. Love's answer was, "The only hope we have right now in terms of dealing with breast cancer is in early detection and that means mammography."[38] The **only** hope. God forbid that should be true. And trust me, it isn't! In fact, not only is early detection **not** your **only** hope, it's barely any hope at all. Relying on early detection as your "only hope" is to give up and admit defeat. **Early detection means you have breast cancer!** Don't accept that.

You know, I read lots of material from the many support groups around the country that work with breast cancer patients and also try to bring an awareness of the seriousness of breast cancer to both the public and those who allocate money for breast cancer research. A theme that seems to run through virtually all of this material is a call to arms for women. They want women to speak up and speak out, to fight back, to get angry and **demand** something be done. Good idea! And if you want something to really get angry about, get angry about being told that your **"only hope"** in dealing with breast cancer is to sit around and wait until you get it, then hope you detect it before it kills you. Because that is precisely what's happening.

After all is said and done, after all the talk and posturing about what's been done and what's being done, after all the billions spent and research conducted, all the most highly advanced and technologically superior medical machine in the world can tell you is, in effect...**nothing!** Your last glimmer of hope, your last resort and refuge, lies in a test with the efficiency and accuracy of a coin toss: mammography.

All attention and focus as relates to the subject of breast cancer is directed toward mammographies. Why? Because there's nothing else to offer. So by creating a big hubbub and to-do around mammographies, it gives the appearance that **something** is being done about breast cancer. And so now there is what is described in the *New York Times* as "One of the most contentious disputes in medicine."[39] Another article in the *Times* describes the controversy surrounding mammography guidelines as a "wrenching" and "impassioned" debate among the experts.[40] And what is this debate that has captured the headlines? Should women **under** fifty have regular mammograms?

According to a number of studies, if women over fifty have mammograms every one to two years, their risk of dying of breast cancer is reduced by one third.[41] But there are no such studies to prove that the same is true for women in their forties. This controversy has flared on and off since the 70's.[42]

The United States stands virtually alone in the world in recommending mammographies for women in their forties.[43] "The eight-nation European Group for Breast Cancer opposes it on the basis that there is no demonstrated benefit."[44] The "experts" here in the United States seem to be equally divided with opponents saying there is no scientific evidence to support mammographies for women in their forties. And since the tissue in a younger woman's breast is far denser than the tissue in the breasts of women in their fifties and older, the possibility of high error rates of false positives is greatly increased which can lead to unnecessary treatments.

Dr. Suzanne W. Fletcher, Co-Editor of the *Annals of Internal Medicine*, and her husband, Dr. Robert H. Fletcher, wrote, "Medical scientists and physicians do not do modern women a service by promulgating a screening practice that medical science has not been able to substantiate after so many tries."[45]

Proponents acknowledge that there are no good scientific studies to prove the value of mammographies for women in their forties, but their argument is that there are no studies proving that they **don't** help either.

And so the dispute rages on. It's interesting that in **all** other matters of health care such as this, medical experts across the board adamantly **insist** that good, hard data from scientifically sound studies be in place first. Why the exception here? If you think about it, women's health issues have always been played kind of fast and loose and this appears to be another example of it. Plus, there's another factor to consider that no one **wants** to believe is influencing the decision to push for mammographies for women under fifty, but it's pretty hard to ignore.

In keeping with my earlier suggestion that the money incentive is something that should always be looked at when you're talking about a trillion dollar industry, I came across an interesting comment from Dr. Howard Ozer, Chief of Medical Oncology at the University of North Carolina

School of Medicine. He was being interviewed about the debate over the screening guidelines for women in their forties and amongst several points he was making, he said that, "...the mammography business has become highly lucrative and younger women are the best customers."[46] No need to embellish on that, he makes the point better than I.

You know what gets me about all this? It's a smoke screen that clouds the more important issues. By keeping the ongoing controversy of mammographies for early detection in the public eye, it keeps women thinking about that and which side they should take as regards when they should start getting mammographies. In the meantime, they lose sight of the bigger, more important issue of prevention! Never allow the fact to drift from your mind that the use of mammographies for early detection concerns itself with only one thing: finding a cancerous tumor in your breast. Let's not lose sight of your goal **here**, which isn't to **locate** a tumor in your breast, but to avoid ever **developing** one.

Actually, it would be one thing if mammographies performed the service they are intended to with dependability and preciseness, but there is an unsettling irony in all of this. On the one hand you are being told, in the clearest possible language, that there is no way to prevent or cure breast cancer, so all of your faith and trust should be focused on mammographies for early detection which is being held up as your final bastion of hope. On the other hand, mammography's track record of reliability isn't exactly something that will fill you with confidence. Mammography fails to detect as much as 20% of all breast cancers and as much as 40% in women under the age of fifty,[46] and that is in the best of circumstances when all procedures involved are being performed with high efficiency.

Examples of how treatment was either withheld when it should have been given, or given when it should have been withheld could fill this book.

Primetime Live gives an example of a woman who had soreness in her breast so she had a mammography and was told, "Everything is normal." But within eight months, the cancer that was missed grew and spread. The breast had to be removed.[47]

Good Morning America tells the story of a woman told she had cancer based on a laboratory examination of tissue from her breast by a pathologist who had thirty years experience. She had both breasts removed only to find out later that she didn't have cancer.[48]

In April 1994, a Florida woman whose left breast was removed after a misdiagnosis of cancer was awarded 2.7 million dollars. The jury ruled that **all four** of the doctors who were involved were negligent. Astonishingly, the mistake was discovered **two weeks before** her mastectomy, but no one spoke up.[49]

As Jane Pauley stated on a program she hosted, "The fact is, some women do everything right, they find it early, they get treatment, but they still die from the disease."[21]

The problem with placing so much reliance on mammographies for early detection lies in the fact that there are several variables that come into play at once and influence the ultimate diagnosis. If **any one** of these variables are inaccurate or performed incorrectly, the probability of a **mis**diagnosis goes way up. There are three factors that are of extreme importance: the machine taking the X-ray picture or mammography, the technician operating the machine and the interpretation of the film.

In 1992, ABC's *Prime Time Live* conducted a four-month investigation that canvassed the country interviewing surgeons, radiologists, cancer patients and experts in the field. What they discovered is that "there is a crisis in the quality of mammography in this country."[50] Unlike Western Europe, where there are federal regulations, the mammography business in the United States has proliferated with virtually no rules. Until very recently, there were no national quality standards.

Many of the machines simply do not take good pictures and they are being used every day. In Michigan, it was discovered that **35-50%** of the facilities doing mammographies were doing unacceptable work. Michigan cracked down on these faulty facilities and now has the toughest laws in the country. **But only nine states have tough laws governing mammographies**. That means forty-one states do not!

The operators of these machines, who are called technologists, should have what can amount to two years of study in X-ray technology. This, according to Dr. Ed Hendrick, Professor at the University of Colorado and top physicist at The American College of Radiology. A crucial and complicated part of the mammography is the careful placement of the breast. Since each patient is different, a technologist has to know how to compress the breast, not to mention test the machine and check the processing of the film. *Prime Time's* hidden cameras showed in one instance, a nurse with only **two days'** training in mammography, doubling as a technologist. In another office, the **receptionist** did mammographies and she, too, had only two days' training. In twenty-one states, technologists don't even have to be licensed. Diane Sawyer, the co-anchor of the *Prime Time* show, said, "In a lot of states there's more supervision of pizza parlors than mammographies."[47] And this, so you are told, is your "only hope" in dealing with breast cancer.

Here is a rather astonishing piece of information that too few women are even aware of and which seriously weakens the premise that early detection is the key in avoiding becoming a breast cancer statistic. Cancer cells grow at a very slow pace. It takes one year for a single cancer cell to become twelve cells. At that rate of growth, it will take six years for the cancer to be the size of a pencil point,[51] and about **ten** years to even be detectable in a mammogram.[52] At that point, it is one centimeter, about the size of a pea. I want to be sure you see the full import of what I am saying. You can religiously get a mammogram every year and not have a cancer show up that has been growing in your breast for **ten years**.

And then there is the all-important issue of interpretation. A new study has raised serious questions about radiologists' reliability in reading mammograms and making recommendations about what to do when a suspicious lesion is found in the breast. The study, by researchers at Yale University School of Medicine and published in *The New England Journal of Medicine*, found that interpretations and advice given based on those interpretations vary greatly. Where one radiologist might recommend an immediate biopsy, another, looking at the same mammogram might suggest a repeat X-ray in three months, and still another might suggest waiting a year to do another mammogram.[52A]

In November, 1992, the landmark Canadian study on mammography—the largest study ever conducted in the world—involving ninety thousand women, showed "no benefit for women under forty-nine" and it "fails to reduce breast cancer deaths among women between fifty and fifty-nine."[53] Consider the words of physician and best selling author, Dr. John McDougall, when he writes, "Because most of the years of cancer growth are hidden at microscopic levels, efforts toward early detection are unlikely to ever yield much success in saving lives."[54] "To be quite realistic, in most cases the only real beneficiaries from early detection are the health professionals. Early detection gets the patient going to the doctor earlier and, thereby, a longer total time period is available for more expensive doctor visits, hospitalizations and tests. And the patient lives no longer or better from all this well meaning effort."[55]

As more ingenious techniques are developed to detect smaller and smaller cancers, some investigators are voicing their concerns. They point out that studies show that many, if not most, early cancers do not grow large and dangerous and would never be noticed unless doctors with an early detection method went looking for them. Tiny cancers are so common that autopsy studies of middle-aged and older people have found that almost everyone's body contains them. No one can tell which early cancers are dangerous and which ones are not, and no one understands enough about the natural history of cancer to know what it means to find a tumor so small. This led Dr. Barry Kramer, Associate Director of the Early Detection and Community Oncology Program at the National Cancer Institute, to state, "We have to meticulously avoid the tendency to assume that early diagnosis in and of itself will make a difference."[55A] After all the hoopla centered around early detection, this specialist is saying that early detection **makes no difference!**

Do you know what I think of every time I hear about people depending on mammographies and early detection to save them from dying of breast cancer? I imagine two people out in mountain wilderness and one slips off the edge of a cliff and is stranded on a small ledge jutting over a two thousand foot drop. The person up above throws down a tired old rope that is all frayed and which looks like it was left over from the Spanish American War. The person on the ledge yells up that the rope doesn't look like it will hold any weight and the person throwing the rope down says, "It's all we have, just grab hold and hope for the best." That's what you're being asked to do with mammographies and early detection.

Fortunately, for the purposes of this book at least, mammographies are irrelevant. We're not looking to detect, we're looking to prevent. And mammographies have absolutely nothing to do with prevention. **Nothing!**

Once again, the words of Dr. Susan Love: "What we really need is some kind of prevention of breast cancer, not finding it. We need to prevent it from happening."[55.1] By implementing the information in this book, you're going to take a giant step toward preventing ever developing cancerous lumps in your breasts. Mammographies will go from being a life raft thrown to a drowning person to a monitoring device to validate your success.

I do not wish to imply that this book is going to wipe out breast cancer. There are no such guarantees from **anyone**. There are some women that no matter what they do, and no matter how conscientious they are, **will** get breast cancer and die from it. That's a cold, hard fact of life. What I am saying is that a lot of women, **a lot**, are going to be able to avoid that fate from following the recommendations in this book.

Just so there are no misunderstandings that may lead me to be accused of suggesting that women stop getting regular mammographies, I want to state clearly and categorically that I am **not** saying that. I am saying that I want mammography to become something else in your consciousness rather than being viewed as a tool to detect cancer so that you can go to work on it. I want you to see it as a means by which you prove to yourself that you are successfully preventing cancer from getting a foothold.

I could easily understand if you were to feel upset about some of what you have read in this chapter. After all, finding out that the experts you are relying on for direction are as baffled about breast cancer as you are can be disconcerting, to put it mildly. But I want you to be very clear about something. I did not share that revelation with you in order to alarm you, but rather to **alert** you to the fact that complacency on your part in the form of reliance on the experts is not going to serve you well, at this time.

I live in South Florida where the danger of a hurricane coming through and wiping me out is a very real possibility. When I'm warned of a hurricane approaching, it is not done to scare me, it's done to give me the opportunity to take the measures necessary to save my life. It's true, I may have given you information that is upsetting, but more importantly, I am also going to give you what you need to save **your** life.

Dr. I. Craig Henderson is a breast cancer researcher who is Chief of Medical Oncology at the University of California in San Francisco. In an interview with the *New York Times*, he stated that, "Science often made its leaps from unexpected directions, which means that the next great advance in breast cancer may not come from breast cancer research. It is important for us to follow the clues wherever they are and to realize that the answer may not be in breast cancer directed funds."[56]

Thank you, Dr. Henderson, those are my sentiments exactly. And this book is my contribution to proving you right.

Chapter Three

THE NATURAL SUPERIORITY OF WOMEN?

This is going to be a short chapter consisting of a subject matter that must be addressed, but not dwelled upon. There is really no easy or polite way to bring it up, so I'm just going to blurt it out, brick-in-the-face style. In the vast majority of cases, the decision to cut off women's breasts are being made by men. Now, this statement is not intended to start an argument, or to suggest that there are male physicians sitting around deciding to cut off women's breasts for any reason other than an attempt to save their lives. But the plain fact is that for millennia, in every area of life when it came to rights and fairness in acknowledging and respecting those rights, women have gotten the short end of the stick and men have been instrumental in bringing that about. Period. Anyone not aware of that has been on an extended leave of absence from reality.

This is not a book, or even a chapter, that is a treatise on feminism, but the subject can hardly be ignored. Besides, many a writer far more capable than I have already made the case for equal rights and made it well. But I have to discuss, briefly, the effect of male domination on the subject at hand. The history of the world is rife with examples of men making decisions that negatively effect women's lives.

It was the male-dominated church that instigated the infamous witch hunts. Millions of women were burned at the stake, accused by the church of being witches, when in actual fact their only crime was being able to help people heal themselves. It was believed at the time that God brought on disease and only God could heal it. Women, who were in touch with their own biologically-encoded ability to nurture and used that wisdom to instruct others on how to recapture their health were declared to be witches and killed.

Even today male-dominated churches refuse to allow women to be ordained as priests. In early 1994, when the Church of England broke with tradition and voted to allow thirty-two women in the priesthood, there were bitter objections resulting in at least seven hundred clergymen quitting in protest and indicating an intention to convert to Roman Catholicism.[57] I can't help but wonder if any of these seven hundred gentlemen would have quit if the women they were protesting against were the ones who carried them in their wombs for nine months before giving them life.

The Vatican reacted sharply to the ordination reasserting its opposition to women priests and that the Church of England's decision was a setback. One priest compared female priests to "witches and dogs." Another placed an ad on a billboard reading "the Church of England murdered today."[58]

Also, in early 1994, the Vatican granted permission for priests to have girls assist them at mass, a task traditionally restricted to males. It's only small tasks like lighting candles and pouring wine and water, but even this outraged male members of the church. The Vatican, however, quickly pointed out that the move did not signal a change in its "ban on the ordination of women to the priesthood."[59]

Right here in the good ol' U.S.A., in the male-dominated political arena, women were not "allowed" to vote until 1920.

Women are still trying to receive equal pay for equal work in the male-dominated work force.

And, of course, there's the male-dominated medical profession. Today women physicians are commonplace, but that was not always the case, not by a long shot. Women had to fight long and hard just to earn the **right** to study medicine. Women were **banned** from entering medical colleges. In 1852 Dr. Russell Trall, a medical doctor turned Natural Hygienist, founded the first medical college to admit women. There were also colleges **founded** by women, but established colleges would only accept men. In the late 1800's, Johns Hopkins University had been trying to open a medical school but lacked the funding. A half a million dollar endowment, raised **solely by women**, was given to the University on the condition that women be admitted on the same terms as men. In 1893, when the Johns Hopkins Medical School opened, most of the other medical schools in the country started to adopt coeducation policies.

In 1873, Dr. Edward H. Clark, a physician and Harvard professor, cautioned against a college education for women, as it would cause "uterine atrophy."[60] Harvard had a resolution prohibiting the admission of women as medical students until **1946**.

As recently as 1970 there was a quota that limited women to **10%** of the student body in most medical schools.[61]

Throughout the history of medicine, which up until the mid-1800's was the sole domain of the male practitioner, women have been treated by men with disdain, arrogance, elitism, condescension, ridicule and superiority. Men's overall contempt for women was best illustrated by the words of Hippocrates, referred to as the "Father of Medicine," when asked the question, "What is woman?" he answered with one word: "Disease."[62]

One of the most egregious injustices ever perpetrated directly against women by men is the hysterectomy. Many a book could be, and **has been**, written about this procedure that got its start based on ignorance of the highest order.

There are references of hysterectomies being performed in ancient Greece. Menstruation was thought of as a monthly blood letting that automatically "rendered women weak and inferior creatures."[63] Up until 1846, when anesthesia was introduced by a Massachusetts dentist named William T. G. Morton, hysterectomies were conducted with no pain killer. After the introduction of anesthesia, it was literally "open season" on the female internal organs[64] and a woman was likely to find herself on the operating table for just about anything her father, husband or doctor might decide was wrong with her. This could include headaches, epilepsy, indigestion, backaches, liver trouble, overeating, attempted suicide, painful menstruation and, most particularly, masturbation, erotic behavior or excessive sexual desire.

Women were socialized to be docile, feeble and subservient to men. If they were not, that's when medicine had to intervene and, despite their importance to the sanctity of childbearing, the female organs had to be sacrificed. Doctors of the day were convinced that hysterectomies had a calming effect that would render women more "tractable, orderly, industrious and cleanly."[65]

Believe me when I tell you that it is no accident that the word hysterectomy comes from the word hysteria, which is the Greek term for uterus. Let a woman become emotional about something, and lord knows she certainly has had ample reason, and she was pronounced hysterical and separated from her sexual organs. If I'm not mistaken, there are a significant number of instances of men becoming hysterical over one thing or another. I wonder how the suggestion would be received that when men exhibit hysteria, **their** sexual organs are removed to render them more "tractable and orderly." Why is it appropriate for the female of the species and not the male? Just a rhetorical question guys, don't get nervous.

Perhaps one of the most outrageous examples of male arrogance on this subject was put forth in the early 1970's by a Connecticut physician named Ralph W. Wright. He set forth in a paper that, "After the last planned pregnancy, the uterus becomes a useless, symptom-producing, potentially cancer-bearing organ and therefore should be removed."[66] His proposal was actually taken seriously enough to be debated at a 1971 meeting of the American College of Obstetrics and Gynecology, and those who agreed outnumbered opponents. Wouldn't you like to know how many women were in the group that were in favor? Me too.

As recently as 1977, James H. Sammons, M.D., Executive Vice President of the American Medical Association, took the position that hysterectomy was "beneficial to women with excessive anxiety."[67]

Today there are over 600,000 hysterectomies performed a year, over sixteen-hundred **every day**.[68] According to Dr. Stanley West, noted surgeon, infertility specialist and Chief of Reproductive Endocrinology at St. Vincent's Hospital in New York, in his eye opening book, *The Hysterectomy Hoax*, no more than ten percent of hysterectomies are truly necessary. Dr. West takes a public stand against hysterectomies in virtually all circumstances except when a woman has cancer. In fact, he contends, there is compelling evidence that the operation does more harm than good and therefore presents an unacceptable risk except in the face of life-threatening illness. In every other instance when a hysterectomy is routinely performed, there is an alternative treatment that is much less dangerous and devastating. Too bad Dr. West wasn't in attendance when Dr. Wright put forth his premise.

My point with all of this is that the attitude toward sacrificing women's body parts, from the male-dominated medical perspective, has been one of ignorance and routine. I fear that women's breasts have fallen into that category of expendability and, as is the case with hysterectomies, their mutilation and/or removal is, in the majority of cases, unnecessary.

I was once speaking with a woman in her forties who planned to have no more children and who was having a lot of pain and discomfort with her breasts; not cancer, but lumps that were uncomfortable, especially around the time of her period. Her doctor told her something to the effect that her breasts were just these hunks of flesh no longer serving any useful purpose. Since they were causing her discomfort, pain and anxiety, she should just get rid of them. Those are words unlikely to ever be uttered from the mouth of a woman, but are indicative of an attitude, a belief system that is buried deep in the psyche of men. Oh, it's not overt, but it's there. It's been part of male thinking going back so many thousands of years, that to **some** degree, 1%, 3%, more, who knows, it has to play a role.

The interesting thing is, that the idea of men's superiority over women has very little to do with reality, especially when we are discussing the area of health.

All available research on the matter of health care clearly indicates that men are far more prone to suffer the consequences of a negative life-style than are women. This appears to be the result of an inner "knowing" possessed by women as to how best to achieve and maintain a high level of health. And although this trait also exists in men to some degree, the evidence seems to indicate that it is nowhere near that of women. It always has been, and is now, women who represent the best chance we have of learning and implementing life-styles that will insure the high level of health to which we all aspire.

When you think of the strongest animals on earth, which do you perceive to be the very strongest of all? Most people rightly name the elephant as the strongest animal and, aside from some whales, the elephant is also the largest. These impressive beasts can stand over ten feet tall and weigh over twelve thousand pounds! The largest known elephant, an African bull, measured over thirteen feet tall and weighed twelve **tons!** They can perform phenomenal feats of strength, carrying cargos of six hundred pounds with ease, or moving logs that weigh up to two tons! When lions were proclaimed "King of the Jungle," there must have been a weight and size restriction to enter the running, for elephants are truly the masters of the animal kingdom in terms of size and shear power. An enraged elephant on a full run can strike fear into the heart of **any** animal in its path.

Dr. Depak Chopra tells of a most interesting aspect of the elephant's personality. He points out that elephants in India have been used extensively for centuries to perform heavy tasks after they are tamed and trained. The process of taming begins at a young age when they are shackled to huge trees with very heavy iron chains. No matter how hard the young elephant tries to break away, it can't. Finally, it gives up trying. As soon as it reaches the full length of its chain, it simply stops right there and makes no other attempt to go further. As time goes by, both the size of the tree and the strength of the chains are decreased until the elephant cannot escape from even a flimsy, little rope tied to a small twig. Having grown up with the inability to wander further than the length of its chains, the moment the elephant feels resistance upon its leg, it stops, thinking it can go no further. Even though it could easily pull away from the flimsy rope that has it tethered to a peg in the ground, it has been convinced that it does not have the power to do so, and so it remains captive even though it could easily go anywhere it wanted, whenever it pleased.

Whatever could this all have to do with the subject at hand? Glad you asked. I can't help but compare the plight of the elephant who, although possessing extraordinary power and strength yet is effectively subdued, to the plight of women who have the same thing done to them. Women, **all women**, have been endowed with incredible powers as part of their biological makeup. Yet, over time, the knowledge of these innate abilities has been so successfully buried that precious few women today are even aware of the remarkable power they possess to bring about health in themselves **and** their loved ones.

Over the course of the last several years, during which time I did the research for this book, it has become unwaveringly clear to me that women in nearly all areas of life are superior to men. This will undoubtedly elicit some pshaws and grumbles from many men and even perhaps some women. But, at the least, biologically, psychologically and emotionally, women have it all over men. And in all other areas, intellectually, creatively, in fact in everything except actual physical strength, women are, if not superior, at least equal to men. Throughout the modern world, cultures are different, diets are different, ways of life and causes of death are different, but one thing is the same—women outlive men. In the United States, **80%** of the population over sixty-five years old and living alone are women,[69] and the most provocative statistic of all is that **five out of six widowed Americans are women**.[70]

Women are 25% less likely to smoke cigarettes than men.[71] 42% more men than women drink alcohol and men are 250% more likely to drink once a week.[72] Men are 55% more likely to take an elicit drug than women.[73] One of the leading causes of ill health is the heavy consumption of meat (this is discussed in depth in Chapter 7). Women eat less than half as much meat as men.[74] They eat approximately four ounces, while men go for twelve ounces and eat other's leftovers as well.[75] Women do over 80% of the day-to-day shopping[76] and typically buy a twelve ounce cut of beef for their husbands while choosing a four to five ounce piece for themselves.[77] If they buy pork chops, they buy two for their husbands and one for themselves.[78]

The importance of exercise for health and longevity is disputed by no one. The United States Center for Health Statistics regards "regular exercise" as any exercise done on a **weekly** basis. Even under this rather generous definition, fewer than half of the nation's men exercise regularly. Women are far more likely to exercise than men.[79]

Men are 11% more likely to die of diabetes than women,[80] 77% more likely to die of pneumonia[81] and 100% more likely to die of chronic lung or liver conditions.[82] The death rate from cancer is 47% higher among men on an age-adjusted basis[83] and the age-adjusted death rate from heart disease or stroke is 75% higher among men than women.[84] Whoever classified women as "the weaker sex" obviously had no occasion to review these figures. **On the whole, the death rate for men is 73% higher than it is for women of the same age.**[85]

The facts proving women's superiority over men have been available for a very long time. But in our male-dominated world, where preservation of the myth of male superiority must be maintained at all costs in order to keep the male ego sufficiently inflated, women have been depicted as some form of subspecies to the male. Although **nothing** could be further from the truth, beliefs and prejudices that have been fixed in the mind with age are apparently accepted more readily than fact, effectively perpetuating the myth.

The book that most clearly and convincingly supports the idea that women are superior to men and which shifted my own thinking on the subject is *The Natural Superiority of Women* by Ashley Montagu. Mr. Montagu is a prolific writer and ex-Chairman of the Department of Anthropology at Rutgers University. In the opening of his book, which was first written in 1952 and revised and re-released in 1993, Mr. Montagu makes the statement that, "If in these pages the natural superiority of women is emphasized, it is because the fact has thus far received far too little attention and the time is long overdue that both men and women become aware of it."[86] He then proceeds to demolish every one of the unfounded stereotypes about women that were both brought into existence and perpetuated over the ages by, who else? Men.

It appears that men, **all** men, whether they are aware of it or not, have a deep rooted jealousy of women. This jealousy stems from the fact that it is women who are capable of performing the single most important task in all the world: the creation of new life for the perpetuation of the species. It doesn't matter how smart, successful, powerful, productive or macho a man is, he still can't do the **one** thing that surpasses all other things in importance, no matter what, and that is give birth!

Only women can do that, and men have been looking for ways to measure up since our biblical Adam first learned to think for himself, thanks to the efforts of Eve. And through it all, even if men were to somehow be given the ability to give birth, jealous or not, they'd probably turn down the chance. It's been said many times over that if men had to have babies, few of them would survive the process. I know that I wouldn't race to the front of the line if volunteers were being called upon to see just how well men would fare with pregnancy and childbirth.

So from time immemorial, men have been trying to make the grade and, since they can't conceive and give birth to babies, they instead try to compensate by demonstrating their productive prowess in other areas of endeavor. Haven't we all heard men make statements such as, "this is my brain **child**," or "I **conceived** of an idea and **nursed** it along until I gave **birth** to a plan?" And after having created some great piece of work or come up with some great idea, haven't men stood back and proudly exclaimed, **"That's my baby!"** Why would men, who ordinarily go to such great pains to use masculine phraseology while avoiding anything that would even **suggest** femininity, use these obstetrical expressions with such regularity?

For how long have we heard the standard drivel that women are just too darned emotional to be trusted with important positions? That, unlike men who can repress emotions that are unpleasant to them and stoically maintain "control" and press on with the job at hand, women are crippled by their inability to keep their emotions in check? Men are depicted as the "strong, silent ones" standing with arms crossed, defiantly suppressing their emotions while ministering to the frail "little woman" who, unable to control herself, is reduced to whimpers, unable to cope and in need of sympathy.

Dr. Edgar Berman, whose most famous patient was the late Vice-President Hubert H. Humphrey, once declared that women were not fit to be President because of "raging hormonal imbalances" that rendered them unfit for decision making.[87]

Perhaps you recall in 1988 when Congresswoman Pat Schroeder decided, for personal reasons, not to seek the Presidency of the United States and tearfully told her supporters of her decision at a press conference. There she was on national television wiping tears from her eyes as she shared her innermost feelings. Well, the political pundits (the male ones, of course) had a real field day in their newspaper columns and television commentaries. How on earth could a **woman**, too weak to even maintain her composure for such a minor situation, possibly keep it together when having to deal with the rigors of high-level, world-impacting decisions that would have to be made on a daily basis? Yes, it was far better that she leave these things to the men and their steely dispositions that serve as a coat of armor and prevent them from ever falling victim to an emotion.

It was the classic, typical reaction of those steeped in the myth of male superiority. Are women more emotional than men? **You bet they are!** And it is just one more clear example of their innate sense of what is healthy. Emotions are a natural, **healthy** part of human existence. It's not "unmanly" to display emotions. It's **unhealthy** not to. Women, of course, know this, being far more tuned in to what is necessary to live a life that builds health, not disease.

It should, therefore, come as a surprise to no one that emotionally, all statistics point to the fact that more men suffer from the functional disorders of emotional illness than do women.[88] Men suffer from more ulcers than women.[89] They have more nervous breakdowns than women.[90] There are more men in mental institutions than women,[91] and they commit suicide **four times** more frequently than women.[92] Most men would rather get kicked in the testicles by a mule than exhibit a public display of emotion. Much better to let it seethe and ferment inside until it boils over resulting in some emotional disorder or prostate cancer, but at least they wouldn't have to endure the humiliation of shedding a tear in public.*

I am counting on that certain "something" women possess—that innate, instinctive ability to **know** the best course of action to take in order to insure their well-being. **You have it.** I am convinced! It is part of your biological makeup.

As you read on and learn of what you can do to prevent breast cancer, I know that on a deep level you will be

* I have long been an ardent fan of sarcastic wit. It has, on occasion, gotten me in trouble so I tend to leave it alone. But there's so much fodder here, I couldn't resist. I hope you'll bear with me.

able to grasp and understand the importance of what you need to do and why. You have been systematically convinced that the subject is "over your head" and that you must leave it all up to the experts. That, obviously has not worked to date so it's time now to trust yourself—the **real** expert.

Be absolutely clear that I am **not** asking you to blindly follow my recommendations. I am confident that once you see what I'm suggesting and what it entails to incorporate it into your life-style, that your common-sense, your logic, your inborn wisdom and instinct for self-preservation will all combine to make it clear to you what you need to do. You are so much more capable of taking a more dominant role and making the right decisions for yourself than you may think. As a woman, know how special you are, know how powerful you are. Know that you **can** prevent breast cancer.

Chapter Four

THE WORD
NO ONE WANTS TO HEAR

Cancer. The mere mention of the word is unnerving and understandably so. The only thing as sociated with cancer is pain, suffering and death. Former first lady Betty Ford, a breast cancer victor, says, "To hear the word cancer is almost like hearing the word death."[93]

As stated by the world-renowned health columnist for the *New York Times*, Jane Brody, "Women worry far more about breast cancer than about any other health threat."[93A] Sonya Freedman, host of *Sonya Live*, says it succinctly when she states, "It's every woman's nightmare."[94]

Although the typical breast cancer patient is a woman over age fifty, from 1983 to 1993, cases have risen steadily in all age groups. More young women than ever have gotten the disease. Now, each year eleven thousand American women in their twenties and thirties develop breast cancer. One such woman to develop breast cancer at a young age says, "In the moment of diagnosis, in that one sentence when the doctor says, 'You have cancer,' it's as though everything that matters—every dream, every prayer, every vision, every hope—suddenly has been stomped on and stamped out."[95]

We're all aware of the existence of cancer and all hope and pray in the back of our minds that we never have to deal with it. As I said earlier, it's the disease that people fear the most. But you know, very few people know what cancer is. Do you know? I mean **really** know. You ask your friends if they know what cancer is and they'll all say something to the effect, "of course I know what it is, who doesn't?" But when it comes right down to it, people **don't** know. They know the **results of** cancer and its treatment, but not unless they work in the health field in some capacity do they know what it actually is. And guess what? **Those** people, the researchers, the scientists, the ones who are **supposed** to know, don't know either. That's right. Oh, there are suppositions, presumptions, inferences, theories and hypotheses galore, but when it gets right down to it, the "experts" are still trying to fully understand cancer.

In 1971, then President Nixon inaugurated the formal "War on Cancer" with the National Cancer Act, passed by Congress on December 23, 1971, as a Christmas present to the nation. The National Cancer Institute's budget was more than doubled for the year of 1972,[96] and it was confidently proclaimed that we would have a cure by America's two hundredth birthday celebration in 1976.

The first major assessment of the "War" was fourteen years later. In 1971, one in four developed cancer. Fourteen years later, it increased to one in three.[97] In 1971, two in three families were affected. Fourteen years later, it was three in four.[98] In 1971, the mortality rate, which is truly the most important number of all, was one in six. Fourteen years later, it went to one in five—a twenty-two percent increase.[99]

Dr. John Bailor, a biostatistician at Harvard, was editor of the *Journal of the National Cancer Institute* and worked at the Institute for twenty-five years. In 1986, in the *New England Journal of Medicine*, he coauthored a study of the results of the fight against cancer during the years from 1950 to 1985.[100] According to the researchers, the data they reviewed:

"... provided no evidence that some thirty-five years of intense and growing efforts to improve the treatment of cancer had much overall effect on the most fundamental measure of clinical outcome— death. Indeed, with respect to cancer as a whole, we have slowly lost ground. Incidence of cancer is also increasing, suggesting a failure to prevent or control new or current causes of cancer."

They summed up their report with, "the main conclusion we draw is that some thirty-five years of intense efforts focused largely on improving treatment must be judged a qualified failure." It doesn't get any clearer than that.

Today, over twenty years later, with over thirty-five billion dollars spent on research (that's only federal money, much more than that was spent in private money), one trillion dollars spent on treatment, over seven million deaths, and no closer to a "cure" now than when we were then, it is blatantly obvious that the best and smartest minds medical science has to offer have been confounded and bewildered by cancer. When Carl Rochelle, CNN correspondent, asked if we are **losing** the battle against cancer, Dr. Samuel Epstein, at the University of Chicago Medical Center, answered with sobering directness when he said, "Oh, I think we've really lost the fight against cancer. There have been major increases in cancer rates over the last four decades."[101]

Since President Nixon declared the war on cancer in 1971 until the end of 1994, more than $23 billion has been spent and the overall mortality rate is 8% higher. This has led cancer experts to tell congress that the war against cancer has stalled and that without major changes, it will become the nation's **top killer** in five years.[101A]

The seriousness of all these grim facts make it all the more essential that we focus on prevention. And since prevention is precisely what this book is about, there is no need for me to go into a long, technical, hard-to-under-stand explanation of what cancer is. Quite frankly, what difference does it make if you know exactly what it is or is not. I do, however, have to describe briefly the nature of what cancer is, but only to the extent that it will help you understand how and why the principles which are to follow will help prevent breast cancer. And I promise you, it will be the simplest, most nontechnical, succinct and easily understood description you have ever read.

Many people would probably think it a most daunting challenge to try to demystify and simplify cancer. It has been buried beneath such an avalanche of confusion and jargon that most people perceive it to be too complicated, bewildering and obscure to even try to understand. It's a deep, dark mystery surrounded in perplexity and best left to the professionals who can wade through the quagmire and make some sense of it all. Wrong. That kind of thinking may be convenient for the professionals, but it keeps you out of the decision-making process that could affect your **very life**. It's simply too darned important to be left up to the cancer establishment and the "experts" who, as we have learned, are more baffled by cancer than anything else.

When it comes to anything having to do with health care, your body and medicine, there are two ways you can be given information. One is in an incomprehensible, convoluted way, the other is with straightforward, unencumbered talk. Unfortunately, the former is the standard approach. Allow me to illustrate. I could tell you that I have antecubital and retropopliteal urticaria with pruritus, or I could simply say my arms and legs itch. I could tell you I'm experiencing orthostatic hypotension, or I could tell you I'm dizzy. See the difference? Guess which approach has been used to tell you about cancer? No wonder you may be thinking that it's a subject out of your realm of understanding.

There are probably going to be those unable to accept my contention that cancer, which has been misunderstood and overly complicated, is actually quite a bit more uncomplicated and understandable than we've been led to believe. It all depends on which point of view you choose to consider.

The medical explanation, which is likely the only one you have ever been exposed to, is quite different from that of Natural Hygiene, the field of health care I chose to study. Unless you read about it in *FIT FOR LIFE*, chances are you've never heard of Natural Hygiene. No matter—you get to learn of it now.

Your body is made up of cells. Lots of them. One hundred trillion of them. That's a one with fourteen zeros! Absolutely every part of you is made up of cells, joined together to form your skin, bones, muscles, organs, teeth, hair, fingernails, vocal cords, eyeballs—**everything**. All of these cells, right down to the very last one, are under the jurisdiction and direction of the brain.

To me, the most astounding fact in all of the universe is that every last one of these hundred trillion cells are constantly sending messages to the brain asking for instructions, as it were, and the brain remarkably receives and answers each and every message. The trillions of messages are sent up and back twenty-four hours a day, without stop and all the myriad functions of the body are performed with pinpoint perfection, all **simultaneously!**

Each cell is like a soldier in the army awaiting orders. Every activity, no matter how minuscule, is performed under the direction and supervision of the brain. It is orderly and it is predictable. No cell ever does **anything** unilaterally. And, as is the case with most things in life, there are exceptions. The exception here is....cancer.

This will likely be the most simplistic definition of cancer you have ever encountered. It is straightforward, nontechnical, easy to understand and, as stated, all you will need to know about it in order to see the reasoning behind how the principles to come later work to prevent breast cancer.

A cancer cell is a normal cell so deranged by toxic substances that it loses contact with and is no longer controlled by the brain. It has literally been driven "crazy" by poisoning, and it is "out there on its own." Whereas normal cells divide and stop dividing after a certain fixed time, cancer cells do not. Instead, they proliferate in a disorderly fashion. Two normal cells, placed on a slide will stop growing as soon as they touch each other. Cancer cells, in the same conditions, keep on growing; wildly, and out of control. In **most** cases of cancer, unrestrained cell growth leads to the buildup of tumors which will invade and destroy normal cells.

Obviously, what all the world wants to know is what drives the normal cells crazy. Figure that out and you've figured out cancer. According to the concepts of Natural Hygiene, toxins, or poisons that normal cells are relentlessly forced to come into contact with for years on end, finally drive the normal cells crazy. I will explain this more fully later, but our bodies produce toxins from within as a result of metabolism and we take in toxins from the food and drink we consume. Cancer is the end result in a long, pathological evolution that had its beginning long before any chemical signs of cancer showed up. In other words, what is crucially important for you to realize is that **cancer does not attack, it evolves.**

In all life matters, whether discussing cancer or anything else, we have to operate under the laws of cause and effect. Actions produce reactions. **Cancer will never just happen.** It will inevitably be the result of causes that were not removed over a very long period of time.

Traditional therapies of surgery, radiation and chemotherapy attack the problem at the end stages of its growth, **after the fact**. It is attacking the effect while ignoring the cause. If a woman has a tumor removed from her breast or has a mastectomy and goes right back to the same life-style that brought on the problem in the first place without addressing the cause, health will not be restored and her cancerous condition will then "come back." You will hear, "You've relapsed," or "It's returned," or "We must not have gotten it all." It didn't "come back," it never left! Cutting off a breast and removing a bunch of lymph nodes without removing the **cause** of cancer and thinking that the cancer will not return is like thinking that by picking all the apples off a tree, no more apples will grow.

When the toxic conditions that resulted in abnormal cell growth are removed, then, and only then, will health begin to be restored. This is provided, of course, that the condition has not advanced so far that irreparable harm has been done. Irreparable harm means that negative conditions existed without let up for so long that the diseased state finally resulted in cancer. If that cancer metastasizes, which means it breaks lose from the original site and spreads to other areas of the body, then, obviously, preventive measures are futile and another course of action must be undertaken. This, of course, is the downside in all of this. There **is** an upside as well.

Remember my revealing to you the fact that before cancer could even be detected, the disease had to be progressing for some ten years first? You're not well one day and sick the next. You don't go to sleep in health and wake up with cancer. Disease has seven distinct stages. They take a very long time to develop, and if the cause of the problem is corrected during any of the first six stages, health will be restored and cancer, the seventh stage, **will not develop**. In other words, you have **years** to turn things around, and do what is necessary to prevent cancer from ever developing.

Plus! Your body always, **always**, is striving for the very highest level of health possible. The human body is self-repairing, self-healing and self-maintaining, and as a matter of course persistently martials its forces in a tireless quest to achieve and maintain health. Health is the normal, natural state of your body. Ill health is abnormal and unnatural. When you are healthy, your body automatically directs its efforts toward maintaining that state. When you're in a state of ill health, the body diligently strives to restore health. Every one of the trillions of functions your body performs every day and night without letup are performed as part of the never ending effort to procure and preserve its health.

The same way a ball full of air will shoot up to the surface if submerged in water and then let go, your body strives for optimum health under any and all circumstances. Once the ball is released under water, it can do one thing and one thing only—get up to the surface in as direct a route and quickly as possible. There's no hesitation, it doesn't move side to side, down or stay put, it makes a beeline for the surface. **It can do nothing else**. Your body, in its quest for health, is the same. It is always trying to achieve health in the quickest, most efficient way. The ball in the analogy, can only be kept from rising quickly to the top if it is held down. The only way your body can be prevented from achieving its goal of health is if it is forced to handle more than it can contend with and its defenses are overwhelmed. Even then, it does not give up trying. As long as the body is alive, it is striving for health.

Fortunately for us all, the body has a built in mechanism that warns us when its health is in jeopardy. The more critical the problem, the more intense are the warnings. It has been my experience that most people do not realize that their bodies are trying to get their attention to alert them of impending danger. Because the warnings are not recognized as such, they are either ignored or masked over with drugs. What starts out as a situation that could have been corrected before becoming life threatening is allowed to progress and deteriorate, all too frequently culminating in cancer.

All during the first six stages of disease the body initiates these warnings, and it is absolutely crucial that you don't miss them by failing to realize what they are and what they mean. If you are able to recognize the warnings for what they are, you can take the appropriate measures necessary to protect yourself and prevent the end result of continued neglect which is cancer.

As you read over the description of the seven stages of disease and the warning signs they produce, know that familiarizing yourself with them can not only save you untold heartache, anguish, pain and suffering, but also **your life**.

Chapter Five

THE SEVEN STAGES OF DISEASE

Have you ever heard someone commenting on the severe illness or death of some person by saying something to the effect of, "I can't believe it, he was so healthy." Or, "I just saw her the other day, she looked so great, so healthy."

Be very clear about something, disease, especially cancer, never, **ever** just sneaks up on people and strikes them down. It doesn't happen that way. It takes a long time and a great deal of neglect and abuse for cancer to finally occur. From the first stage of disease to the seventh, cancer, we can be talking about many years. At any step, you can stop its progress. By familiarizing yourself with the seven stages and their warning signals, you put yourself in the position of knowing where you stand in terms of your health so that you can take charge and take control of the situation.

One—ENERVATION

The word enervation comes from the word energy. Energy is the essence of all life. Your very existence is dependent upon how much energy is available at any given time, to carry out **all** of the functions of your body. Enervation is a condition in which the body is either not generating sufficient energy for the tasks it must perform, **or** the tasks the body must perform are greater than the normal energy supply can cope with. When this occurs, the body becomes impaired and generates even less energy. In fact, **all** of the body's functions are impaired and this includes the processes of elimination of the toxic by-products of both metabolism and the residue of foods taken into the body. A certain amount of toxins in the body is totally natural. It is when there are more being produced than are being eliminated that problems arise. This situation results not only in the further inability of the body to restore depleted energy, but it also allows the body to become overladen with this toxic material. (This subject is discussed in more detail in the next chapter.) Since energy is restored when you sleep, the first warning sign you'll receive that you are becoming enervated is that you will become tired and sluggish or require naps and/or more sleep at night. Enervation leads directly to the second stage of disease.

Two—TOXEMIA

(Also referred to as Toxicosis or Autointoxication)

Quite simply, toxemia occurs when the uneliminated toxic material described above starts to saturate the blood, lymph and tissues of the body. The body, of course, recognizes this situation that **must** be remedied and, in an attempt to cleanse itself and maintain its integrity, it initiates a flushing out of the toxins. Two results can be expected when this happens. First, more recognizable warnings in the form of discomfort occurs, and second, the process places an even greater burden on the body's energy supply. If a person is also overworked, or under stress or getting insufficient rest and sleep—all energy sappers—the feelings of tiredness and sluggishness become more pronounced. At a certain level of toxemia when the toxins must be forced out, the next stage of disease develops.

Three—IRRITATION

Whereas with enervation the only recognizable warning sign is a feeling of tiredness or fatigue, toxemia and the resulting irritation brings forth other more recognizable warning symptoms. In fact, the entire purpose of this stage is designed to make you aware of the rising

72

level of toxemia in your body in the hope you will pay heed to the warnings and take the appropriate corrective steps to remove them.

Irritation is a condition where the body sets in motion its defensive mechanisms and speeds up its internal activities for the purpose of unloading toxins that have been stored up. This can happen at various points in the body. Although irritation is not so painful that you would go to a doctor for treatment, it is sufficiently unpleasant to make us seek out a way to relieve ourselves of the discomfort it produces. It is the body's way of prodding us into action.

An obvious example of irritation is the urge to urinate or have a bowel movement. This is not painful, unless of course it is ignored for a long time, and then it becomes so painful you can think of nothing else but relieving yourself. The bowels and bladder are clearly a most obvious means by which waste and toxins are removed from the body. Less obvious is when toxins are removed at other sites in the body. Unless we are specifically educated to acknowledge the warnings given to us by our bodies for what they are, we are likely apt to dismiss them as merely the minor discomforts of daily life instead of recognizing them as the valuable gifts they are.

Examples of classic warning symptoms produced by irritation will be totally familiar to you. That is because since we have all managed, at one time or another, to toxify our systems, we've all had the opportunity to experience the results of doing so.

A common warning signal of irritation due to toxemia within the body, is itchiness. The skin is not only the body's largest organ, it is also an organ of elimination. The body freely and regularly uses the four billion-some pores that make up our skin to remove toxins from within the body, from the top of your head to the bottom of your feet and everywhere in between. If **any** part of your skin becomes itchy, that is a classic sign that toxins are being removed, and when they reach the surface of the skin that area becomes irritated and itchy. It's not serious or even particularly painful, but it is bothersome, which is the body's way of getting your attention. At this stage only if it is ignored and nothing is done to remove the cause of the problem, does the itchiness progress to something far more troublesome. This will be discussed in stage four.

Not everyone experiences itchy skin in a state of irritation. Others feel queasy or nauseous for no apparent reason and at all different times of day, but particularly in the morning when the body is in its elimination cycle. You may feel a persistent tickle in the nose which is another form of irritation. Yet another is to feel jumpy or uneasy or on edge, so that you "fly off the handle" for no apparent reason. If you find yourself uncharacteristically short tempered or easily aggravated, those are signs of irritation. Certainly you've heard people say things like, "She's so irritable all the time," or "Don't irritate him, he's in a bad mood." People feel irritated because their bodies are in a state of irritation. It's that simple.

Other warning signs include nervousness, depression, anxiety and worry, especially when those traits are usually out of character for you. You may start to have more frequent headaches, or have minor aches and pains in other areas of your body. If you find it more difficult to fall asleep or sleep fitfully, that is another indication of irritation. So is putting on weight. Other classic indicators are coated tongue, bad breath, increased body odor and sallow complexion, especially dark circles under the eyes. Women may experience out of the ordinary menstrual problems or heavier menstrual flow.

You may be thinking, "Good grief, is anything **not** a warning signal?" That's pretty accurate. When the body is toxemic it will try anything to get your attention.

Unfortunately, people live **years** in a state of irritation without ever knowing what's beating them up. It's not serious enough to go for treatment so they just "live with it." But when the effects of enervation, toxemia and irritation are ignored long enough and the toxic residue that started the whole thing in motion in the first place builds to a higher concentration, the forth stage of disease ultimately results.

Four—INFLAMMATION

Inflammation is the body's most intense effort to cleanse and restore itself. This is when you become keenly aware of a problem, for it involves pain. Pain is not something that occurs haphazardly or without cause. It is not punishment for some indiscretion. **Pain has purpose**. It's the body's **most** effective warning signal. It is specifically designed to alert you to the fact that without corrective measures you are endangering yourself. The body is now more desperately attempting to get rid of the ever increasing level of toxemia before it causes devastating damage.

Precious few people realize that this is a cleansing, **healing** mode of the body as it tries to fix itself. It is instead looked upon as an "attack" against your well-being, so it is off to the doctor in search of relief. And sure enough, the doctor **will** find signs of pathology, which, more often than not, will be treated with drugs. The drugs do **nothing** to remove the **cause** of the problem. They serve only to lessen the pain of the problem. Unfortunately, in doing so, they add to the level of toxemia while giving the false impression that the problem is being handled.

With inflammation the toxins in the system have usually been concentrated in a particular organ or a particular area of the body (the breasts perhaps) for a massive eliminative effort. The area becomes inflamed due to the constant irritation from toxic material. When inflammation exists, we are diagnosed with one or more of the "itises." "Itis" at the end of a word literally means "inflammation of." So tonsillitis means inflammation of the tonsils. Appendicitis—inflammation of the appendix. Hepatitis—inflammation of the liver. Nephritis—inflammation of the kidneys. Arthritis—inflammation of the joints. Colitis—inflammation of the colon. A cold with inflammation of the sinus cavities is rhinitis with sinusitis. The list of "itises" goes on interminably. When a lymph node becomes inflamed, it enlarges and becomes tender. It is called "lymphadenitis."[102] A swollen lymph node or gland is one of the body's most obvious warnings that a cleansing of built up toxins is long overdue. (The lymph system is discussed more fully in the next chapter.)

I spoke in stage three about the irritation of the skin. When that is allowed to progress, it results in dermatitis—inflammation of the skin. Eczema and psoriasis are particularly severe types of dermatitis and are most obvious and recognizable examples of the body using its reparative powers to forcibly push toxins right out through the skin. Corrective measures at this juncture that lower toxic levels in the body will invariably clear up this malady. I have seen it first hand on numerous occasions.

Sadly, however, that is often not the course of action taken. Rather, the painful symptoms are suppressed with drugs. The pain may temporarily go away, but the problem doesn't. When the cleansing efforts of the body **are** suppressed with drugs, the level of toxicity increases until other organs become effected as well—not only with the toxins already in the body but also with the added toxicity of the drugs that are administered.

This stage is a most pivotal juncture in terms of whether or not you are going to recover your health or fall deeper into the diseased state. You are right in the middle of the seven stages and your actions now are crucial. If the condition of the body's general toxification is unceasing, it will result in the next stage of disease.

Five—ULCERATION

The fifth stage means that the body has been under assault for such a long time that massive amounts of cells and tissue are being destroyed. This condition is often intensely painful for there are exposed nerves. Lesions or ulcers can occur inside or outside of the body. An example of an ulcer on the inside is the classic ulcer in the stomach, a hole is literally opened up. Those who have experienced this type of ulcer know all too well how much pain is associated with it. An example of an ulcer on the outside of the body is a canker sore on the mouth, or an open, oozing sore on the arm or leg. While the body may use an ulcer as an outlet to rid itself of toxins, it will heal the ulcer if the level of toxemia is sufficiently lowered. Following on the heels of ulceration is the process the body goes through to seal these wounds.

Six—INDURATION

Scarring is a form of induration, which is a hardening of tissue or the filling in of tissue where it has been lost, such as with an ulcer. But this hardening has real direction and purpose. The toxic material that is threatening the well-being of the body is encapsulated in a sack of hardened tissue. This is a way of quarantining the toxic material, holding it in one place so it will not spread freely throughout the body. The sack is what is referred to as a tumor and is very often diagnosed as cancer when, in fact, no cancer exists.

Induration is the last stage during which the body is still in control of its cells. Should the destructive practices discussed so far which brought matters to this stage be continued, cells will start to "go crazy." They will become parasitic, living off of whatever nutrients they can obtain, but contributing nothing to the body in return. The constant poisoning has finally altered their genetic encoding and they become wild and disorganized. When cells go wild in this manner, the condition is called cancer.

Seven—CANCER

This is the end point in the long evolution of disease and if the causes that brought it about to begin with are continued it is usually fatal. Body vitality is at a very low level, cells are no longer under the control of the brain, but are rather multiplying wildly in an unorganized manner. Although in the best of circumstances, with a most healthy regimen, cancer **can** be arrested and reversed, it would take a diligent, concentrated effort. The entire purpose of this book is to show you how to prevent this stage from ever occurring.

Contrary to what a staggering number of women think, especially those who have been diagnosed with cancer, your very best friend, your greatest ally in your quest for health and the prevention of breast cancer, is your body. **Never, ever doubt that.** I cannot tell you how many times I have heard women describe their breasts as their enemy. As though they were somehow separate and apart from their bodies and acting on their own. Look at the following statement made by a woman interviewed on a program on breast cancer aired on PBS: "I had a feeling of wanting very much to get rid of my breasts—they had become my enemies. I wanted rid of them, they were something that was going to kill me."[103] Nothing in all of the universe, could be further from the truth. **Nothing!**

People may view the human body as a lot of different parts that are separate from each other, but the body does no such thing. Every part of the body is as sacred and as important and as cherished and as protected as any other. The breasts are just as important and receive just as much healing attention as any other part of the body, be it the heart, lungs, teeth, skin, eyes, intestines or any other part. No part receives more or less attention than any other. If something is amiss somewhere in the body, energy is sent to that area in an attempt to correct the problem. And as part of the wisdom inherent in every cell, the body sends messages to us to alert us of any impending problem.

All through the first six stages of disease just described, the body gives incessant warnings. If the warnings are understood and corrective measures are taken, the warnings stop. If they are not understood and the same habits are persisted in, the warnings become progressively more acute. This built-in mechanism is as automatic as the eyes blinking when necessary or blood flowing through the veins. This warning system is yet one more beautiful example of the magnificence of the human body. But all the body can do is warn us to make a change, it can't make the changes for us.

Have you ever been driving down the road and all of a sudden you notice a red light flashing on your dash board indicating a problem of some sort? What do you do when you see that red light? Do you ignore it in the hope that it will just go away? Do you cover it with tape so you don't have to see it? Or do you take the car into the repair shop as soon as possible to see what the problem is?

The people who build cars have managed to figure out how to put a built-in warning system into them to prevent the destruction of the car. In your wildest imaginations do you think that God forgot to do the same for us? **No! She didn't!*** No way that God, in her infinite, limitless wisdom would forget such a crucially important

---

* Periodically throughout this book I refer to God. Some people see God as a male, some as a female and some as a force or power that encompasses both. But it always creates a bit of a problem knowing whether to refer to God as he or she. So, for the purposes of this book, which will probably be read by far more women than men, I'm going to refer to God in the feminine. Hope you don't mind. Thanks.

component in our bodies as a warning system to protect us from harm.

You must keep in mind that health is natural and illness is not. The body always strives to maintain a healthy state. If health is threatened and warnings appear, it means that the body has not been provided the best circumstances for maintaining its health and is trying to deal with an overload of toxins. At this point, if the causes of the warnings are corrected and the requirements of health are provided, illness will progress no further, the warnings will cease and health will again return. On the other hand, if the warning signals are suppressed or ignored, the toxic overload will not be removed. More serious illness will ensue with the final end point being cancer.

Make it a priority to become sensitive to the warnings that have been described and to the steps you need to take to remove them, which I will be delineating shortly, and you are well on your way to learning how you **can** prevent breast cancer.

Chapter Six

THE CLEAN MACHINE

If you could be granted **one** gift, what would it be? Imagine being given the opportunity to have **one** wish fulfilled, no matter what it was. What would you request? Perhaps your immediate reaction might be to wish for some mind-boggling amount of money, more than could be spent in a lifetime. But upon reflection, most people invariably say that they would wish for uninterrupted, unwavering health. Think about it; to not only be free of any illness whatsoever, but also free of the **fear** of developing an illness. After all, what good is a lot of money if you're too sick to enjoy it? If money could buy health, there would be no sick rich people.

Everybody wants to be healthy! And of late there has been an encouraging surge in the number of people taking personal responsibility for their health. It's not what science or medicine has done for them, it's what they have done for **themselves.** The last ten years have produced a literal army of people who have discovered the benefits of upgrading their diets and participating in some regular form of exercise.

If you have not yet joined them, this is your time, your opportunity. You **can** have control over your level of health. You **can** have a say in the length and quality of your life. You **can** prevent breast cancer. You **can!** And more and more women are becoming aware of that fact every day. The beauty of this revelation is that **taking** control and **being** in charge of your health is not all that complicated. Oh, I know you've been conditioned to

81

believe that it is, but it **isn't!** Plus, you can turn the tide in your favor almost immediately, depending upon how long it takes you to finish this book.

I know that the entire subject of breast cancer has been complicated to the point of mass confusion and frustration, so I can easily relate to some who may be skeptical of my promise to show you how you can learn how to prevent it with the reading of one book. No problem. I can handle skepticism. It's apathy born of frustration that I have to conquer. But if you will give it a chance and just **try** what is suggested, I will succeed, as will you.

You are going to learn not only **what** you need to do and **why**, but also **how**. There is a component in the quest to prevent breast cancer that is absolutely essential, possibly more crucial than any other, but that has somehow, astonishingly, been overlooked.

Of course, you must be eager to know exactly what I am talking about. What **is** this certain something, this **special ingredient** that will make your goal to live free of the fear of breast cancer so much easier to attain? To introduce it to you, I would like to use an analogy. This analogy has to do with your car. Since practically everyone either has a car or relies somehow on cars, it is likely that there will be no difficulty in relating to the analogy.

In one respect, understanding the intricacies of the engine of a car and how all the parts interact to make the car run can be a real challenge. On the other hand, its basic operation is rather simple: put in fuel and the car will continue to run and serve its owner in an endless number of ways for a very long time. Your body is like the car in that you give it fuel (food) which it converts into energy which it uses to perform the myriad functions necessary to accomplish all the activities of life.

In order to keep the car in good running condition, periodically you **must** change the oil. If you didn't, the inner workings of the car would quickly become silted up with sludge and break down. Neglected long enough, the oil would ultimately become so thick with this sludge that it would become solid. The car cannot run under these circumstances. The dirty oil must be replaced with clean oil on a regular basis. There is no amount of **external** cleaning that will substitute for this **inner** cleaning. You can wash, shine, polish, paint or detail the car until it is the best **looking** car on the block. But it won't run if the inside of the engine is filthy.

Precisely the same scenario holds true for the human body, and understanding this is the key in preventing breast cancer. **The inside of your body must also be cleansed regularly or it too will become silted up.** The result can be not only breast cancer but all manner of ill health. Just as the oil in your car's engine becomes dirtier and dirtier as time passes, a certain amount of toxic residue is continuously generated in your system as a normal and natural result of your body's biological processes and your daily living habits. This waste **must** be eliminated from every area of the body.

Fortunately, your body **does** have the mechanism to expel it. But it **can**, under certain commonly experienced circumstances, be overwhelmed. The result is a dangerous and harmful buildup of this toxic matter. Where exactly does the waste come from? Some is produced inside the body by the replacement of billions of old cells with new ones every day. The old cells are toxic, **highly** poisonous, and they **must not** remain in the body. The rest is produced from the food and drink that is consumed daily. The residue that is not incorporated into new cell structure is waste that must be cleansed from your system.

Like anything else you can think of, the cleaner the body is, the better it works. We clean our houses, our tools, our closets, our garages, our typewriters, our stoves, our offices, our clothes, our cars, and we fanatically, in some cases, clean the **outside** of our bodies. It is peculiar in the extreme that such a simple and essential prerequisite of a healthy life, that of cleansing the inside of the body, has so consistently been ignored. It's not taught in school. It's not taught in college. **It's not taught!**

Hundreds of billions of dollars are spent a year on health care, but the entire expenditure revolves around expensive screening tests, expensive drugs and other exorbitant treatments, all of which are designed to address problems **after they** occur. The entire subject of prevention to which there is continuous lip service paid and of which the detoxification or cleansing from the body of accumulated toxins and waste matter is the centerpiece, is completely neglected.

This is a tragedy of considerable proportion because detoxifying the body, or "cleansing," the word I prefer to use because it is easier to relate to, will do more to lay the groundwork for prevention than practically any other measure you as an individual can take. **If there is, in fact, such a thing as a "secret" or a "key" to health, the cleansing of the inner body is surely it.** That is one of the reasons why organizations that attempt to assist people in overcoming drug and alcohol addiction call their programs "detoxification programs." They are literally eliminating their patients' dependencies on drugs by **cleansing** the drugs from their bodies.

My goal is to get you to understand that until the inside of your body is cleansed and rejuvenated, you remain at risk of developing breast cancer. Once this cleansing **has** been accomplished and you start to enjoy the rewards it brings, it will make you wonder with genuine curiosity how you could ever have missed a tool of such inestimable value.

Isn't it fascinating that whenever the subject of caring for the body comes up, it's **always** in the context of what should or should not be put into the body? Put in more fiber. Don't put in so much fat. Put in pure water. Don't put in chemicals, additives and pesticides. Put in this or that nutritional supplement. Don't put in refined salt or sugar. Ever notice that there's **never** a discussion about what should come **out**?

The missing link in experiencing the radiant health that we all strive for and which is still eluding so many is yours for the asking. You merely have to grasp the value of **doing** what is necessary to cleanse and rejuvenate the **inside** of your body. Interesting, isn't it, that I used the analogy of the car and the letters **C A R** are the first letters of **Cleanse And Rejuvenate**, the three-word phrase I am now emphasizing and will be explaining further throughout this book? Whenever you use your car, let the fact that it must periodically have the old, dirty oil replaced with clean oil be a reminder to you that your body deserves at **least** as much attention as your car. And don't worry, by the end of the book you'll have all the tools you need to show you what steps you can take to minimize the harmful buildup of waste in your body, and you will see exactly how to accomplish the regular **C**leansing **A**nd **R**ejuvenation I am so strongly suggesting.

In order to accomplish the goal of cleansing, or in order to accomplish **any goal**, for that matter, there is one decisive element that must always be present. It is the one commodity that everyone knowingly or unknowingly wants, the one that will allow you to do everything you wish to do in life, the one that you can never have too much of. No, it's not money. It's **energy!** Energy is the very essence of your life. When it is plentiful, all things are possible. You feel you are omnipotent. When it dwindles, life becomes an ordeal and you find yourself at the mercy of all the forces around you. When energy is completely absent, life is over.

Amazing stuff, this energy. You can't see it or hold it in your hands, but you sure as heaven know when someone around you has it. And you certainly know when **you** have it. As human beings, we literally **are** energy systems. The truth is, there is not one activity or process of the body that can or will be performed without energy. Everything that you do and everything that your body does requires energy.

Back to the car analogy. What good would your car be to you if it had no engine? What good would the engine be to you if you had no car to put it in? Cleansing and energy levels are **that** interrelated. So much so that we are practically dealing with a "catch 22" in that we **must** have energy to cleanse and we must cleanse to have more energy. Just as the body in its unfathomable wisdom allots energy to circulation and the constant beating of your heart, it is also acutely in tune with the need to regularly cleanse itself of deleterious waste and it automatically allots or conserves a certain amount of energy to do this.

Throughout nature, all forms of life herald the spring season with signs of rebirth. Flowers bloom, hibernating animals awaken, new life appears everywhere. And spring also invokes the age old tradition of house cleaning or "spring cleaning," when we go from the attic to the cellar getting rid of the old and starting fresh. This commendable industriousness must also be extended to the most precious possession of all: your body. I am sure you have at some time thought of a real "spring cleaning" for your home. My goal is to convince you to care about your body in the same way. When you care for your body, it cares for you. That caring is best exemplified by allowing it to function at its greatest level of efficiency. And that is **only** possible when it is cleansed of that which would interfere with its smooth operation.

Isn't the word CARE a beautiful word? It can be used to express so much feeling or concern:

"I care about what you are feeling."

"My mother is such a caring person."

"She took such good care of me."

"I care for you."

"He sure does take good care of himself."

There is something about the word CARE that brings to mind positive feelings: help, empathy, compassion, concern, love.

I now wish to introduce you to a brand new meaning for the word CARE, and this meaning is a major reason why this book was written. I have presented how crucial it is in your quest to prevent breast cancer to cleanse and rejuvenate the inside of your body. I have also touched on the pivotal role energy plays in the cleansing process. Remember the car analogy and the observation that C A R was also the three first letters of Cleanse And Rejuvenate? Now take the "E" from the beginning of the word energy and put it at the end of the word car. You have **CARE— CLEANSE AND REJUVENATE ENERGETICALLY**. That is the new meaning of the word care that will insure for you a long and healthy life. **CAREing** for your body is the best possible health insurance you'll ever have. This process that I call **CARE**—**C**leansing **A**nd **R**ejuvenating **E**nergetically—is the ultimate tool in preventing breast cancer. Understanding the dynamics of how toxins are stored up and removed from your body is the key to understanding the importance of making CARE an integral part of your everyday life-style.

The accumulation and elimination of a considerable amount of toxic waste matter in the body is a physiological fact of life. The question of the moment is:

where does all this waste come from and, more importantly, when more is built up than is removed, where does it go? There are two sources that produce toxins in the body. The first is generated entirely from internal sources, the second from external sources. The body is essentially a machine that requires fuel, turns that fuel into energy in order to carry out its many functions, and generates waste in the process. Just like a car.

When I speak of internal waste, I am referring to the regeneration of the trillions of cells in our bodies. Literally hundreds of billions of old cells are replaced with new cells every single day! The worn out, spent cells are toxic and must be eliminated, and the body, knowing this, uses the eliminative organs, the bowels, bladder, lungs and skin, to get rid of them. This cell replacement process is an automatic phenomenon. It is as spontaneous a process as is the circulation of blood or the digestion of food. We have no control over this internal waste production. It is involuntary and independent of our involvement.

It is in the area of the waste generated as a result of what we put into our bodies that we have the most control. This waste is the end product of all the metabolic activities occurring in every cell of the body. Every cell is a miniature "body" in its own right, taking in what it requires and excreting its wastes. Problems only arise when the buildup of toxins exceeds that which the body can eliminate via the eliminative organs. It's very simple. If, on a daily basis, more toxins are produced than are removed, the excess remains in the body where all manner of problems can develop because of it. (The extent to which this relates to lumps in the breasts and breast cancer will be expounded upon in the next chapter.)

How sad it is that the prevailing opinion of traditional medicine ignores entirely the need for inner cleansing. This tragic oversight of the basic process of cleansing results in all the clogged, choked off and self-poisoned bodies that are unnecessarily treated with drugs and surgery. If only it were true that our bodies do not get dirty, and that cleansing is not an issue! However, the proof that that is not the case is all around us.

It is an undeniable fact that millions of people are walking around with distended abdomens due to a buildup of waste that has not been eliminated. They spend a fortune on laxatives each year because they cannot have something so natural and basic as regular bowel movements without drugs. Millions of others have skin problems or high blood pressure. Others have sinus and respiratory problems. All are the result of dirty bodies. It is terribly naive to think that all wastes are removed from the body.

The body can only get rid of so much. It **can** be overburdened. Think of a bathtub full of water. If you pull the plug but leave the water running and more is going into the tub than is leaving it, what is the only inevitable result? The tub will overflow. When this happens inside the body with toxins, it spells disease. If it were true that the body always rids itself of that which is harmful or inappropriate, it is unlikely that nearly a million people a year would be losing their lives due to **clogged** arteries. These arteries are not clogged with good intentions! They're clogged with sticky, toxic waste matter that the body **wanted** to get rid of and **should** have gotten rid of but couldn't.

If you lived in a house in which you did not clean the floors, did not empty the garbage, did not wash the bedding, did not wash the dishes or the windows or periodically dust, you **could** survive there, but what would it be like? Perhaps you are saying right now, "Who in their right mind would ever let a house go like that?" Right! But you must understand that far too many people are unknowingly allowing this kind of neglect right inside their own bodies. The principles of **CARE** presented later in this book are going to make sure that you are not one of those people. It is designed to allow your cleansing mechanism to operate at optimum efficiency so you will not suffer from breast cancer, one of the consequences of a body overwhelmed by toxins.

Chapter Seven

YOUR VERY BEST FRIEND

I sincerely hope you realize how exquisite you are, how magnificent your body is, what wisdom it possesses. It is capable of performing tasks in such prodigious numbers, and with such perfection, that to even try to comprehend the extent of the intelligence of your body is fruitless. You are a marvel of creation.

There are those in the biological and physiological sciences who are convinced that we will **never** fully fathom the depth of the intelligence of the human body. The brain alone is beyond comprehension. The most sophisticated computer ever devised doesn't hold a candle to the intricacies of the brain. Joined with the other components of your structure, your body is unmatched in power, capacity and adaptability.

Did you know that your body is comprised of one hundred **trillion** cells all working in perfect harmony with one another? Each organ is a marvel in itself. The heart pumping six quarts of blood through 96,000 miles of blood vessels. The digestive tract turning food into flesh and blood. Balance always being maintained, temperature always being kept stable. Lungs supplying oxygen to the cells. Over two hundred bones and over six hundred muscles working together to enable you to move in any direction at any time you wish. Hearing that allows you to enjoy music. Eyes to behold the glories of a sunset. Sense of smell to marvel at the scent of a rose. Taste buds to take pleasure from food. And more activities, too numerous to list, all proceeding with extraordinary precision, **simultaneously** for one hundred years or more, if need be.

It is staggering to try to grasp the infinite intelligence necessary to coordinate the activities and precision of the human body. We can only stand in humble awe of it.

There is a force, an energy, that resides in each of us that directs and governs all of the functions described above and more. It is that energy that was able to transform you from an almost infinitesimal bit of protoplasm into the astonishing being you are today.

It is that energy that "knows" instantaneously what to do if you should cut your finger. Without any stimulation on your part, the blood coagulates, a scab forms, the wound seals itself, the scab falls off and presto, no more cut. What is it that heals a broken bone after a fracture? Is it the cast and sling? Of course not. It is the wisdom and power of the body that heals. A complicated process involving the creation of brand new structure which is identical to the process that produced the bone originally is carried out.

The body does it for itself automatically as part of its never ending quest for self-preservation. A substance more powerful than any glue is secreted by the bone at both points of fracture, and the two segments are reunited as strongly or stronger than before the break. This process is neither chemical nor physical. It is biological! Even if you were to fall and break several bones and receive several cuts, **all** of them would be healed simultaneously, while all the other myriad functions of the body were also being performed. Such is the power inherent in the energy that directs the activities of the human body.

This energy, this force that has been with you since the beginning of your life, **never leaves you** as long as you are alive. It is an integral part of your very existence. This energy that miraculously heals wounds is **always** there to carry out other, even more serious healing. From this point on you can be totally confident that whether you are in a state of exuberant health or failing health this energy is **automatically** striving for your highest possible level of health under **all** circumstances. **It can do nothing else!** It is why it exists. It is with you **fully** at this very moment and always will be. My goal is to create in you a sense of reverence for this powerful energy, reverence that will lead you to support your body in its ability and effort to prevent breast cancer.

It is precisely in this area of acknowledgment of, and appreciation for, the remarkable power of the body to protect and heal itself that the "experts" have somehow managed to commit the most astonishing oversight in all the history of the healing professions. Do you recall in Chapter Two all the statements that were made declaring "We don't know, we don't know, we don't know?" **This chapter is what they don't know!** What boggles the mind so, is that what they have missed is so glaringly obvious that there's really no accounting for **why** it has been missed. It's just one of those unexplained mysteries.

I wonder if you happen to have a recollection similar to one I have that goes something like this: as a youngster I was asked by my mother to get the butter from the refrigerator and bring it to the dinner table. "Sure, Mom," I said as I jumped up from the table and headed for the fridge. After opening the refrigerator door this conversation ensued up and back from the kitchen to the dining room in loud voices:

"It's not here, Mom."

"It certainly is. I put it there myself."

"I'm looking all over. It's not here."

"Open your eyes. It's right in the front."

"I'm tellin' you, Mom, my eyes are open. It's not here!"

"Don't make me come in there and get it myself."

"Mom! Somebody must have taken it already."

At this point she strode into the kitchen, walked up to me and the open refrigerator and, without so much as a glance, reached in and picked up the butter dish which was on the middle shelf **right in front!** I couldn't believe I was looking right at it and didn't see it. If it were any closer to me, it would have stained my shirt.*

It may not be the most appropriate analogy in the world, but what the authorities in breast cancer have missed should have been as obvious to them as the butter dish should have been to me. The only difference is that my oversight has not resulted in the unnecessary loss of life.

By now you must be asking, "My God, what is it? What did they miss?" Only the single most important factor we have in the prevention of breast cancer. It falls under the category of "the dynamics of the human body." Herein lies the most fundamental difference between the standard medical approach and that of Natural Hygiene. Hygiene looks at the human body as dynamic and capable, always aware of problems that may exist and constantly on top of dealing with them. Medicine looks at the human body as a hapless victim, forever at the mercy of any and all malevolent beasts that may attack it.

Specifically, I am talking about the body's lymph system. This magnificent system's purpose has been misunderstood and its activities have been misinterpreted. As part of the incredible intelligence of the human body there are several systems that perform seemingly miraculous functions. The nervous system, cardiovascular system, respiratory system, digestive system, reproductive system, musculoskeletal system and the lymph system which is an integral part of the body's defense system. Your body is infinitely capable of defending and protecting itself.

---

* I don't think I'll ever forget the look on my mom's face when she picked up that butter dish. She gave me the kind of look that was a cross between annoyance and disgust that she might give if she saw someone pick his nose and wipe it on his sleeve.

Our creator thought of absolutely **everything** when She made our bodies. She didn't forget something as critically important and essential as a mechanism to protect itself against disease. That is the defense system, erroneously referred to as the "immune system." There is no such thing as an "immune system." It would be lovely if we could be made to be "immune," but it doesn't work that way. And you may think I am merely splitting hairs by calling it the "defense system" rather than the "immune system." Not so.

If you hold a loaded gun to your head and pull the trigger, there is no immunity to blowing your brains out. And there is no immunity to violating the laws of nature for years on end and not having to pay the price for doing so. People have been convinced that they can regularly live a life, the only possible consequence being ill health, and then run to the doctor for a pill or shot that will make everything O.K., as if all past transgressions can be swept away by some potion. That's delusionary thinking that ultimately leads to one's demise.

So throughout the book, whenever I refer to what is called the "immune system," I will be calling it the "defense system." If I do need to use the term "immune system" because it is more convenient, I will be putting the words in quotes so that you will know what I am referring to is the "defense system."

As far as preventing breast cancer is concerned, your success in doing so lies in understanding the lymph system which is the heart and soul of the body's defense mechanism. It is not at all complicated. You already know something of it. Most of what you know about the "immune system" is actually the work of the lymph system. And I am sure you are well aware of the fact that whenever there is a discussion of breast cancer, lymph nodes are invariably involved. You can be certain that that is no coincidence.

I have mentioned the words "toxins" or "toxic waste" or "toxicity" so many times already in this book that you may be getting tired of reading them. But it is for a very good reason that they have been mentioned so many times.

If you recall the chapter where the seven stages of disease were discussed; right from the second stage on, the role that toxins play all along the way in the development of cancer was made abundantly clear. Toxins are a **major** contributing factor in the development of cancer and there is just no getting around this fact. No understanding of cancer will ever be reached if the role played by toxemia is not also understood.

If toxins are allowed to build up and remain in your body, they **will** eventually cause harm to some degree— anything from general aches and pains all the way to cancer. If, however, they are removed from the body on a regular basis so that what is being built up is not allowed to exceed what is eliminated, your system will be kept sufficiently clean to prevent cancer from ever getting started. Does it not, therefore, make all the sense in the world to do whatever you possibly can to assist and facilitate the mechanism in your body responsible for removing toxins?

How fortunate we are that our bodies are equipped with such supreme intelligence. You may not have ever thought specifically about it before, but isn't it absolutely amazing that your body knows how to turn an apple into blood? It's really quite a remarkable feat if you think about it. In this highly technologically-advanced world, there is no scientist anywhere on earth that can go into a laboratory and turn a food into blood. Yet our bodies accomplish this formidable task as a matter of course right along with all of the other equally impressive feats they perform. It is with the same intelligence, ability and precision that the body performs **all** of its functions, **including the removal of toxins from the body**. Enter the lymph system.

Do you remember a few years back when the New York City Department of Sanitation went on strike and refused to pick up any garbage? I don't recall how long the strike lasted, but I do know it was long enough to become an abominable situation for New Yorkers. The mere sight of huge stockpiles of garbage virtually everywhere you looked was depressing enough, but such a prodigious amount of garbage accumulated that it actually blocked sidewalks for pedestrians and, in some instances, spewed out into the streets impeding traffic. Worse yet, was the sickening stench which was horrendous enough to take the enamel off your teeth.

Every day the news on television brought us pictures of the ever worsening crisis and the comments of frustrated and disgusted New Yorkers. It was, in no uncertain terms, a great big ugly, stinking mess that if not corrected would have eventually shut down the city. Guess what I'm getting at? **The lymph system is, quite literally, your body's garbage collector.** Although it **can** be overwhelmed and forced to try to contend with more than it possibly can, fortunately for us, **our** garbage collector **never** goes on strike. It is hard at work twenty-four hours a day in its never-ending effort to keep the inside of the body clean and healthy.

I have tried the best I can to give you a sense of the magnificence of your body, of the incomprehensible wisdom by which it is governed. And you can be totally confident that the incomparable intelligence with which the lymph system carries out its many functions is no exception. The lymph system is an astounding network of fluid, organs, nodes and nodules, ducts, glands and vessels that continuously and aggressively cleanse the system of waste matter. Millions upon millions of nodes, some minuscule, some large, guard the passages into the body against the intrusion of destructive substances. Placed end to end in a straight line all the lymph vessels in the body would cover a distance in excess of 100,000 miles. They would circle the globe **four times!**[104] There is three times as much lymph fluid in your body as there is blood.[104.1] That should tell you something of its importance.

Unlike the circulatory blood system, the lymph system carries fluid only **away** from the tissues.[105] It picks up wastes from all the cells and, through a complex series of processes, breaks them down and arranges their elimination from the body. It is also involved in the production of white blood cells (lymphocytes) that seek out, capture and destroy foreign substances such as bacteria and other "invaders," and removes them from the body as well.

Except for cartilage, nails and hair, your entire body is bathed in lymph. If you could somehow see a picture of the inside of your body and the network of glands and nodes, you would see what looked like an extremely fine sheath of lace totally covering and saturating everything. You can actually feel some lymph nodes where they are close to the surface of your skin. On the sides of your neck, under your chin, under your arms and where your legs meet your torso are places where you can most easily feel lymph nodes.

If you would like to actually see some unusually large lymph nodules, open your mouth and look at your tonsils. This, of course, will not be possible for a huge segment of the population, because before it was realized how extremely important and beneficial the tonsils were, they were unceremoniously removed willy-nilly as though they were some mistake of nature. Now that it is known what an integral part of the lymph system they are and that they form a protective ring of lymph tissue around the opening between the nasal and oral cavities that provide protection against bacteria and other potentially harmful materials,[106] they are allowed to stay where God put them.

The tonsils, represent a perfect illustration of the lack of understanding of and respect for the lymph system that it most assuredly deserves. The attitude of expendability of the tonsils, which does not recognize the crucial role they play, speaks loudly of the accuracy of my contention that this marvel of creation—the lymph system—has been minimized and overlooked as the protector of our health that it is.

I remember travelling through London in 1988 and, while reading the local newspaper there, I saw an article with the headline, "Tonsils Bargain." Evidently in an effort to facilitate the removal of these troublesome and obviously useless organs, physicians gave their time free and set up an assembly line so that over two weekends 152 children could have their tonsils removed at a very low cost. According to the head of the health department who arranged the "Tonsils Bargain," "We did 128 operations last Easter and it was such a success we thought we would repeat the exercise."[107]

I myself had my tonsils summarily removed at age three. In those days (late 1940's), it was almost automatic. The tonsils were looked upon as some sort of affliction that God stuck in our throats as a kind of practical joke. The attitude was that of "good riddance." Tragic, really.

It's ironic when you think about the fact that when the tonsils enlarge it's very uncomfortable to swallow. It's almost as though the body is trying to tell us something like, "Hey, will you stop eating for a while so I can catch up and clear things out?" And, instead of us being educated to understand the message our tonsils are sending us and taking the appropriate action, we tear them out at the roots and get a big bowl of ice cream as a reward for being co-operative while they were being removed. It makes me sad.

It's not important for you to have an in depth, highly technical understanding of all the physiological functions of the lymph system. In fact, for the purposes of being able to prevent breast cancer, you practically know all that you need to know about it. The main thing is to know that toxins build up in your body. If not removed, the toxins will eventually drive certain cells crazy, making them cancer cells, and that is the explicit function of the infinitely capable lymph system: to break down and remove toxins from the body before they can cause harm.

There is an area that I do want to be more specific about so that you not only have a full grasp and understanding of it but also feel comfortable with implementing the three principles of CARE to be given later. There are two subjects that invariably come up when discussing breast cancer: lumps in the breasts and lymph nodes.

First, let me tell you that finding a lump in your breast is no reason to panic.

Let me say quickly here that I am not trying in any way to make light of or minimize any aspect of breast cancer. Far too many women have suffered far too much for me to do that. No. What I mean is, because of the nature of and dynamics of the lymph system, it is very likely indeed that you have had many lumps in your breasts come and go without you ever having the slightest awareness of them.

Lymph nodes fill up and empty all the time, the frequency depending upon the level of toxemia in your body and the amount of vital energy your body has to empty them. That is why Dr. Susan Love, who I have quoted several times in this book, says, "If you feel a lump (in your breast), the first thing you should do is take a deep breath. There is no rush. Even the diagnosis of breast cancer is not an emergency. And certainly the diagnosis of a lump is not an emergency. There are twelve benign lumps for every cancer."[108]

I find it criminal that women in this country have been whipped into such a frenzy of fear over searching out and finding lumps in their breasts that, when they actually find one, their lives pass before them. Women have actually been taught to fear the normal activities of their bodies rather than to understand and appreciate them. We fear the unknown. Once you know what the lumps are, why they have appeared and how simply you can facilitate their removal, fear will no longer have a hold over you.

As I am a devoted fan of the analogy as a learning tool, I would like to use one here to explain about lumps and lymph nodes. I am thinking of a type of decorative fountain that has water forced up its center and when it reaches the top the water cascades down onto a series of shallow, bowl-shaped ledges. It looks somewhat like a Christmas tree in shape in that the top ledge has a small diameter and all the ledges below increase in diameter. As the water fills the top bowl-like ledge, it spills over into the next ledge below it. As it fills, it spills over into the larger one below it and so on until all the ledges are filled and the last one at the bottom spills over into the pool and a pump sends the water back up the center of the fountain. I've seen miniature versions of this at parties where fruit punch is dispensed this way. You simply hold your glass under one of the ledges where the punch is overflowing.

It is a simplistic comparison, but the activities of the lymph system with its network of lymph nodes works similarly to that of the fountain, with waste matter in your body represented by the water and lymph nodes represented by the ledges that fill and overflow.

Now remember, waste matter, toxins, are constantly being produced and built up, picked up by the lymph system, and removed from the body. Lymph nodes are truly amazing little processing plants. As an indispensable component of the body's defense system, lymph nodes filter out bacteria and other foreign material from lymph fluid which constantly flows through the nodes. This waste material is broken down, degraded, and sent on its way for elimination. When the level of waste in the body builds at a greater pace than it is eliminated, the lymph nodes are overburdened and they enlarge. They simply cannot keep pace. As lymph nodes swell up and fill to their capacity, the waste moves on to the next available node. Frequently, these swollen lymph nodes are surgically removed, especially if cancerous cells are detected in them. But **removing the nodes is not removing the problem**. The problem is the ever-increasing level of toxemic waste, not the nodes that are trying to contain it.

In the description above of the fountain, do you think for one fleeting moment that if you removed one of the ledges near the top of the fountain that is filling with water that it would prevent the water from getting to the other ledges? Even the removal of **all** the ledges would not impede the water one iota. The only way to prevent the ledges from filling with water is not to remove them, but to stem the flow of water.

The only way to prevent lymph nodes from enlarging is not to remove them, but to stem the flow of wastes flowing into them. Imagine the dire consequences of removing **all** the lymph nodes in the body because they became enlarged. The defense system would be so severely impaired that premature death would inevitably follow as poisons would be allowed to flow freely throughout any and all parts of your body. Your body is your citadel of life. Your lymph nodes are your warriors, your guardians, performing an indispensable service protecting you from harm. **You can't live without them!**

There is something I wish to share with you. All during the writing of this book, whenever I needed some bit of information or some help, as though by some divine grace, I got exactly what I needed when I needed it, in the most unusual fashion. I don't want to sound airy-fairy here, but what I needed came to me in totally unexpected ways so many times that I simply can't help but think that it was more than mere coincidence. For example, this book was one of three that I was contemplating writing and I was having difficulty deciding which I should focus on. It was either a book on weight loss, AIDS, or breast cancer.

Right when I was trying to decide which to do, and I was looking for some sign to direct me, ABC-TV aired a most provocative show on breast cancer. Less than two weeks later, *60 Minutes* aired a great segment on breast cancer. Two weeks later, PBS aired an equally thought provoking show on breast cancer and five days later PBS aired yet another information-packed show on breast cancer. I taped them all, watched them all twice and my head was so full of what was happening with breast cancer that I couldn't think of anything else.

Right then, I met and had the conversation with the woman whose story is related in the opening of this book. My course was set, no doubt about it. It kept happening. I won't relate all the instances because there are simply too many big and small. I would need a certain piece of information and it would show up in the mail, sent to me by someone who was merely sending me an article that he or she thought I would be interested in. Or I would need a certain quote and I would see what I was looking for on the cover of a magazine in a book store.

Once I was anguishing over the fact that I didn't have enough information on a certain aspect of what I was working on and that very day I happened to call someone on a completely unrelated issue and wound up with a number to call for a service that screened television talk shows for various subjects and provided transcripts. I wound up with a four-inch high stack of precisely what I was looking for.

At one point, I remember thinking that it was all too much. They were the most remarkable string of coincidences of my life. That very day that I was ruminating on whether it was coincidence or divine intervention, a friend told me about a book that she thought I would enjoy. It was called *The Celestine Prophecy* by James Redfield. I wasn't doing a lot of reading outside of the subject I was working on, but I picked up the book to take a look at it because I was beginning to get the hint that these *coincidences* weren't coincidences. The book describes nine key insights into life that will help those who read them have a deeper spiritual awareness. The first of the insights described how everything happens in life on schedule, with purpose—**that there are no coincidences**. You could have knocked me over with a feather.

"So what does all this have to do with my lymph system?" you are probably asking. And, I don't blame you. I knew from the very beginning of this project that this particular chapter was going to be one of **the** most important and pivotal chapters in the book. Important for two reasons. First of all, it explains what lumps in the breasts are, why they appear and the incredible lymph system that governs the coming and going of lumps and swollen lymph nodes. Understanding the dynamics of the body's activities is crucial to seeing how the three principles of CARE you are to learn will help you prevent breast cancer. Secondly, it is no small matter to state that the experts in charge have somehow missed something as significant as the lymph system's role in **preventing** breast cancer rather than being a victim of it.

I have to build a very clear, logical, unassailable case to prove my point. Of course, the most convincing evidence is the frequency with which lymph nodes are routinely removed from a woman's chest, side and arms, and how little provocation is needed to do so. I know **many** women whose physicians convinced them to allow the removal of lymph nodes from under their arms as a "safety measure." That would be like tearing out your alarm system at home as a safety measure against burglary.

Anyway, one day I'm at my desk writing **this chapter** and I receive a phone call from a friend who I had not spoken to for some time and who lives far from me. We're chatting along and it gets around to what I'm working on. After I tell him, he mentions, almost as an afterthought, that he's been looking through a really first rate physiology book. It's used as a textbook and is beautifully written and illustrated. He said he remembered reading some interesting material on the lymph system. After all of the similar experiences I had had, I definitely looked upon his call and the mention of this book as another of these "coincidences." Because it's more of a teaching book, it was not available in any book stores in my town. But I found a store somewhere in the state willing to FedEx one to me.

Immediately upon receipt the next day, I sat down and read the chapter entitled "Lymphatic Organs and Immunity." Have you ever been watching a movie, a taut, suspense thriller where someone is trying to find some lost or hidden piece of evidence to solve some mystery? There comes a time after following numerous leads that the information being searched for is finally found. The suspense has built to a nervous crescendo and at the moment when the realization hits, that what has been searched for has been found, the camera moves in for a close-up of the hero's face, a sudden flourish of music starts to play and the person who has been searching so long and hard pumps a clenched fist in the air and yells, "**YES!**" I came to a passage in the chapter on the lymph system that made me feel so much like that, that I looked around for the movie camera, fully expecting to hear music start to play. At that moment, I would not have been the least bit surprised if Steven Spielberg himself stood up behind me and said, "Cut! That's a wrap!"

I came to a passage, a short, simple passage that spoke volumes. At first I couldn't believe what my eyes saw, so I read it over carefully again and again. It was as if all my work and effort had been rewarded with one simple sentence found in probably the last place on earth I would expect, or even hope, to find it; in a defining text used to **teach** the subject.

Here is the passage which was set off from the rest of the text and printed on a different colored background in order to set it off from the rest of the information on that page.

"Cancer cells can spread from a tumor site to other areas of the body through the lymphatic system. At first, however, as the cancer cells pass through the lymph system, they are trapped in the lymph nodes, which filter the lymph. During cancer surgery, malignant (cancerous) lymph nodes are often removed, and their vessels are cut and tied off to prevent the spread of the cancer."[109]

Now in all likelihood, there's nothing so momentous there that you would equate it with finding the lost Holy Grail as I have. But let me highlight the sentence that jumped off the page at me like a pit bull going after a steak and explain why it is of such significance:

"At first, however, as the cells pass through the lymph system **THEY ARE TRAPPED IN THE LYMPH NODES** which filter the lymph."

This one sentence proves so much of what I have been stating.

As I am writing this right now, I'm so excited I hardly know where to begin in showing you the magnitude of this statement. First of all, it shows that although there may be a masterful understanding of the **technical** functions of the lymph system, there is no understanding of the **practical** functions it performs. Earlier I stated that Natural Hygiene sees the body as dynamic, as the actor. Traditional medicine sees the body as passive, as a victim. We so often hear about how cancer spreads and works itself into a lymph node requiring the node's removal. But it is made very clear, totally clear in the passage from the teaching text that cancer cells don't work their way into a lymph node, the cancer cells are "**trapped by**" the lymph nodes.

A cancer cell works its way into a lymph node in the same way a piece of dirt "works its way" into a vacuum cleaner. The lymph node is doing something to the cancer cells. It's not the other way around. No wonder "they don't know." They have reversed the entire order of things. Talk about not seeing the butter in the refrigerator, how about not even seeing the refrigerator in the kitchen? It would be like describing our solar system, noting that the sun is at the center with the planets circling around it, then stating that the sun actually does move across the sky because you can see it do so. It only **looks** like the sun is moving, in actual fact it isn't. It only **looks** like cancer cells are attacking lymph nodes, in actual fact they aren't.

As cancer cells are carried by the lymph fluid, they are **brought** to lymph nodes where they are trapped. Let's look at this more closely. I have made the point over and over how magnificently intelligent the human body is. It "knows" what it's doing. Performing trillions of actions and reactions, no activity is wasted, none are superfluous, all have an absolute reason for taking place. The body has far too much to do to busy itself with activities that don't directly contribute to its own survival. So you can be sure beyond even the most infinitesimal shadow of doubt that if the body traps cancer cells in its lymph nodes, it has a damn good reason for doing so!

Within the lymph nodes there are what are called phagocytic cells. Phago means eat and cytic means cell. Eating cells gobble up and degrade foreign substances. Cancer cells are trapped there as the body's last line of defense. Remember, cancer is the seventh and last stage of disease. All during the first six stages when cancer could have been prevented by certain life-style changes, but wasn't, the next stage kept inevitably following the previous one until cancer appeared. As a last ditch effort to deal with the cancer that had obviously broken away from its original site and started to spread through the lymph system, the body traps them, to deal with them.

There is no other possible reason why the body would make this effort. The body never gives up the fight no matter how bad things are, no matter how serious the situation, no matter how long-standing has been the neglect. As long as it is alive, the body strives for homeostasis—balance. Like water in a jar that seeks its own level no matter what position the jar is in, the body seeks to normalize, correct and maintain balance no matter what the circumstances. Even in the face of such long-standing abuse and neglect that cancer finally develops, the body still has the wherewithal to call to arms its last sentinels guarding the integrity of the body: those amazing, cancer-trapping, protective lymph nodes.

And how are these precious lymph nodes treated by those who "don't know?" **They are cut out!** And why? **For performing the very function they were created and intended to perform!**

Nothing, and I mean **nothing**, could be more backwards. Would you allow your bladder to be cut out because of the presence of urine? Would you allow your colon to be cut out because of the presence of feces? Would you allow your lungs to be cut out because of the presence of carbon dioxide? Can you imagine a more preposterous suggestion than that? The removal of one of your vital organs for doing the very job it was put there to do? It is every bit as preposterous to remove a lymph node for doing its job as it is to remove the bladder, colon or lungs for doing their job.

We look back in amazement and disbelief that our medical ancestors could have been so blind to the dynamics of the body that they would routinely drain blood from the sick. Bleeding patients was a standard, universally accepted practice performed with the idea that as the blood ran out of the body, so would the sickness. Removing lymph nodes, for doing the job they were created to do, at the very moment when what they are doing is most needed; preventing the wild, uncontrolled spread of cancer cells, makes bleeding look like the cornerstone of scientific wisdom.

And just where, pray tell, will the waste and cancer cells go when these lymph nodes are removed? To the next available lymph nodes, that's where. Removing one of the ledges in the fountain won't stop the water from going to the next available ledge, and removing a bunch of lymph nodes won't stop the cancer from going to the next available node. That's why it is so common to hear the two famous statements, either, "You've relapsed," or "We didn't get it all." Because until the buildup and flow of wastes and toxins in the body are curtailed, you can cut every lymph node in the body out and it will be to no avail. That is because the swollen lymph node is only the symptom of a cause that is not being addressed. Under those conditions, "relapse" is inevitable.

Do you happen to recall when O.J. Simpson was in custody awaiting his trial, that he had a lymph node removed from under his arm to see if it was cancerous? It turned out that it wasn't. The attending physician diagnosed the swollen lymph node as, "benign reactive lymphocytic hyperplasia." Translated into English, that is the abnormal growth of normal white blood cells that results in the increased size of the node.

Now, even the most elemental understanding of the role lymph nodes play in the lymph system's job of keeping the body clean, tells us what was happening. It indicates that the body increased production of white blood cells to deal with an overload of toxins in the body that had started to accumulate in the lymph nodes. It's the body's defense system in action. Simple. Obvious. **Elemental**. But on the news and in the papers, it was stated that, "further studies" were going to be conducted to try to "determine the cause of the swelling" of the node.[109.1] Studies? That would be like pulling a floundering person out of a swimming pool and then doing "further studies" to determine why the person was soaking wet.

I was deeply saddened by the passing of Jacqueline Kennedy Onassis. Not so much because she was the widow of one of our Presidents of the United States or that she was a woman of great courage, style and dignity who had gone through so much in her private and public life. I was saddened by the fact that she became yet one more victim in a long and heart-rending line of victims to lose their lives because of a lack of understanding of the basic needs of the human body. The history books will record that Jacqueline Kennedy Onassis died of cancer. And most assuredly the cancer in her body contributed to her demise. But I would be shirking my obligation and responsibility to not at least make mention of the fact that ignorance of the dynamics of her lymph system certainly hastened her to her grave.

There is a simple, obvious, logical, common-sense axiom in Natural Hygiene. It is **so** obvious that one might think that it is ludicrous to even mention. "You cannot be poisoned back to health." Does that seem reasonable to you? But lo and behold there is also a medical axiom. In Latin it is *Ubi virus ibi virtus*. Translation: "Where there is poison there is virtue." Would you, if you were in a book store, be captivated and sufficiently interested to spend your money on a book entitled "How To Poison Yourself Back To Health?" Probably every fiber in your being would revolt against such a suggestion; yet, by some inexplicable fluke of reasoning, medical treatment dictates that those who are sickest are poisoned the most.

Radiation and chemotherapy are poisons. They poison and kill both cancer cells and **healthy** cells. Plus, these treatments are themselves carcinogenic. That's right, the treatment for cancer **causes** cancer. Back in the early 80's, health care workers who were involved with the preparation and administration of anticancer drugs were warned to take special precautions when handling the drugs because of the risk of developing cancer from being in contact with them. In an article in a journal published by the American Cancer Society, it stated that the increased risk, "should be of great concern to those handling anticancer agents."[110]

Now, get this: Those **handling** the drugs should be greatly concerned. What about the people having it injected **directly into their veins!?** No need for concern there? If a strong, healthy, fit and vibrant woman were to be given intense radiation and chemotherapy, she would quickly become debilitated, devitalized and sick. How then could the same treatment given to one who is **already** sick be expected to make her well? Where's the reason? The logic? The common-sense? If something will make a well person sick, it will surely make a sick person sicker. How could it possibly be otherwise?

As I read the articles in the newspapers describing the cancer and the treatment given Mrs. Onassis, I was filled with sorrow and dread. I remember commenting to a friend in the midst of the assault she was under, she couldn't possibly live out the week. She died the next day.

Although it was not breast cancer with which Mrs. Onassis was dealing, it was cancer so very similar that I cannot resist using her case to make my point here. Mrs. Onassis had lymphoma. "Oma" means tumor, so what she had was a tumor in her lymph system, meaning one or more of her lymph nodes were found to have cancer cells in them. **Trapped there**, no doubt, by her body as it struggled the best it could to deal with the results of years of toxemia within her system. Had the affected lymph nodes been in her breasts, she would have been told that she had breast cancer. If cancer is diagnosed in a lymph node it is described as a lymphoma. In actual fact, a tumorous lymph node in the breast could be called a lymphoma as well.

Some of the newspaper accounts of her predicament described her particular cancer and the treatment she was receiving. We were told that her cancer, "attacked" the lymph system and that "tumors can arise anywhere there are lymph nodes and lymphatic channels."[111] She became acutely aware of her problem when, in December, 1993, she "noted a swelling in her right groin."[112] A physician diagnosed a swollen lymph node. A few weeks later she developed a "cough, swollen lymph nodes in her neck and pain in her abdomen."[113] She flew to New York to be examined and her doctor there found "enlarged lymph nodes in her neck and in her armpit."[114] A CAT scan (a computerized X-ray) showed that "there were swollen lymph nodes in her chest and in an area deep in her abdomen."[115]

To a Natural Hygienist, in tune with the dynamics of the body and the knowledge of the important role the lymph system plays, these signals could not have been more clear. She needed to allow her system to be cleansed of toxins and waste and she needed it **fast**. Unfortunately, she did not have the benefit of that point of view. If she did, she could very well be alive today.

Instead of realizing that cancer cells had been trapped in the lymph nodes as an attempt to cordon them off from the rest of the body until they could be dealt with, the lymph nodes were looked upon as helpless victims under attack by marauding cancer cells and in response to that view, a course of very aggressive radiation and chemotherapy was undertaken and her fate was sealed. She was literally bombarded with drugs. Lots of powerful, virulent, energy-sapping, life-diminishing drugs. It was stated that she "initially responded to therapy, but it came back in her brain and spread through her body."[116]

For the unrelenting pain in her neck, she received more drugs. For the acute pneumonia she developed in her weakened state, she received more drugs. Steroids were part of the mixture in her chemotherapy which caused a perforated ulcer in her stomach. In the middle of her ordeal, she had to be operated on to sew up the hole in her stomach. She went from bad to worse and, as a final assault on her body, she was subjected to even more radiation and chemotherapy. Only this time it was shot **directly into her brain**. It spread to her spinal chord, her liver and throughout her body. She became weak, disoriented, lost weight, developed shaking chills, her speech slowed and she had difficulty walking.

How she held on for as long as she did under such a barrage of poisonous chemicals is testimony to her strength and will to live, The fact is that her body was already weak from her own internal struggle to deal with the cancer in her lymph system. Add to that an unrelenting assault with the most virulent poisons on earth and she didn't have an ice cube's chance on the sun. After the assault on Mrs. Onassis's body culminated and it was apparent that all hope of recovery was gone, the headline in the *New York Times* read, "Doctors Told Mrs. Onassis That There Was Nothing More They Could Do." I'd say!

How ironic it is that the constant contact with toxins—poisons—is what turns cells cancerous in the first place and it is **more** poisons that are then used to try and destroy those cells. It is the elements of **health** that will produce good health, recapture it if it is lost, and maintain it once found—not poisons.

I watched the same scenario unfold with my father in 1963 when he was only fifty-seven years old. The cancer was bad, but it was nothing compared to the aftermath of his treatment with radiation and chemotherapy. I was only eighteen at the time and had not yet learned what I know now, so obviously I couldn't exert any influence on the decisions being made on his behalf. He is one reason why my life's work is to help people avoid a similar fate to his.

A few days after Mrs. Onassis's passing, there was a big article in the *New York Times* with a headline that made me shake my head in exasperation. It read, "Lymphomas Are On the Rise In U.S., and No One Knows Why."[117] In the article, there were statements like, "No one knows precisely why." "Experts are stymied." "Doctors know little." "Reasons are poorly understood." It always amazes me that whenever medical scientists don't know something, they immediately declare that "no one knows." It's not true.

I am very fortunate to have several friends who are medical doctors who are not threatened by the fact that I am not medically trained, yet I can sufficiently challenge their thinking on certain aspects of traditional medical treatment to make them stop and think. One such friend, who I have known for over a dozen years and with whom I am very close, was asking me about what track I was going to take in telling women how they can prevent breast cancer.

I said it revolves around an understanding of the lymph system, how it works and how to keep it sufficiently clean so as to not allow tumors to appear. After explaining to him certain aspects of how the lymph system operates, I asked him point blank, "How is it that medical doctors, **including you**, can go to school for twelve years and come away with no understanding of the crucial role the lymph system plays in preventing breast cancer?"

He thought for a few moments and said, "You know what, Harvey? I don't know why. It's just not stressed. We learn the mechanics of it, but not its practical application." And it is this epic oversight that is the very reason why so many of the experts "don't know" how to deal with breast cancer.

Here is my message to you, dear reader: not to worry. By applying the three principles of CARE, you **will** know how to deal with breast cancer because by understanding and respecting the activities and needs of your lymph system, you will be taking the steps to prevent it from ever occurring in the first place.

Chapter Eight

TOO FAT OR NOT TOO FAT

I love to eat. I love food and I **love** to eat. Always have, too. I love everything about the eating expe rience. I enjoy thinking about it, looking at it, talking about it, preparing it, smelling it, tasting it and eating it. Going to a new restaurant that I have not been to before and sampling their cuisine is as exciting an adventure for me as going to a thrilling sports event may be for someone else. So I am not the least bit surprised my life revolves around the study and teaching of the effect of food on the human body which I consider to be a great gift in my life. I don't mind telling you that I feel blessed to have been given the ability to grasp the importance of nutrition as it relates to good health. Because, quite frankly, had I **not** grasped it, considering the road I was on, I would probably be dead or as close to it as one can be and still be breathing.

In terms of my health, the difference between the first twenty-five years of my life and the second twenty-five years, is like the difference between a barren strip-mine site and a lush rain forest. The first twenty-five years was an ongoing battle against pain, excess weight and lethargy. I suffered from excruciating stomach pains, frequent headaches, including migraines, numerous colds and sinus problems, a perennial lack of energy and ultimately reached a weight of just over two hundred pounds. That is because my love for eating had no bounds. I was never raised with or ever taught **anything** about the effect of food on my health. My only prerequisite for what I would eat was, could I get it down my throat?

At age twenty-five, I had the immeasurable good fortune to be introduced to Natural Hygiene and since that time (1970), I have had no stomach-aches, headaches or sinus problems. I have an abundance of energy and the fifty pounds I quickly lost have stayed off in all this time. And the really **good** news, for me anyway, is that I achieved all this while still reveling in the joys of eating. The difference is, I learned how to fully enjoy the eating experience **and** have my health.

There are **many** factors involved in the development of disease, be it breast cancer or anything else. Most prominent are quality of food, air and water, exercise, rest and sleep, sunshine, loving relationships, self-love and inner peace and how we think. I know that all of these variables, and more, play a role in whether or not we become ill, but I am certain beyond any possible doubt that far and away the number one factor is the food we eat. This is not a **belief** that I hold, but rather, based on my own extensive experience and both scientific and observational evidence, something that I am **convinced** is so.

If we were to compare **all** foods that we consume, **everything**, to measure its worth, obviously **something** would have to be the very **best** food for our health, and something would have to be the most detrimental, with everything else falling somewhere in between. Later on I'm going to talk about the very best, but right now it is essential that I talk about the one at the other end of the scale. That food which, if eaten in excess, will do more to increase your chances of developing breast cancer than any other.

This is the fifth book I have written since 1978. In all of my books, I address what I feel has been and continues to be the greatest threat to your health: animal products. Animal products are all meat, chicken, fish, eggs and dairy products, and I am convinced that the **overconsumption**

118

of them is the leading cause of a clogged body, excess weight, pain, ill health, disease, suffering and death in this country.

Of course, these are words that make organizations like the Cattlemen's Association and Diary Council have fits of apoplexy. The animal products industries take in over a quarter of a **trillion** dollars a year, so they hardly want you to find out the truth about their products. One major strategy they use is to call out their hired "experts" to scare the blood out of the veins of anyone who would even contemplate **investigating** a diet with little or no animal products. The people making the billions of dollars selling animal products would have you believe that the next three generations of your offspring will be condemned to all manner of deficiencies and disease if you skipped meat or milk at even one meal. A **slight exaggeration**, but they do get a bit carried away when our quest for health starts to interfere with their profits.

Actually, their attempts to dissuade us from eating less of their products are becoming increasingly more difficult because of the vast amount of data coming forth on a very consistent basis that **proves** that our love affair with animal products has been and remains a major contributor to our ill health. Before going even one word further, to clarify my position and head off any campaign by the animal products industry to label me as something I'm not, I wish to spell out, in terms no one will be able to misinterpret, precisely where I stand in relation to vegetarianism.

In short, vegetarianism is **ideally** the healthiest way to eat, but vegetarianism is simply not for everyone. I know vegetarians who have had their lives saved by cutting meat and dairy from their diet. I also know people who became strict vegetarians whose health suffered until they reintroduced some animal products back into their diets. Anyone who insists that vegetarianism is the **only** way to eat to be truly healthy is just as off base as someone who insists you can't be truly healthy if you **are** a vegetarian.

There are those who discover **intellectually** that cutting meat and dairy from their diets is best, but because they were **raised** on those foods and have eaten them for decades, they're up against a tremendous amount of physical and emotional conditioning. Being a vegetarian is an exceedingly personal choice and depends on many variables that relate to each individual's characteristics and circumstances. Just because a vegetarian diet works well for some people does not automatically mean it will work for everyone. It is as objectionable to demand of people that they embrace vegetarianism as it would be to tell someone to change religions.

There **is**, however, something that everyone **can** do and that many people are already doing, to take advantage of the most up-to-date research on the subject, **cut** back! For decades we have been overeating animal products. Research on the effect of this over consumption is overwhelmingly conclusive: it is **killing** us!

In *FIT FOR LIFE*, and especially in *FIT FOR LIFE II*, I discussed in great detail the full extent to which animal products contribute to every major disease. At that time, I challenged several dietary myths: the four food group mentality; the daily need for huge amounts of protein; that meat is the best source of protein; and that dairy was essential for calcium and protection against osteoporosis.

Today discussions no longer revolve around whether or not we **should** reduce our intake, but rather the **extent** to which we should reduce it. As with other matters of such import, opinions on how much vary all the way from a conservative cutback of 15% or 20% to total abstention of all animal products. What you as a person motivated to prevent breast cancer must decide is what would be most comfortable and work best in **your** life. One thing is certain beyond any possible doubt: lowering your intake of animal products is going to have a beneficial effect on your health commensurate with the extent to which you reduce these foods in your diet. Why? What has happened to so dramatically alter the landscape of nutritional studies that would have so many people in agreement on this issue?

Do the words "cholesterol" and "saturated fat" sound familiar? One short decade ago, you hardly, if ever, heard these terms. Today it is nearly impossible to go through a single day without hearing or reading **something** about them, and with good reason. They kill people! **Lots** of people. In fact, the argument is very strong that, together, cholesterol and fat kill more people than any other single cause of death in the United States.

Where do these killers come from? Absolutely **all** cholesterol comes from animal products. Cholesterol is produced in the liver and cells of **animals** and **nowhere else in the world**. It is **impossible** to ingest cholesterol from the plant kingdom. There are, however, still people who are confused about this fact. They will ask, "What about avocados, nuts and oils?" Since none of these has a liver, they contain no cholesterol. If you have any concern with or present problem with cholesterol, know that it is the result of the animal foods in your diet. Reduce them and you reduce your level of cholesterol. A simple formula.

The vast, **vast** majority of fat, including saturated fats, comes from these foods as well. And although cholesterol is an important contributing factor, it is now well understood that fat in the American diet is as much or more of a cause for concern.

Before revealing to you how animal products contribute to breast cancer, I would be remiss if I didn't, at least briefly, comment on the impact animal products have on the biggest killer this country has ever known. Cardiovascular disease which includes heart disease, all atherosclerotic diseases of the blood vessels and stroke, kills more people than all other causes of death **combined!**[118] It kills nearly one million people a year, two and a half thousand **every day!** When blood is constricted and unable to get to the heart, a heart attack is the result. When the blood is prevented from reaching the brain, a stroke or "heart attack of the brain" occurs.

What causes the veins to be blocked? Plaque. What is plaque? A thick coating of cholesterol and fat trapped in the arteries which the body has been unable to remove. And you can be sure that if these substances are overburdening the cardiovascular system, they are doing the same to the lymph system, as we will see shortly. Certainly there are many other factors involved in cardiovascular disease, and animal products are not the exclusive cause, but they are unquestionably the **major cause**.

The abundance of research corroborating the direct link between fat and cholesterol levels and heart disease is irrefutable. It is **the leading** predictor of atherosclerosis and subsequent heart disease.[119-150] Let me introduce you to Dr. Marc Sorenson, the incredibly fit and healthy founder of the National Institute of Fitness in Ivins, Utah (where he is known as "Doctor Fit" and where thousands of people from all over the world go to recapture their health). He is the author of three highly comprehensive and informative books and has this to say on the subject of heart disease:

"Heart disease is an insidious and unnecessary malady which is caused explicitly by the consumption of animal products and saturated fat. It is predictable, preventable, reversible and wholly unnecessary."[151]

And yet about 50% of Americans die from heart disease,[152] while twelve billion dollars are spent on bypass surgery a year[153] which, amazingly, is actually **worse than doing nothing!**[154] What is imperative for you to know and never lose sight of is that while animal proteins definitely raise cholesterol levels, **vegetable protein can reduce them!**[155]

The second leading cause of death in the United States is cancer. There is a widespread misconception about cancer which I have to clear up right now. Most simply put, cancer is cancer—regardless of what part of the body it affects. A cancer cell is a cell gone crazy and that can happen **anywhere** in the body. The **area** of the body in which cancer manifests is incidental to the fact that it did actually develop. People talk of breast cancer or colon cancer or prostate cancer or cancers in other areas of the body as though they were all separate and distinct diseases. They aren't. **Cancer is cancer** regardless of where it appears. If people live their lives in such a way that the cells in their bodies are forced to contend with a relentless barrage of toxins for years, **decades** on end, then there is a strong likelihood that some cells somewhere in the body will go crazy.

Where that happens isn't the most important thing. **Why** it happens is the issue. That is why it's such a tragedy for some women to have their healthy breasts removed with no sign whatsoever of cancer or even swollen lymph nodes. If a woman removes her breasts, she won't have cancer of the breasts, it is true, but she hasn't removed the possibility of developing cancer. Only a life-style built around a cleansed and healthy lymph system will do that. To say that breast cancer is a different disease than lymph cancer which is a different disease from colon cancer would be exactly like saying that rain, snow, ice, sleet, frost, dew and hail all have separate and different essences when in fact they are all water in different degrees of consistency. Rain and snow may be different in appearance, but they are both water in different forms. Breast cancer and colon cancer may be different in appearance, but they are both cancers in different forms.

In my local newspaper there was an article describing the experiences of three women who had breast cancer. One woman spoke of her "three kinds of cancer."[156] She lost a lung to cancer in 1983, lost a breast to cancer in 1986 and had a skin cancer excised in 1992. The article stated that she took responsibility for getting the lung cancer because she smoked for thirty-four years. However, in her words, "But my breast cancer—what did I do to get breast cancer? What did I do?"

Earlier in the article she also said that, "Smoking was probably the cruelest thing she ever did to her body." That is the key, although she didn't realize it. **What she did to her body.** The smoking, which in my opinion is singularly the most toxic offense against life and health in existence, containing **hundreds** of toxic substances, affected her **whole** body, not only her lungs. Of course, the lungs would be the most likely area of the body to be affected by smoking, but it is a person's entire life-style that determines whether or not cancer will manifest. Something as inherently poisonous as smoking affects **all** the cells of the body, not only cells of the lungs. Her smoking was a factor, a **major** factor, in her cancer of the lungs, cancer of the skin and cancer of the breast. Because of smoking, **together** with other negative life-style habits, her body simply started to break down at its weakest points.

It's been my experience that people who smoke also have dietary indiscretions that contribute greatly to their ill health as well. By the way, in a study by the American Cancer Society conducted on more than **600,000** women, it was concluded that smoking escalates a woman's risk of dying from breast cancer by at least 25%. The more cigarettes a woman smokes and the longer she smokes, the greater her risk. The study also said that the risk is eliminated by quitting.[157]

It is exceedingly important that you understand that breast cancer is not a separate entity unto itself. It's not something that somehow gets into your body and goes to your breasts. Whatever factors are involved in causing cancer in one area of your body can cause cancer in **any** area of your body.

Right behind lung cancer, colon cancer is the second leading cause of cancer deaths. In 1990, two major studies were published that dealt with diet and colon cancer. Both looked at large numbers of people over a long period of time. Both reached similar conclusions. They indicated meat eating as a major risk factor in this disease.[158] One of the studies reported in the *New England Journal of Medicine* followed more than **88,000 subjects for six years**. The findings indicated that the more animal fat eaten, the more likely it was that colon cancer would result. Those eating the most animal fat were nearly twice as likely to develop colon cancer as those eating the least animal fat.

Dr. Walter Willet, who directed the study, concluded: "If you step back and look at the data, the optimum amount of red meat you eat should be zero."[159] That's not a lot of red meat. Typical of the studies I see, this study made no mention of the importance of **cleansing** the colon. That is the one most effective measure an individual can use to prevent all cancers, including that of the colon. Animal products, which are very high in fat and devoid of fiber, serve only to block and toxify the colon. High fiber plant foods are the colon's best protection against cancer. Plus, **women who consume the highest amount of vegetables have one tenth the breast cancer as those who eat the least**.[160]

In the late 1980's, the case against animal products really took off. In October 1988, the Surgeon General's *Report on Health and Nutrition* exploded on the front page of newspapers all over the country. After reviewing over **2,500** scientific studies on the subject, the nation's top medical doctor removed any hope the animal products industry might have had of not being incriminated. In the report itself, and in interview after interview, the message from the Surgeon General was clear: Cholesterol and fat (animal products) are reeking havoc. His advice; cut back on these foods and add more fiber in the form of fruits, vegetables, whole grains and legumes. Although he did not label them as such, these, of course, are the **cleansing foods.**

The Surgeon General's report was followed up by recommendations from the National Academy of Sciences in 1989. After taking three years to review **six thousand** research studies, they released what they call the "most definitive dietary recommendations in the history of the organization."[161] It was the Surgeon General's recommendations all over again.

Then the National Institutes of Health released their recommendations. Same again. Plus there were the recommendations of the Senate Select Committee on Nutrition and Human Needs in 1977, the American Heart Association in 1979, the National Cancer Institute in 1979, the American Cancer Society in 1984, and at least twenty other authoritative agencies and organizations in the United States and abroad. All said the same thing.

When you have that kind of unanimity among top authorities, it's **time to pay attention.** For so many in the medical community to now so strongly and so unanimously concur with the very findings they denied as recently as the late 1980's sends the clearest possible message: the amount of evidence supporting the recommendation to reduce our intake of animal products has to be titanic. And when they finally link up the case for reducing animal products with the individual's ability to prevent illness by cleansing the body, they will have the **whole** picture and we will begin to have an approach to health care that is **truly grounded in prevention.**

Whenever I attempt to impart information that may be new for some people, I have always preferred to ask my readers to rely as much on their common-sense as on the so-called "scientific proof." Because, quite frankly, under the right circumstances and with "proper funding," scientists can "prove" anything they want. Medical libraries are rife with examples of "scientific studies" either proving what isn't, to be so, or proving the opposite of something that has already been proven in a different study.

I already gave you the example earlier of the two studies in the same journal "proving" estrogen to both prevent **and** cause heart disease. As another quick example, consider the incredible, terrible egg. Eggs contain one of the highest concentrations of cholesterol of any food. Data abounds showing that this is so. Eggs are the choice of researchers when they want to study their subjects' staggering increases in cholesterol levels.[162] In fact, eggs will increase blood cholesterol levels more effectively than **pure cholesterol dissolved in oil!**[163] Yet the egg industry is quick to cloud the issue with confusion by constantly referring to five "scientific" studies that "prove," of all things, that eggs **don't** raise blood cholesterol levels.[164] The five studies just happened to be funded by the egg industry.[165]

These examples are why it is so difficult to rely solely on scientific studies and scientific experts, and why observation and common-sense have to be given equal weight when making decisions about what actions you're going to take in your own behalf. This is particularly important in regards to the issue of fat in the diet as a major risk factor in the development of breast cancer. There is at present a controversy raging in the scientific community about this very subject.

Once again, the "experts" are divided, half thinking there is conclusive evidence and half thinking there is inconclusive evidence. How this can be, absolutely boggles my mind. To me, there is about as much doubt that fat is indeed a risk factor as there is doubt that the world is round, not flat. And I will try as best I can to prove this to you using both scientific data and common-sense.

Those who **are** convinced feel that there is sufficient evidence incriminating fat to reduce intake of it **now** so as not to take any added chances. Those who are not convinced agree that there is evidence pointing to fat as a possible villain but since there are no studies that absolutely and definitively prove that to be so, they want more research to be conducted before they can feel certain that it is so and make recommendations accordingly. Since I am one of those who needs no further proof, I am going to give you all those reasons why I think you **should** reduce your fat intake **now**. Then you can decide for yourself.

As it stands, there already are numerous studies that make a compelling correlation between breast cancer and the consumption of dietary fat.[166-182] And, fat intake also impacts a couple of the other suspected risk factors as well. One of those suspected risk factors is the female sex hormone estrogen. According to an article in *Science News*,[183] "Scientists don't understand exactly how estrogen fosters breast cancer," but the consensus is that the more estrogen there is in the blood, the more likelihood there is of developing breast cancer. High fat diets cause high levels of estrogen in women.[184] Comparisons reveal that women who eat meat have significantly higher levels of estrogen in their blood than vegetarian women.[185] And when women switch to low fat diets, the levels of estrogen drop sharply.[186-190]

Another suspected risk factor is late menopause. A correlation has been shown between late menopause and excessive fats in the diet.[191-195]

One very convincing piece of evidence incriminating dietary fat as a risk factor that promotes breast cancer is the incidence of breast cancer in Japanese women who either come to the United States and change their diet or stay home and change their traditional diet to one more like women in the United States. An article in the magazine *FDA Consumer*[196] stated that, "The death rate from breast cancer is the highest in countries like the United States where the intake of fat and animal protein is high." It commented further that, Japanese women historically have a low risk for breast cancer but that risk has been rising dramatically, concurrent with a "westernization" of eating habits; that is, from a low fat to high fat diet. Other studies looking into fat consumption of women living in Japan or coming to the United States and increasing their fat intake also confirm that the more fat eaten, the more breast cancer.[197-202]

An article in *Newsweek* magazine commented on the hazard to Japanese health because of a western diet, namely beef, dairy and other fat-laden foods. The article was titled, "Death By Fried Chicken."[203]

Adding to this rather conclusive evidence is the fact that Japanese women are not alone in this. A quick look at the chart on the next page illustrates clearly the association between fat intake and breast cancer in various countries. It is no accident that the incidence of breast cancer goes up commensurately with the increase in consumption of fat.

Researchers at the National Cancer Institute reanalyzed one hundred animal experiments pertaining to fats, calories and breast cancer and concluded that each excess fat-derived calorie posed 67% more risk than calories from other sources.[204] A study of Finnish women found that the participants who later developed breast cancer showed a "consistently higher" average percent of fat-derived calories.[205]

As important as it is to become aware of those foods that put you at risk of breast cancer, such as animal products, it is every bit as important to know what foods, if any, contain compounds capable of retarding cancer. The more researchers understand about the ingredients in fruits, vegetables and other plant-based foods, the more impressed

Relationship of Dietary Fat Consumption
To Death from Breast Cancer

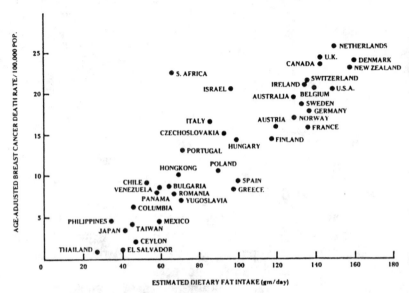

they are with the power of these compounds to retard the bodily breakdown that results in cancer.[206] Consider this comment from an editorial in the *New York Times*: "Nutritionists and epidemiologists have long observed that people who eat a plant rich diet suffer lower rates of cancer than do meat loyalists."[207]

I can tell you categorically that you will not see headlines proclaiming to isolate some special ingredient in a pork chop or a hamburger that has been found to fight breast cancer. All of those names of constituents of food that are ever more frequently being used in the news and that are becoming more and more familiar to people **all** come from plant foods, not animal foods. Words like flavonoids, carotenes, antioxidants, and fiber, and many, many more are **all** derived from foods. Every time you hear about some newly discovered multi-syllabled compound that fights disease, it is derived from fruits, vegetables, grains or some other plant food.

Have you heard of sulforaphane? Its discovery resulted in a headline in the newspaper that read: **"Broccoli Extract Shown to Block Breast Cancer."**[208] Researchers at Johns Hopkins University made the discovery and reported it to the media. Sulforaphane is to be found in what are called cruciferous vegetables: broccoli, cauliflower, Brussels sprouts and cabbage. They didn't find any in steak.

Gladys Block, Ph.D., of the University of California at Berkeley, reviewed approximately ninety studies relating Vitamin C intake and cancer. She indicated that "There is overwhelming evidence of the protective effect of Vitamin C and other antioxidants against cancer of the breast."[209] Fruits and vegetables such as citrus fruits, tomatoes, green leafy vegetables and potatoes are, of course, rich sources of Vitamin C and other nutrients. Additionally, Dr. Block reviewed 170 studies from seventeen nations and came to the conclusion that people everywhere who eat the most fruit and vegetables, compared with those who eat the least, slash their expectations of cancer by about **50%!**[209A] She mentioned breast cancer specifically. The evidence is so overwhelming that Dr. Block views fruits and vegetables as a powerful preventive that could substantially wipe out the scourge of cancer, just as cleaning up the water supply eliminated past epidemics such as cholera.

Dr. Peter Greenwald, director of the Division of Cancer Prevention and Control at the National Cancer Institute, has this to say: "The more fruit and vegetables people eat, the less likely they are to get cancer, from colon and stomach cancer to **breast** and even lung cancer. For many cancers, persons with high fruit and vegetable intake have about **half the risk of people with low intake**."[209B]

David Kritchevsky, Ph.D., in the journal *Cancer*, states that, "Breast cancer might be prevented if more women were to get sufficient amounts of Vitamin A, beta carotene and the other carotenoids."[210] Carotenoids are to be found in parsley, carrots, winter squash, sweet potatoes, yams, cantaloupe, apricots, spinach, kale, turnip greens and citrus fruits.

Geoffrey R. Howe of the National Cancer Institute of Canada reviewed twelve case-controlled studies of diet and breast cancer and reported that fruits and vegetables provided a protective effect. Vitamin C had the most consistent statistically significant inverse association with breast cancer risk in all women.[211]

In an issue of *Medical Tribune*, two studies were reviewed indicating that nutrients, fiber and antioxidants in fruits and vegetables protect women from cancer. In one study it was found that of 310 women with breast cancer and 316 women without breast cancer, those without cancer ate more fruits and vegetables.[212]

Dr. Bruce N. Ames is a member of the National Academy of Sciences. He is a biochemist and molecular biologist at the University of California at Berkeley, where he directs the National Institute of Environmental Health Center. Dr. Ames is one of the two dozen most-often cited scientists in the world.[212.1] His colleagues refer to him as "one of the most innovative thinkers in the world of science."[212.2] Dr. Ames states that the antioxidant nutrients in fruits and vegetables "can suppress all stages of the cancer process," and that, "Diet is at least as important as smoking as a cause of cancer."[212.3]

The most recent study on cancer prevention that I can include in this book was conducted at the Memorial Sloan-Kettering Cancer Center in New York, and appeared in the *Journal of the National Cancer Institute* in October, 1995. Dr. William R. Fair, at Sloan-Kettering said, "What we found was astonishing to us."[212.4] And what was it that Dr. Fair found so astonishing? Human prostate cancer tumors grew only **half** as fast in mice eating diets with about 21% fat as those eating diets with about 40% fat.

Are you starting to see the picture here? Could there be any doubt in **anyone's** mind that it is at the very least **probably** a good idea to minimize intake of fat and maximize intake of plant foods? How much proof is enough?

Once again, here are a few comments from people involved in research on one level or another:

"Women on low fat diets have less breast cancer than women on high fat diets, and women on high fiber diets have less breast cancer than women on low fiber diets."

> Dr. Lawrence Power, *Author and Syndicated Food and Fitness Columnist*[213]

"If I were to blame anything for the modest increase in breast cancer that is not related to early detection, I'd point to dietary fat."

> Dr. Ernst Winder, *President of the American Health Foundation*[214]

"In terms of fat in the diet, there are several different types of evidence—none of them completely conclusive, but all of them pointing in the same direction—that link a very low fat diet, really about half of what the average American woman eats now, 20% of the total calories, to a lower incidence of breast cancer."

> Cindy Pearson, *National Women's Health Network*[215]

"As far as diet is concerned, while various investigators have looked into the question of fat in relation to breast cancer, none of them have examined the very much more important question that fat and fatty meat contain high concentrations of pesticides and sex hormones, steroids, which are clearly known to induce cancer, including cancer of the breast."

Samuel Epstein, M.D., Professor of Medicine, University of Chicago Medical Center[216]

"There is no such thing as a 'Cancer Personality,' although certain life-style choices—choosing to smoke or eat a fatty diet, for instance—do make a difference."

Jimmie Holland, M.D., Memorial Sloan-Kettering Cancer Center[217]

One study monitored over 14,000 women for six years, focusing on their consumption of meat, fat, protein and other animal products. Mr. Paolo Toniolo, of the New York University Medical Center, who headed up the study, said, "It seems that frequent meat consumers are at more of a risk for breast cancer. I don't know if it's fat or other elements of one's diet. But I know it's diet."[217.1]

And this final one made on the nationally televised show Nightline by Dr. Timothy Johnson—truly the voice of common-sense and reason:

"You can probably lower your risk (of breast cancer) by cutting down on the fat in your diet. And even if we can't prove that either way, it makes sense to do it for all kinds of other reasons, so why not do it?"[218]

Hear, hear. Why not, indeed?

Michael Sporn, Director of a new National Cancer Institute laboratory devoted to intervening in pre-cancerous stages of the disease using a combination of new therapies, states that, "Over the next twenty-five years, breast cancer will disappear like the Cheshire cat."[219] I'm all for positive thinking, but breast cancer is not going to just "disappear." There is no magic bullet. It may very well be gone in twenty-five years, but that will be because of the actions women take **now** to protect themselves and prevent it.

I have told you that studies are studies and any premise can be "proven." But every once in a while, one study comes along that simply cannot be ignored.

Over the years, there have been thousands of studies supporting what is now becoming common knowledge about animal products' negative role in the human diet. There are various requirements that are taken into consideration when determining whether a study will be established as credible and reliable. For example, how large the study is, the length of the study, the number of people studied, the preciseness of the data collected, the means by which it is classified, the exactness with which the entire study is conducted and to what extent each variable the overall outcome.

Because it is so difficult to have all of the prerequisites met in one study, for decades it has been hoped that there would be **one** study that linked diet to health that was so large scale and definitive in every aspect that it would be viewed by everyone as absolutely precise and unquestionably accurate. The days of wishing and hoping are over. Just such a study was inaugurated in 1983, and in mid-1990 the first seven years of its data were released. It is called The Cornell Oxford China Project on Nutrition, Health and Environment, known simply as the China Health Project (CHP).[220] In the many reviews of this extraordinary study, it has been referred to as the "Grand Prix of Epidemiology,"[221] "The Champion Diet,"[222] and in one it was hailed as "One of the most rigorous and conclusive studies in the history of health research."[223]

At my seminars, I always ask my audiences how many have heard of the China Health Project. Even in audiences of over a thousand people, more often than not only a smattering of hands go up. What an injustice! What a tragedy! How deeply saddened I am by this situation. Considering its importance and potential benefit to the American people, this study literally should have been headlined on the front page of every newspaper in this country and been the lead story on every news program for at least a week, or for however long it took to be certain that every American citizen was aware of it.

If Americans have a true hero in the area of research linking diet to health, it is surely Dr. T. Colin Campbell, a nutritional biochemist at Cornell University. He was the mastermind and coordinator of the China Health Project.

Dr. Campbell has been studying diet and health for over a quarter of a century. He was instrumental in producing the National Academy of Science's landmark 1982 report "Diet, Nutrition and Cancer," which was the first "official" recommendation to reduce fat intake some 25% and which led to the guidelines adopted by the National Cancer Institute, the American Cancer Society, and the American Institute for Cancer Research.

Although his innovative and ground-breaking research over the years was frequently met with opposition, his perseverance and commitment never wavered. Those traits brought him to the forefront of this area of research and made him one of the leading nutritional experts in the world. Dr. Campbell is one of the most concerned and dedicated individuals I have ever had the privilege of knowing.

One of the factors making the China Health Project unique is the sheer scope of the study. Dr. Campbell, together with researchers from Oxford University in Great Britain and researchers commissioned by the Chinese government, observed 6,500 Chinese citizens for six years to obtain the widest possible range of data on death rates for over fifty diseases, making it the most complex study ever conducted of a single large population.

What is undoubtedly the most striking aspect of the study and what has made it so reliable has to do with the living habits of the Chinese people who were studied. They have two very interesting traits that helped make the entire study as exacting as it is. First, the Chinese people generally do not move around. They are born, live and die in the same locale. Second, their eating habits do not vary. They eat essentially the same foods their entire lives with very little, if any, variation. Their diets are simple and basic, determined by the season. These factors allowed the researchers for the first time to study a **human laboratory** on a very large scale for a very long time.

Perhaps you are familiar with the term, "diseases of affluence." These include heart disease, cancer, diabetes, osteoporosis and obesity. Throughout the world, wherever there is enough wealth to allow people to move away from the basic needs of existence, the prevalence of these diseases increase. In the United States, diseases of affluence are rampant.

In China, they are either practically nonexistent or notably uncommon. It is not a secret that the more affluent and industrialized the society, the more animal products and refined foods its people consume. We Americans consume sixteen million animals, 165 million eggs, eleven million pounds of fish, and 345 million pounds of dairy products **every single day!**[224-225] We lead the world in the diseases of affluence.

The Chinese eat primarily the **cleansing** foods: vegetables, grains and legumes, some fish and **no** dairy. What is of inestimable importance is the fact that they obtain **7%** of their protein from animal products, while Americans obtain **70%** of their protein from animal products. **Ten times as much!**

137

The main reason why we Americans eat so much animal protein is because we have been effectively conditioned over the years to believe that protein every single day, indeed every single meal, is absolutely essential, and that animal products are the very best source of that protein. It would be as though a car manufacturer, say General Motors, or Ford, were to somehow convince you through erroneous propaganda that you couldn't get a safe car unless you bought one of theirs. And the propaganda works so well that you're actually scared to buy a car from anywhere else, even though you might be able to buy a car as safe or **safer** than the one you are conditioned to buy.

The idea that it is difficult to obtain sufficient protein from the plant kingdom is an outright falsehood, constantly perpetuated by the industries who make money selling animal products and by their hired "experts." Hundreds of millions of dollars have been spent over the years to condition you to automatically think of meat and other animal products whenever the subject of protein arises. Without a doubt, the most frequently asked question of a vegetarian is: "Where do you get your protein?" As if by not eating animal products it can't be obtained. The conditioning has worked all too well.

The China Health Project rather soundly obliterates that particular profit-driven nutritional myth. In *Eat For Life: The Food & Nutrition Board's Guide to Reducing Your Risk of Chronic Disease*, a book recently released by the prestigious National Academy of Sciences, Dr. Paul R. Thomas, one of the book's editors, says, "There is nothing nutritionally unique about meat products that other foods cannot supply."

Dr. William E. Connor, author and head of the Division of Endocrinology, Metabolism and Nutrition at Oregon's Health Science University in Portland, sums it up well by saying, "The public has been sold on the idea that protein from animals is best and doesn't realize that plants contain high quality protein. **Everything that grows has protein.**"[226] After all, **isn't that where the animals we eat get theirs?**

Heart disease in China declines to an almost negligible level when fat and cholesterol levels are low. The study shows that low fat and cholesterol not only protects against heart disease, but also protects against cancer of the colon. The more animal products eaten, the greater the risk.

Obesity is a rarity in China. Although the Chinese consume twenty percent **more** calories than Americans do, Americans are **25% fatter!** I have long maintained that calories are not significant in whether you get fat or not. I was even attacked for saying so. The China Project and other data (*T-Factor Diet*) certainly substantiate my point. After all, a calorie is nothing more than a measure of heat. Heat does not make you fat. **Fat makes you fat.** Unfortunately, it is being consistently shown that it can also make you **dead!** Researchers show that as obesity goes up, so does the death rate.

Another area of great concern in this country and many other countries around the world, especially for women, is osteoporosis, the loss of calcium from the bones until they become so porous and weak that a rib or hip can be broken merely by going over a bump in the road in a car. In the same way, we have been conditioned to think of meat whenever the word protein is mentioned. Similar conditioning has been utilized to foster the idea that dairy products are without doubt not only the finest source of calcium for us, but also the best means by which to prevent osteoporosis.

Once again, that is precisely what the dairy industry, which makes billions of dollars selling dairy products, wants you to believe and once again it is patently untrue. It is a well established fact that the high protein content of meat and dairy products turns the blood acidic which draws calcium out of the bones. This **causes** the body to lose or excrete more calcium than it takes in. The deficit must be made up from the body's calcium reserve which is primarily the bones. Result—osteoporosis. This is not new information either. It's been known since 1920 that protein from meat consumption causes a net loss of calcium.[227] Fortunately, protein from vegetable sources does not cause a negative calcium balance and, in fact, can actually have a protective effect against bone loss.[228-229]

Women who are eating dairy products to prevent osteoporosis must pay attention to this well-documented fact: The countries of the world that consume the greatest amount of dairy products have the highest incidence of osteoporosis! The countries that consume the lowest amount of dairy products have the least incidence of osteoporosis.[230-233] The United States is among the leading consumers of dairy products in the world and has the highest incidence of osteoporosis affecting between fifteen and twenty million people and taking at least twenty thousand lives a year from hip fractures alone.[235]

The Chinese don't even have a **word** for osteoporosis in their language! It simply isn't a problem there. And how much dairy products do the Chinese people eat? According to Dr. Tierry Brun, an Agricultural and Nutritional Scientist from the National Institute of Health and Medical Research in France, "The Chinese consume no cow's milk or dairy products, yet they have among the lowest rates of osteoporosis in the world."[236]

Dr. Campbell points out that, "Dairy calcium is not needed to prevent osteoporosis. Most Chinese consume no dairy products and, instead, get all their calcium from vegetables. The Chinese data indicate that people need less calcium than we think and can get adequate amounts from vegetables."[237] **Isn't that where the animals we eat get theirs?**

For how many years have you been subjected to the aggressive propaganda by the dairy industry and their paid "experts" to frighten you, especially if you are a woman, into consuming dairy products lest you suffer the horror of osteoporosis? How much more sinister do those deceptive advertisements turn out to be now that it is becoming more obvious every day that the protein and dairy products sold **contribute** to osteoporosis?

Yet another scare tactic employed by the animal products industries has been to claim that red meat and other animal products are the best source of iron and that without animal products, one risks developing anemia. The truth is that even in vegetarians and vegans, iron deficiency anemia is rare with studies revealing them to have iron levels as high or **higher** than those who eat an animal- laden diet.[238-241] Also, Vitamin C, which **increases** iron absorption from food, is in plant foods, not animal foods.[242]

The China Health Project has shed some much needed light on this subject as well. Those in the study "with the highest fiber intake also had the most iron rich blood."[243] You must understand that red meat, or any animal product for that matter, contains **no fiber**. The study also shows that "consumption of meat is not needed to prevent iron deficiency anemia. The average Chinese who shows no evidence of anemia consumes twice the iron Americans do, but the vast majority comes from the iron in plants."[244] **Isn't that where the animals we eat get theirs?**

The results of this extraordinary study could not be clearer. The massive amount of industry-initiated, profit-driven propaganda that has deluged us over the years extolling the virtues of a diet laden with animal products has been instrumental in the toxification of your body and the deterioration of your health. The industries have been well served. You haven't. The more animal products you eat, the more ill health ensues. In the China Health Project, Dr. Campbell reveals that,

"In those few regions in China where meat and dairy consumption has begun to increase—notably the heavily westernized cities—it has been closely followed by a higher incidence of cancer, heart disease and diabetes. **Once these people start eating more animal products, that's when all the mischief starts.**"[245]

What has been demonstrated most clearly by the meticulously conducted China Health Project and what cannot be altered by the animal products industry's posturing and propaganda is that those who eat the least amount of animal products exhibit the least risk of disease. Those who eat the most animal products have the highest rate of diseases of affluence. It is interesting to note that complex carbohydrates, which are only to be found in plant foods and never in animal foods, are the only food category not in some way linked to dread diseases.[245A]

The recommendations we are receiving from every quarter are to **decrease** our intake of foods high in cholesterol and fat (animal products) and **increase** our consumption of foods high in fiber (fruit, vegetables, legumes and whole grains). Remember that animal products are extremely **high** in cholesterol and fat, which clog you up, and are virtually **devoid** of fiber which cleans you out! In other words, animal products could not be in more direct opposition to what researchers the world over are recommending we eat.

Having masterminded the China Health Project, having spent seven years in close contact with the accumulation and deciphering of its data, and having seen firsthand the result of this project, what does Dr. Campbell suggest we do to best prevent disease and preserve our health? As relates to diet, he says, "Change the diet so that 80% to 90% of protein comes from plant products, only 10% to 20% from animal products. Build meals around plant foods such as fruits, vegetables, grains and pasta.

The idea is to use animal products to flavor and as an accompaniment, not as the main focus."[246]

As relates to exercise, he says, "Exercise more. Chinese people are more physically active than people in the United States. They ride bicycles every day."[247] These are the basic guidelines of the program you will soon be following.

Dr. Campbell sums up what he learned from the China Health Project thusly: "We must come to realize that we are basically a vegetarian species. The study suggests that whether industrialized societies such as ours can cure themselves of their meat addiction, may ultimately be a greater factor in world health than all the doctors, health insurance policies and drugs put together."[248]

Of course, the number one reason why I am relating so much about the China Health Project to you has to do with Dr. Campbell's findings on breast cancer. Remember, Chinese women obtain **7%** of their protein from animal products, while American women obtain **70%** of their protein from animal products. The breast cancer death rate for American women is not double, triple or even quadruple what it is for their Chinese counterpart, but a whopping **five times** the number of deaths. That is a **500%** higher death rate. It is not time to sit around and wait for further evidence. It is time to take action and take the steps to protect yourself **now!**

As part of the National Institute of Health's Women's Health Initiative, some four thousand women will be tested to see if cutting dietary fat by half can lower breast cancer rates. They expect their results in the year 2006.[249] **YOU CAN'T WAIT THAT LONG!** The time is **now!**

All you have to do is ask questions of those around you and it will quickly become apparent that a change in thinking and habit as relates to the eating of animal products is taking place. Many of you are already cutting back.

Whether it's due to an instinctive "knowing" that you should eat less meat and dairy, or the fact that more forward thinking physicians are now regularly encouraging it, or that news from the numerous studies supporting such a change is filtering down to the public, it is clear that you are eating fewer animal products. How often do you hear others say, and how many of you can yourselves say, "I have definitely cut down on red meat and I'm eating more fish and chicken?" That is part of the trend, and that trend is validated and encouraged by a rapidly growing number of authorities both outside and inside the medical community.

If you have not yet joined this trend because you feel the issue is not quite settled or that the "experts" are still at odds, your time has arrived. It would be a formidable challenge to find **anyone** other than those making money from their sale not in agreement that reducing animal products in the diet is a wise decision. When it comes to matters of diet, many people choose to follow the direction of the American Dietetic Association. In their position paper on vegetarianism, they make it quite clear that even if you wanted to become a strict vegetarian, you could do so confidently by eating from a wide range of non-animal foods.[250] If the journey **all the way** to vegetarianism is safe, obviously only cutting back would pose no problem.

Comments on vegetarianism from places where not even ten years ago you would ever have expected to hear them are beginning to surface. Where do you think the following comes from?

"Although we think we are one, and we act as if we are one, human beings are not natural carnivores. When we kill animals to eat them, they wind up killing us because their flesh was never intended for human beings who are natural herbivores."[251]

Are these the words of someone clinging to the "sixties?" Are they the words of the head of one of the many animal rights groups in America?

They are the words of Dr. William C. Roberts, Professor of Clinical Medicine at Georgetown University and Chief Cardiology Pathologist for the National Institutes of Health. He also happens to be the Editor-in-Chief of the *American Journal of Cardiology,* a conservative, mainstream medical journal. His words appear in an editorial in that journal and they should prompt us to wonder how we ever could have been so misled.

Sometimes change is difficult. It certainly is when the change runs counter to what we have done for years, **decades**, but the change of lessening the overall amount of animal products in your diet can have but one long-term effect: a longer, healthier, disease-free life. That is why one of the principles of CARE deals directly with how to easily accomplish this in the most effective and convenient way possible.

Before leaving this chapter, I want to point out a most intriguing aspect of what I have been talking about here as it relates to your lymph system. I have already made a strong case for the invaluable role your lymph system plays in the prevention of breast cancer. That being so, there are two things that should be paramount in your mind. First, you should strive to do whatever you can to lessen the burden of your lymph system's activities, and second, you should strive to do whatever you can to improve the lymph system's functionability.

As regards the first, one of the major, basic functions of the lymph system is to **absorb fats from the digestive tract**.[253] The more fat you eat, the harder your lymph system has to work, the more clogged it becomes, and the less energy it has for the cleansing and removal of wastes. It is no accident that a primary function of the lymph system is to remove fat, so the less it has to remove, the better.

As regards your efforts to optimize the workings of your lymph system, there **is** something **you** can do to directly assist and support its optimum operation and effectiveness. It is an ingredient that is inseparable from a healthy life-style and imperative for the activities of the lymph system. That ingredient is, of course....

Chapter Nine

EXERCISE

Hold it! Before you pass up this chapter with something like: "Yeah, yeah, I should exercise. I know. I'll read this later," just read a little of it now, please. Later has a funny way of turning into never, and I promise not to beat you over the head with a celebrity workout tape. I know darn good and well that if you're not exercising, one more admonishment that you'd better start is probably not going to get you out huffing and puffing.

So what I'd like to do is tell you something about exercising that you are probably not aware of and offer you such a simple, yet effective means of supplying your exercising needs, that you just **couldn't** stay sedentary. Besides, I could hardly write a book on health care and **not** include exercise. After all, exercisers have death rates less than one-third those of non-exercisers.[253]

Here is the most important reason why I'm bugging you about exercise: some form of regular physical activity, even if it is a very mild form of activity, is crucial in the effort to prevent breast cancer. Here's why, and I hinted at it at the end of the last chapter. It has to do with your lymph system functioning at optimum level.

Unlike the cardiovascular system, that has at its center the heart which acts as a pump to keep the flow of blood going, the lymph system has no such pump. But lymph fluid must constantly be flowing throughout the body, in the same way that **blood** has to constantly be flowing throughout the body. What is it that does for the lymph system what the heart does for the cardiovascular system?

147

Physical activity. **Exercise!**[254] Also contributing to the flow of lymph through the body are muscles in the walls of lymph vessels and respiration (breathing in and out), but the importance of exercise cannot be minimized in any way. This puts the need for regular physical activity in a whole new light.

Most people, whether they exercise or not, are aware of the value of it in supporting a healthy life-style. One of the most important and convincing studies ever conducted showing this to be so and reported in the *Journal of the American Medical Association* by a group of highly respected researchers (including Dr. Kenneth H. Cooper, considered by many to be America's exercise guru) followed more than thirteen thousand men and women for more than eight years. Their physical fitness was measured by a treadmill exercise task. The death rate of the least fit men was three times that of the most fit and with women it was five times higher. The data showed that an unfit man could reduce his risk of death by nearly 37% by becoming fit, and an unfit woman could reduce her risk by about 48%![255] Those are figures that are hard to ignore.

Yet, with this and so many other studies **proving** the life extension benefits of exercise, at last count, **less than 10% of the nation's adults exercise vigorously at least three times a week.**[256] **WHY NOT?** It's not simply a communication problem, to be sure. Non-exercisers **know** they need to exercise.

How often have you heard, or even said yourself, "I know I need to exercise, but...." Let's face it, there are probably many reasons, physical, emotional and psychological, why people don't exercise. It's not necessary to delve into all the reasons why. What is important is to somehow get those people who are the most sedentary, sufficiently motivated to do at least **something**. If you are already doing some form of exercise, no matter how little or how much, that's fine. What I wish to accomplish here is to get those of you doing practically nothing, up and moving. You see, it doesn't take that much. There's no reason to feel intimidated. You don't have to join a gym or take aerobic classes. Really, I'm not talking about becoming a world class athlete. But I will tell you this, and I won't soften what I'm about to say.

Are you concerned about breast cancer? Are you serious about doing what you can to prevent the pain, anguish and suffering breast cancer can wreak? If your answer is yes, and you are serious, and I mean really serious, then you must do everything you can to keep your lymph system operating at its highest possible efficiency, and some form of regular physical exercise is a major contributing factor in that effort. Period! There's no way around it.

The one vigorous, physical activity that can bring you all the benefits afforded by exercise, can be done practically anywhere at any time, by nearly anyone, regardless of physical condition, doesn't require elaborate facilities or equipment, is convenient and **easy**, is **walking!** According to the National Sporting Goods Manufacturing Association, walking is the fastest growing participation sport on the continent.[257]

What is it about walking that has captured the interest of between seventy and a hundred million people? Probably the single most important factor is the fact that walking will produce results in short term training and in long term health benefits equal to any other aerobic exercise. Including jogging![258] When you jog, you land with three or four times your body weight. When you walk, you don't leap, so you always have one foot on the ground and, therefore, land with only one to one and one-half times your body weight. As runners age, they increasingly experience knee, ankle and back injuries. Walking is far easier on the joints and bones.

All around the world, walking has been a popular and recognized means of keeping fit. At the turn of this century, in our own country, one of the most gruelling, competitive events of the day was the "six day race." Edward Payson Weston was undoubtedly the most popular walking champion of the day. He would regularly cover over four hundred miles in those competitions and his fans lined the route and cheered him all the way. In 1904, at age seventy-one, he walked across the United States from San Francisco to New York in 104 days, walking on the average of over forty miles a day. Mr. Weston passed away at age ninety-one, leaving the legacy of the "Evening Constitutional" as a part of the American way of life.[259]

At that same time, Teddy Roosevelt, the President of the United States, was considered to be one of the fittest Presidents ever. Vigorous exercise helped him overcome serious childhood health problems, and he exercised and encouraged exercise throughout his life. In 1909, at the end of his presidency, he exhibited his physical fitness by walking fifty miles in three days.[260]

At the beginning of the century, heart attacks began to be increasingly prevalent. This devastating health problem was so thoroughly misunderstood that doctors actually thought physical activity made the heart **wear out** and, astonishingly, **discouraged** heart attack victims from physical activity.[261] Those afflicted were told to rest and remain inactive, the very worst possible advice. The heart, which is a muscle, requires regular exercise to keep it strong and make it stronger. But more than fifty years would pass before this understanding would take hold.

In 1924, Dr. Paul Dudley White founded the American Heart Association and is considered to be the "father of American cardiology." He also stunned his colleagues by saying that not only was walking **not** dangerous, but it was, in fact, absolutely beneficial and people should be encouraged to take **daily** walks. This was at a time when cardiology patients were forced to lie flat on their backs with as little movement as possible for **six weeks!** Doctors theorized that it would take that long for the heart to heal.

This bed rest theory was disputed by Dr. White because he noticed too many complications from such prolonged inactivity. After all, the human body is beautifully designed for activity and does not deal well with six weeks of forced inactivity. Another **three decades** would pass before changes were actually made in medical treatment. Dr. White, of course, was already encouraging his patients to get out of bed and start a program of walking.

Probably the most well-known studies on risk factors involved in heart disease were the Framingham studies started in the 1950's. There, researchers studied approximately ten thousand people for over thirty years and amassed a wealth of information that began to reveal the important role activity played in preventing heart disease. Many more studies have subsequently been conducted and the inescapable fact today is that the need for regular physical activity to insure good health and prevent heart disease, the number one killer in the country, is acknowledged by virtually everyone. After all, as one study conducted by the Center for Disease Control revealed, people who do not exercise have **twice the risk of developing heart disease as those who do**.[262] In this regard, walking has emerged as one of the most convenient exercises to insure good health.

Walking is the ideal aerobic exercise, one that oxygenates the blood which, in turn, supplies oxygen to all cells of the body. The number one prerequisite of life is air. Weeks can go by without food, days without water, but only a few minutes without air before you die. The literal meaning of the word aerobic is "in the presence of air." The heart, lungs and blood vessels work in harmony to carry this life-giving oxygen to every part of the body.

When you walk, you use your body's large muscles which allow the entire aerobic mechanism of your body to work harder than when you are at rest. If this is done very consistently, over time, the system becomes stronger and evermore efficient and capable of performing the functions it was designed to perform. Over a lifetime, it is the best possible means of reducing the risk of cardiovascular disease. Add to that the fact that walking will stimulate the activity of your lymph system, and you have a real winner in walking.

Truly exciting and encouraging are the recent studies showing that **even the most moderate, unstructured walking program will reap substantial benefits**.[263] Of course, your common-sense will tell you that the more you do, the more vigorously, the more benefit you will enjoy. But the good news, the **great** news, is that even low levels of activity are beneficial. For example, in one of the first clinical studies of its kind, as reported in the *Journal of the American Medical Association*, it was shown that regular hour-long **strolls** will reduce a woman's risk of heart disease.[264] Mile for mile, walking is actually the best fat burner.[265] Walking four miles burns more fat than running the same distance in less time![266]

An editorial in the *Journal of the American Medical Association* makes the point that a brisk walk of twenty minute duration three times a week would produce many benefits.[267] Dr. James Gavin, author of *The Exercise Habit*, states that, **"Ten minutes of extra activity per day can reduce an individual's risk of heart disease by 80%."**[268]

Considering the subject matter of this book, and this chapter, imagine my excitement when I was looking through the *New York Times* one morning and the following jumped off the page at me: **"STUDY LINKS EXERCISE TO DROP IN BREAST CANCER."** The results of the study were published in *The Journal of the*

National Cancer Institute and stated that, "A thorough new study has found that moderate but regular physical activity can reduce a woman's risk of developing premenopausal breast cancer by as much as 60%.[268A] **60%**!

In a discussion of the study on the *NBC Network News*, it was stated that, "The researchers are saying that exercise is the most important step a woman can take to reduce her risk of breast cancer."[268B] There simply is no longer any reason not to do **some** walking.

In this chapter, I am suggesting a program of walking which is very unstructured, quite easy and will satisfy your body's need for exercise and support your efforts to prevent breast cancer. This is **not** a contest, you are not being graded on your effort, and no one will be "looking over your shoulder" to check up on you. This is your chance to do what you know, in your heart, is so important, **without** pressure and **without** guilt. You do as much or as little as you choose for your own comfort. **Anything helps!**

All that is required is an agreement with yourself that you **will do something**. Your goal should be to build up to a thirty to forty-five minute easy walk three or four times a week, **at your own pace**. That's it! Perhaps in the beginning you will find it easier if you make the walks functional. Turn them into an errand to pick up some light weight odds and ends at the store or mail a letter. Sometimes getting used to walking is easier if you have a purpose and destination.

There are other ways to integrate walking into your life-style. If you go to work out of your home, on occasion, you can leave early enough in the morning to park a mile or so from your office and walk the rest of the way. That walk, coupled with the return walk at the end of the day will not only be adequate for your exercise needs but will also allow you to feel invigorated when you arrive at work and perked up when you return home. Or you can incorporate a walk into your lunch routine, especially during the winter, when extreme cold in the morning and darkness after work might tend to keep you indoors.

In addition, whenever you can, **walk** upstairs instead of taking an elevator. Stair climbing is an excellent workout that also helps keep your legs in good shape, and you will benefit from even brief stair climbing efforts. Drive to a park for the sole purpose of taking a walk in the good air and pleasant surroundings. Any way or at any time that you can walk, no matter how much or how little, do it! It all adds up physically, and psychologically the feeling of accomplishment will be immeasurably worthwhile.

To optimize your results, there are some hints to make your walking experience the most enjoyable and productive it can possibly be:

1)   On top of the list, and possibly the most important factor for successful walking are the proper shoes. Contrary to what many people believe, **walking is not merely running at a slower speed**. The motion of walking is very different from that of running. The transfer of weight is not at all the same. It's a much slower rolling motion versus landing on your heel with more weight. Running shoes need to be softer, walking shoes need to be firmer. Just as running, tennis, soccer and other sports have specifically designed shoes, so does walking. Take your walking seriously, and please obtain the proper shoes! Cutting corners will be a big mistake. **This is very important!** Get a good pair, of which there are many, and they will pay for themselves many times over in comfort, enjoyment and benefits.

I personally have found walking shoes made by ASICS to be the best. Although they are relatively new to the walking market, their shoes are clearly the most innovative. Not only are they particularly comfortable, but they also have an exclusive, patented gel system in the soles and heels of the shoes that make them unique.

What really sold me on ASICS shoes was a story told to me by the great Basketball Hall-of-Famer, Rick Barry. Between his playing days and several operations on his knees, Rick was left with absolutely **no** cartilage in his knees. None, just bone against bone. He happens to be very athletic, playing basketball, tennis and jogging. But due to the absence of cartilage in his knees he could only do so for very short periods of time and even that gave him considerable pain requiring rest and ice packs. He told me that he had resigned himself to the fact that he was not going to be able to be as physically active as he would like. But then along came the ASICS gel shoes and Rick can now play for **hours** without discomfort or the need for ice packs.

The gel disburses vertical impact into a horizontal plane, absorbs shock and dissipates vibration. No pain. No damage. Quite amazing, actually, and in Rick Barry's words, "A real miracle" for him.

2)   Walk either in the early morning or late afternoon. Walking in the heat of the day is not a good idea, because you not only absorb the heat directly from the sun, but also from the pavement. Heat also tends to tire you out faster. It has been shown that when exercise is performed in the morning, 75% of participants stick with it versus 75% who drop it when exercise is scheduled for any other time of day.[269]

3)   Don't push it. Take it easy at first. Start slowly and build up strength, especially if you have not been exercising regularly. Perhaps the first week or two, or the first month, you may not even go for thirty minutes or only walk twice a week. You don't have to prove anything to anyone. Remember, less than 10% of the nation's adults exercise vigorously three times a week!

The mere fact that you're doing it at all puts you in a very elite group, and you are to be commended. Your muscles exist to be used. It will not take long before they accustom themselves to the new activity and normalize. Yes, you may feel sore muscles at first, but this is a "good" soreness. You are using muscles that have been deprived of activity and are being "broken in," so to speak. Warm baths do wonders to alleviate initial strain.

4)   If it is windy out, start your walk with the wind in your face and return with it at your back. This prevents getting a chill by the perspiration you've worked up.

5)   Swing your arms. This helps circulate the blood and strengthen the heart. Ever notice how long music conductors live? Every time I hear of a music conductor passing away, they're in their eighties or nineties. They spend their lives swinging their arms, and heart disease is rare amongst them.*

6)   It is best if there is no food in your stomach when you are exercising. Digesting demands energy and detracts from your ability to exercise well. The exception is fruit, which requires very little energy to digest.

7)   Dehydration can be a real problem in any form of exercise. You must drink water to replenish yourself. Your body is approximately 70% water and, as a normal course of events, you lose about two to two and one-half quarts a day. That can go to four quarts if you exercise. Do yourself a favor, drink water, not soda, Gatorade, or any of the other fluids that contain chemical substances that undermine your health. Drink a glass of water before you walk and after you finish your walk. Drink more if you feel the need. It would be better to have a little more than you need than to not have enough.

8)   Stretching is an excellent practice to develop before walking and after walking. Stretching can prepare muscles for exercise, relieve stiffness, increase the range

---

* Leonard Bernstein died in his sixties a few years ago, but he was hopelessly addicted to cigarettes, which killed him.

of motion of your muscles and prevent injuries. Stretching should be performed very slowly and should **never** go to the point of causing pain. Stretching can itself be of enormous benefit, and there are literally dozens of stretches. Here are three to try:

A) Stretch your hamstrings on the back of your leg by bending over and touching your toes. If you can't touch your toes, just go as far as you can. Hold it for fifteen or twenty seconds and come back up. As far as you can go is **fine**. By doing it regularly, you will be amazed at how quickly you **are** able to touch your toes with ease.

B) Stretch your thighs by holding onto something for support with your left hand while, with your right hand, you pull your right foot up behind you towards your lower back. Then reverse.

C) Stretch your calves by standing on the edge of a stair with only the front half of your foot on the stair, then sink your weight down on your heel.

Each of these three exercises can be repeated. You can't stretch too much, so do as much as you like. There are literally hundreds of different stretches.

One of the most attractive aspects of walking is the convenience of it. You can walk **anywhere**—on the street, around your house, near your office, in the woods, parks, or country trails. When you're on vacation, at work, no matter where you are, with no more than a good pair of walking shoes, you're always able to take advantage of this life extending practice. Sometimes, depending upon where you live, it may be too hot or too cold to walk. If you're committed, even this can be overcome. Over the last decade or so, more and more people have been walking in shopping malls. Most malls open their doors quite early, hours before the stores are open. The temperature is always just right. The walking surface is flat and smooth, and malls are well lit and safe. It's almost as if they were **designed** for walking. Any way you look at it, walking is and can be an enormously positive influence in your life. The list of benefits you can reap from walking is definitely impressive.

1)   It helps increase the strength and efficiency of your heart and muscles.[270]

2)   A recent study indicates that walking lowers cholesterol.[271]

3)   Walking, like other exercises, increases both energy level and stamina.[272]

4)   Bones, like muscles, become stronger with regular exercise. It has been well established that the risk of osteoporosis is lowered with regular exercise. Walking actually increases bone mass.[273]

5)   Overall strength, flexibility and balance are improved.[274]

6)   Together with a healthy diet, walking can be instrumental in helping you lose weight. A forty-five minute walk every other day for a year can burn eighteen pounds of fat.[275]

7)   According to Dr. James Rippe, walking reduces the condition associated with hypertension and aids diabetics.[276]

8)   Walking, like other exercise, promotes better sleep.[277]

9)   One study at a medical center in Salt Lake City showed that mild exercise such as walking after eating moved food through the stomach more quickly, helping relieve minor indigestion.[278]

10)   A study at Appalachian State University showed that women who walked forty-five minutes a day recovered

twice as fast from colds than women who did not exercise.[279]

11) According to the *Berkeley Wellness Letter*, walking is the perfect exercise for promoting a healthy back.[280]

12) Walking relieves stress. Researchers at the Center for Health and Fitness at the University of Massachusetts found that those who took a forty-minute, brisk walk, experienced a 14% average drop in anxiety levels. Walks are part of the therapy at the Betty Ford Center for Drug & Alcohol Rehabilitation.[281]

13) A study at the Exercise, Physiology and Human Performance Laboratory at the University of California at San Diego, showed that healthy men age thirty-five to sixty-five who started a regular exercise program, hugged and kissed their wives more often, had more intercourse and more orgasms than those who did not exercise.[282]

14) A growth hormone administered to people over the age of sixty reduces fat, increases bone mass, improves skin condition and reverses many other apparent symptoms of aging. The artificial hormone is very expensive and has serious side effects, but **walking** as little as twenty minutes a day has been shown to stimulate this growth hormone production.[283]

15) Walking lowers blood pressure.[284]

16) Walking reduces the risk for colon cancer.[285]

17) In these days, it should be encouraging to learn that walking even boosts the "immune system."[286]

18) Of course, there is the benefit of stimulating the lymph system, which, as you have learned is essential in the prevention of breast cancer.

One of the greatest rewards to be reaped from a program of regular exercise such as walking is the mental and emotional lift it provides that then spills over into the other areas of your life.

We all know the importance of exercise, and when we don't do any, not only do we suffer physiologically, but we also suffer psychologically. Somewhere inside, we berate ourselves for not doing the right thing. That all changes when you start to walk. Instead of having a negative feeling every time you are reminded of the fact that you don't exercise sufficiently, you feel a surge of pride that you **do**. Your level of esteem grows steadily and a **positive** message resounds through you instead of a negative one. You start to exude happiness and healthfulness because you truly are **happier and healthier**. On every possible level, you are improving your health. The richest person in the world can't **buy** this feeling of well-being for any amount of money because its value transcends money. **You** can have this feeling starting **right now** for the price of a pair of shoes. Make the effort. You're worth it!

With walking or any other form of exercise, consistency is the key. Do it at a pace that suits you and doesn't put pressure on you. Don't let it be something that hangs over you. If you start slowly and engage in it moderately, it will gradually become as normal and natural a part of your life as putting on clothes in the morning. You'll look forward to it. You'll **miss** it if you don't do it. Discover walking. Make it a part of your life, and you will never regret it.

* * * * * *

There are two other ways in which you can further assist the stimulation of your lymph system that deserve mention.

The first is what is called Lymphatic Drainage Massage. Seek out a qualified message therapist familiar with this technique. There are several areas of the body, on the legs, arms, torso and neck, that can be massaged to directly assist the lymph system in its effort to cleanse the body.

160

The second is Rebounding, which I discussed in great detail in *FIT FOR LIFE II*. Rebounders, or "mini-trampolines" as they are commonly called, can be purchased very inexpensively. I have seen perfectly adequate ones for around $20. Considering the extent to which Rebounding can help you prevent breast cancer, that's the greatest deal on Earth. Rebounding is extremely easy. All it calls for is a slight up and down bounce, which subjects the body to a change in velocity and direction twice with each jump. At the bottom of the bounce all the one-way valves of the lymph system are closed because of the pressure above them. At the top of the bounce the valves are open, allowing the lymph to flow up as the body starts down. Every valve opens at the same time, allowing and stimulating the flow of lymph.[287] As little as five or six minutes a day can be of immeasurable value.

Anything you can do to assist your lymph system should be done. A little effort goes a long way.

PART TWO

THE CARE PROGRAM

Chapter Ten

AN INTRODUCTION TO "CARE"

No matter how great sounding a program for prevention is; no matter how convincing the argument to follow it is; no matter how promising the results will be if it is followed, if there is not a way to easily implement it and **see** results, all the swell sounding promises are for naught. For decades, there have been numerous admonitions telling women over and over again **what** they have to do about breast cancer and **why** they have to do it. And although knowing what and why **is** of extreme importance, both are unhelpful, if not useless, unless accompanied by the **how** that will bring about the desired results.

The CARE program is **how** you are going to dramatically reduce your chances of ever developing breast cancer. At the heart of this approach are three principles which, if you put them to use with some regularity, will prove their worthiness to you. Your health **will** change for the better and the evidence of this bold statement will make itself apparent to you in no uncertain terms. You will **feel** better, you will **look** better, and your lymph system will be clean and operating at a highly efficient level.

However, bear in mind that there are no magic formulas, although sometimes when the body is cleansed of wastes and toxins the positive results do appear to be miraculous. But your body automatically brings about these "miracles" when you make the changes to facilitate them. As I said before, for change to occur, changes must be made. It's like the old saying goes, "If there is no change, then there is no change." We are talking about simple logic here. If you want your health to be different from what it has been, then **there must be some changes made** to make that a reality.

More often than not, I have found that people wanting change in their lives put far too much pressure on **themselves**, especially when the change calls for dietary modifications. For some reason, people put themselves in an "all or nothing" mode, diving into new behaviors with great resolve, restricting themselves too severely and burning themselves out in a few weeks, quickly reverting back to the old habits that weren't working. The only thing different in their lives then is some new guilt to deal with from not succeeding in the latest fling with health.

Perhaps there are going to be those who will follow this exact scenario with the three principles which are on the following pages. So before going any further, I want to make a pitch here and now to prevent as many of you as possible from falling into this trap.

These principles are guidelines to help you, not edicts to hinder you. They are tools to assist you, not rules to enslave you.

Your effort to improve your health and prevent breast cancer needn't be a stress-filled journey. It can be a joyous one. **This is not a race! The prize does not go to the one who gets there first. The prize goes to all who join the race! That is because the prize is the journey itself!** It's not how **fast** you travel, it's that you even make the trip at all. You have time. More time than you need. You see, even if you make use of the principles in a very conservative way until you are comfortable with them and they then become an integral part of your life-style, you will have changed your **direction,** and in so doing, breast cancer will become less and less of a possibility in your life. Rather than stagnating or becoming a little unhealthier every day, allowing the disease process to progress, you will, with each passing day, know what it means to become a little **healthier. Direction is everything. Speed is nothing.**

Imagine you and your family pulling through the entrance gate at Yellowstone National Park. You could spend a week taking in the beauty of this awe-inspiring national treasure and still not see it all. Or you could race through it in half a day like you were being chased by hungry bears. In either case, you could boast to your friends, "Yeah, we did Yellowstone." But which trip do you do? Which trip do you think would be most uplifting? The one in which you leisurely drink in the natural beauty that feeds your spirit and soul, or the one in which you screech through at breakneck speed throwing yourself and everyone with you into a panic of apprehension?

These principles I am about to share with you should not be viewed as a forced march, but rather as a light along your path. When it is convenient and comfortable to utilize them, do so. When it is not, don't. Know that to whatever degree you use them, however often you choose to implement them, that will be right for who you are and they will serve you exactly as well as they will serve those who embrace them to a fuller or even to a lesser degree than you. It's always better to do a little less at first and then do more as you start to see results, than it is to try to do too much and have to cut back and feel as though you failed.

One thing you can count on if you will use these principles: they will work! I have seen them do so for many people for many years. So ready is your body, so well equipped and capable it is to prevent cancer from getting started when given the opportunity, that even with the most moderate adherence to these principles, you will start to experience the benefits that they can so effectively bring about.

Throughout the book I have praised the nearly unfathomable magnificence and intelligence of the human body. I wish to return to this for just a moment before presenting the CARE principles. I made the point that all of the endless activities of your body are sourced and monitored by the brain. It's amazing when you think about the fact that all of the incredible advances made by the human species, from air flight to electricity, from computers to automobiles, all had their beginnings in the brain, and we only use about **10-15% of our brain.** Wow! So, what is the remaining 85-90% of this spectacular gem of creation doing? You can be sure it's not merely there to take up space in our skulls.

The body's—the brain's—number one priority at any and every given moment, is self-preservation. If the part of the brain used to figure out how to go to the moon at 17,000 miles per hour, play hopscotch and come back is so small, can you even begin to imagine the power working for your well being in the vast majority of your brain? Awesome! Your body will **never** give up on you and all you have to do to benefit from its unparalleled power is not stand in its way and to support its natural inclination to seek out and maintain its highest level of health possible. I am telling you that the three Principles of CARE, which I will be detailing in the next three chapters, provide that support.

Of course you would naturally want some kind of proof that these principles will indeed prevent breast cancer. Actually, I could tell you of plenty of women who use these principles and have not developed breast cancer, but someone could easily say, "Well, how do you know it was the three principles that prevented it? Maybe it was because they liked to garden, or because they took vitamins, or because of any number of other activities they participated in." So, about the only proof I can offer is how the principles fare in either stopping, reversing or banishing breast cancer once it has taken hold.

166

Over the years I have received literally hundreds of thousands of letters from people who have made truly remarkable recoveries in their health. I want to share with you a most extraordinary story that clearly demonstrates the indomitable spirit of one woman and the unparalleled healing ability of the human body. Her name is Anne Frahm. She wrote a book about her experiences. Here is her story.

Anne Frahm is a 40 year old wife and mother of two. In her mid 30's she started to experience an excruciating, unrelenting pain between her shoulder blades. X-rays showed "hot spots" on the bones of her shoulder which her doctor diagnosed as bursitis. It was also diagnosed that her condition was being complicated by a kidney infection.

Along with cortisone shots, she was told to apply daily ice packs for her shoulder and she was administered heavy doses of antibiotics both orally and intravenously for the kidney infection. All that happened was that the pain became progressively worse. It became so bad that she could not roll over in bed or even hug her own children without experiencing unbearable pain.

This went on for seven months, at which time she went to a hospital emergency room to seek another doctor's opinion. This doctor conferred with Mrs. Frahm's family doctor and they wondered if all this pain wasn't really just in her head. She was given a shot of muscle relaxant, a prescription for Valium and sent home.

Still in pain, she **demanded** more definitive answers of her doctor. She was sent for a CAT-scan. A young doctor came into her room with the results and told her she had advanced breast cancer to such a degree that she had to have a mastectomy the very next day! When she asked how bad it was, the doctor answered, "I'm not going to pull any punches, most people who have cancer so advanced die within two years."

It wasn't only hearing that she had breast cancer that so shocked her, it was also the fact that several months before the pain even began she had found a small lump in her breast during a self-examination. Since her grandmother had died of breast cancer and her mother had both breasts removed because of ongoing, troubling cysts in her breasts, Anne wasted no time in getting a mammogram. She was told that there were indeed **two** tiny lumps but they were benign, noncancerous. An additional ultrasound test also confirmed that they were benign. The doctor said, "Nope, no cancer here."

Not only **were** they cancerous, but also the cancer had spread and tumors were found covering her skull, shoulders, ribs, pelvis and up and down her spine.

Her breast was removed along with a tumor that was beneath it, the size of her entire breast. For the next year-and-a-half, her body was subjected to very treatments including high doses of chemotherapy and radiation. She went bald, developed severe pneumonia, and her skin from head to toe broke out into itchy, red splotches.

After all of her pain and suffering from the cancer, the chemotherapy and the radiation, she was told that the cancer was steadily progressing and that her situation was becoming ever worse. She was told that her last possible hope was a bone marrow transplant. I don't even want to begin to tell you what a horrendous experience such a procedure is. Suffice it to say that it is something you **never** want to experience.

A couple of months after the bone marrow transplant, monitoring of her white blood cell count indicated that there was still a lot of cancer in her bone marrow. Any more chemotherapy was out of the question, as it would have killed her outright.

When she inquired about a new experimental drug being tested on some patients to stimulate the growth of white blood cells, she was given the most stunning, mind-numbing response imaginable. Since there was only a limited amount of the drug available, it had to be held in reserve for patients with a more favorable chance of survival. Sorry!

With sadness and regret, she was sent home to die.

It was impossible to read Anne's description of her husband, her children and herself huddled together, mourning her impending death, without weeping.

But Anne Frahm did not know the meaning of the words, "give up." They weren't in her vocabulary. She loved her family and her life and was not ready to leave. Her last ditch effort was to turn to a nutritionist for help. She was counseled, given books to read, put on a very strict, detoxifying diet and she never lost her positive attitude. She **knew** she was going to win. A mere five weeks later, in the most remarkable instance of self-healing I have ever encountered, not even the slightest trace of cancer could be found in her body. **It was gone!** Her doctor, noticeably flabbergasted, said, "When you returned from the transplant with cancer in your marrow, I honestly thought you were doomed!"

As word of Anne's miraculous recovery spread and doctors and lay people alike kept contacting her to hear her story, she decided to put it all down in a book. That book is called *A CANCER BATTLE PLAN*, and it was published in 1993.

Before I heard of either Anne, or her book, she wrote me a letter and sent me a picture of herself. Looking at her smiling face and her full head of lush, black hair filled me with joy, as did her letter, which read:

Dear Harvey,

Thank you! Thank you! Thank you! You have helped save the life of this 40 year old wife and mother—me! Four years ago I was dying of cancer. After 1½ years of chemotherapy, radiation, surgery and even a bone marrow transplant, nothing worked and I was sent home to die. Instead, I consulted a nutritionist. **FIVE WEEKS** later at my next checkup, tests revealed **NO TRACE** of cancer in my body!! I've been cancer free and **HEALTHY** for four years!

One of the first books my nutritionist recommended was FIT FOR LIFE. The simple, common sense approach you use helped me and my husband form a basis of understanding that helped me overcome cancer. **THANK YOU** for standing up in the face of overwhelming opposition to tell the truth!!

Your greatest fan,
Anne Frahm

In order to overcome this severely advanced cancer, Anne detoxified her body through dietary regimentation (Principle One in the CARE program), entirely removed animal products from her diet (variation of Principle Two), and filled her mind with positiveness and prayer (Principle Three). The implications of this should be blatantly obvious to anyone interested in preventing breast cancer. If this woman, who was brought to death's door with no hope of survival, was able to use information similar to that in this book to reverse and banish the cancer from her body, do you fully realize the power and ability you have to **prevent** cancer from ever developing in the first place?

170

I hope you do. I sincerely hope you see the control over your health the concepts in this book give you. If cancer can be reversed, it can be prevented. You **can** prevent breast cancer!

Now I want to ask you a question—a question which you need to ask of yourself. What are you willing to do in support of your body's effort to avoid developing breast cancer? Knowing that your body, with the brain at its helm, is tirelessly working for you, doing for you everything and anything it can to keep you in health, are you willing to also make an effort to help? Or, are you of a mind that you want to just go your merry way and leave it all up to fate? I think when you see how simple the three principles are and how easy they are to incorporate into your life-style, your answer will be a resounding, **"I'm ready to do my part!"** Well....turn the page and I'll show you how you can do that.

Chapter Eleven

THE FIRST PRINCIPLE:

PERIODIC MONO-DIETING

All three of these principles, each working in concert with one another, are important, and all will help you immensely in your effort to prevent breast cancer. But this first one, **periodic mono-dieting**, if used **intelligently**, will do more to cleanse and strengthen your lymph system than any other action you could take other than fasting.*

Periodic mono-dieting is, without question, responsible for my recaptured health and my continued well-being more than any other factor. I have personally benefited immeasurably from it for over twenty-five years and continue today to reap the rewards of its effectiveness in helping maintain the level of health I enjoy. Part of the beauty of this tool is its simplicity. **Anyone** can make use of it to both bring about an immediate improvement in health and insure long term health maintenance. It is the key element in preventing breast cancer.

---

* The subject of fasting is far too complex and is deserving of far more space than can be allotted here. Suffice it to say , however, that there is no activity associated with health care that is more thorough, more effective or more beneficial than a properly conducted fast, and there is no other area of healing that is more neglected, more misunderstood or more un- fairly maligned. Those who call fasting and starvation the same thing are guilty of the most unforgivable ignorance of the physiology of the human body. It would be exactly like calling swimming and drowning the same thing.

Periodic mono-dieting is the eating of fresh fruits and/or vegetables and their juices, **uncooked**, for a specific length of time which can range anywhere from one day to several weeks. Before explaining the reasoning behind it and the benefits that can be expected from it, let me give you a few specific examples of possible mono-diets.

1) Drinking only fresh fruit and vegetable juice for **one to three** days.

2) Drinking only fresh juices and eating whole fruits and vegetables for **three to five** days.

3) Drinking only fresh fruit and vegetable juices and eating only fresh fruits and vegetables and salads for **only one** day to **a week** to **10** days.

In other words, periodic mono-dieting is the taking of any combination of any raw, fresh food or juice for whatever length of time you wish.

The reasoning behind all food during a mono-diet being in its natural, raw state is quite simple and crucial in terms of preventing breast cancer. The purpose of mono-dieting is twofold. First, is to use as little energy as possible on digestion so energy can be freed up and directed toward the cleansing and rejuvenation of your lymph system. Second, it is to obtain the maximum amount of fuel and nutrients from the food being eaten. Raw food fulfills these two requirements more than food that has been cooked or otherwise processed.

Raw food demands less energy to digest because it is in its purest state, its natural state. And **any** cooking of food removes or denatures **some** nutrients. Bear in mind that human beings stand alone in all of nature as the one and only species to eat cooked food, and we lead all species in the degenerative diseases as evidence. It is the most obvious area in which our superior thinking and reasoning abilities has not served us.

Periodic mono-dieting should not be viewed as a diet to be used in a crisis to empty out a swollen lymph gland or to deal with an existing cancer, although in both instances it can be beneficial. To gain the greatest benefit from periodic mono-dieting, **it should become a regular part of your life-style** as a means of long-term **prevention** and **long-term wellness**. It is impossible for me to overemphasize this statement. The extent to which you use it is up to you— there are no specifically prescribed regimens.

There are those who have an all juice or all fruit day once a week. Some eat only raw food one day a week. Some have three straight raw days every month. Dr. Gabriel Cousens suggests that every six months you drink only fresh juices for a week. There is literally an unlimited number of ways to use periodic mono-dieting. The object is, of course, to **use it!** If you must discipline yourself by marking on your calendar exactly when you are going to mono-diet for a day or three days or five days or a week, then do it. Or if you wake up one morning and just say, "I feel like only having juice today," then that's your day. This is a flexible tool, it's not regimented, unless you choose for it to be so because you simply function better that way.

The reason I seem to be harping on this one aspect is because it is my experience that whenever the subject of food is discussed, people tend to look for restrictive rules they **must** follow as justifiable punishment for past indiscretions. I encourage you to cultivate a different viewpoint. The fact is that when periodic mono-dieting becomes an integral part of your life-style, breast cancer is kept at bay.

The entire eating experience becomes so much more freeing. Plus one of the most rewarding results of mono-dieting, besides preventing breast cancer, is the incredible feeling of renewal and positivity that fills you up and spills over into all the other areas of your life. Once you incorporate mono-dieting into your life, you **never** abandon it. Even if that means only mono-dieting three days a **year**, once you've experienced the surge of energy and well-being it produces, you never get it out of your mind. Mono-dieting days are looked forward to with great anticipation. **That is because periodic mono-dieting is not a punishment, it is a joy!**

Throughout this book I have made it clear that the traditional approach toward breast cancer is all involved with after-the-fact treatment. The only way to **prevent** breast cancer is entirely dependent upon what you do **before** such treatment is necessary. Periodic mono-dieting is the cornerstone of a life-style that will prevent breast cancer.

When I first embarked on my journey down the pathway to health, mono-dieting proved to be invaluable to me. At a time of desperate need, it gave me my first glimpse of how good I **could** feel. After starting off with short mono-diets of one, two and three days—as my health steadily improved—I started increasing their duration until I was going ten days or two weeks two or three times a year. Recovery from my health problems was dramatically hastened, and I am convinced that periodic mono-dieting was the major reason why. To this day, it remains my most important tool for health maintenance.

The reasoning behind periodic mono-dieting is simple as simple can be. The message of this book is that you can take charge of your health and prevent breast cancer and improve your general health by cleansing the body of wastes and toxins. The means by which that is accomplished is to CARE—Cleanse And Rejuvenate Energetically. Periodic mono-dieting specifically and dramatically does just that. It greatly facilitates cleansing and skyrockets energy levels.

Let's face it. Energy is everything. Without it, nothing is possible and nothing happens. A car without fuel goes nowhere. Neither does a body without energy. There is no way on earth to discuss energy and energy levels without discussing digestion.

When you take into account the full extent of the digestive activities involved in taking in food, processing it and extracting nutrients and delivering them to the cells; the elimination of wastes and all the interactions of the organs, stomach, intestines, pancreas, liver, kidneys, etc.; and the metabolic processes that take place to turn food into blood, muscle and bone, it is no wonder that the digestive process takes such an enormous amount of energy.

There is precious little you can do that requires more energy than digestion. Surely you have evidence of this. After eating a big meal, of many kinds of foods, which do you look for, a mountain to climb or a sofa on which to recline? Knowing the extreme importance of energy and how crucial it is to the cleansing process, what better place to look to free up some than from the vast amount required for digestion.

There are two ways to free up energy from the digestive process for use in other areas of activity. The first is to streamline digestion, have it work more efficiently. In previous books I introduced the concept of food combining for just that purpose. The second way, the way that has the potential to free up huge amounts of energy, is to **give the digestive track less to do.** With less work to do, energy that is routinely spent on digestion is automatically used by the body to cleanse itself of waste. The body always works on priorities and removing impactions and silted up waste that is interfering with the smooth operation of the system is right up on top of the list. Lymph nodes in your breast or anywhere else in your body will not become swollen with waste if wastes in the body are kept to a minimum.

Thus, by giving the digestive track less to do, periodic mono-dieting becomes probably the most compelling and potent tool you can implement in your life to prevent breast cancer. I know full well what a provocative and bold statement that is to make. And, certainly, there are those who immediately demand proof of such a premise. Although the greatest proof of all is in the doing as the beneficial results of periodic mono-dieting become increasingly evident, there are a couple of supportive pieces of evidence, one scientific, one observational, that I can offer.

Roy Walford is a medical doctor. He has been a UCLA professor since 1966 and is one of the world's eminent gerontologists. In addition to being the director of a sixteen member research laboratory at UCLA for the study of immunology and the aging process, he was also a member of the White House Conference on Aging, a member of the National Academy of Sciences Committee on Aging, and the chairman of the National Institute on Aging Task Force in Immunology. He has authored five books dealing with immunology and aging and is recognized the world over as an expert in his field.

Dr. Walford has conducted numerous long-term experiments on aging with mice and, based on those experiments, he is convinced that he is going to live **healthfully** to about 120 years of age—what he considers should be the average life span of humans. To be sure, his experiments have not been on periodic mono-dieting. That is a term I have coined. But his experiments **have** been on the effect of less work for the digestive tract, over a long term, on health and longevity. His findings fully substantiate my premise that the less work the digestive track has to do, the healthier you will be and the longer you will live.

Dr. Walford puts his mice on what he refers to as "the restricted diet," which means they fast two days a week. Most mice live about two years, but Dr. Walford's mice live **more than twice that long**. They not only live much longer, but they also show significantly lower rates of heart disease and cancer. Further, those small numbers of mice that **do** develop such diseases, do so at a much later age than animals eating without restrictions. His experiments have **consistently** shown this improvement in health and longevity. Dr. Walford is seventy years old and vibrantly fit. He fasts two days a week.[288]

The experiments Dr. Walford has conducted over the years supports what the practitioners of Natural Hygiene have known for quite a long while: that during our life-time, we will each consume approximately 70 tons of food and all of the metabolic activities involved in processing that food, using what is needed and ridding itself of the rest, will take more energy from the body over a lifetime than anything else. Learning how to channel some of that energy toward the cleansing that will ultimately result in the prevention of breast cancer is a gift of immeasurable value. That is the gift of periodic mono-dieting.

The practice of giving the digestive track less work to do in order to free up energy for the healing process is a common occurrence that is seen all throughout nature. Anyone who has ever worked a farm or spent time working with animals in some capacity has seen this over and over. A horse that is lame will "go off its food," as the expression goes. It will hardly eat. Every stockyard worker knows that when a cow or horse or hog or sheep day after day eats much less food than normal, there is something wrong with the animal, and it **instinctively** reduces its food intake so the body will have the energy to correct whatever is wrong. Certainly, pet owners know that when a dog or cat is sick or injured, they either refuse food altogether or hardly eat at all. Even when concerned owners try to entice them with the most tempting food, they will refuse. They find a secluded spot and rest until the body completes its healing work.

A similar reaction can be seen in children. When they are ill, they lose their appetite and won't eat. Parents will frequently try to pressure them into eating by saying things like, "Eat this for Mommy," or, "The doctor says you won't get well if you don't eat." But not having been falsely conditioned to believe that you have to eat when sick, they merely follow the directives of their instincts and refuse food.

Even as an adult, haven't you noticed a loss of appetite when you don't feel well? In a manner of speaking, that loss of appetite is a natural tendency of the body to free up energy from digestion that is needed for other work. And although mono-dieting **is** a smart thing to do to speed recovery when you're not feeling well, the most intelligent use of periodic mono-dieting, indeed its prime use and benefit, is to make it a normal and natural part of your life-style as a means of preventing illness in the first place. It helps us shift the focus from illness to wellness!

I do not recommend that it be used as an emergency measure (the same way you would use a drug) once the effect of continued neglect of the body has finally caught up to you. It should become a **regular part of your healthy life-style**, the same as anything else that you do on a regular basis. Would you ever seriously consider not periodically dusting and cleaning your house? Would you ever dream of **not** periodically changing the old oil in your car, even with the red light on the dash board flashing away? Then you mustn't consider not periodically mono-dieting to cleanse your inner body, because having a clean inner body is easily as important—in fact infinitely **more** important than a clean house or car. Because a clean inner body is what insures your success in preventing breast cancer.

The type, length and frequency of your mono-diets will vary according to your personal needs and wants. From the examples at the beginning of the chapter, you can see that some will be only juices, some will be juices, raw vegetables and salads. Some will be one day in duration, some will be a week or ten days. You may do one every week, every month or every three months. **There is no right or wrong involved in this**. This point cannot be made too frequently. Certainly, decisions on this can't be made **now**. How could they?

The only way to make an intelligent and informed decision on how and when to mono-diet on a regular basis would have to come **after** you have experienced what is involved in it and what benefits can be reasonably expected. In my experience, any amount of mono-dieting is beneficial, but mono-diets of three days and more are where you **really** start to see the power behind this practice. However, even one day mono-diets will get you started and give you an experience of mono-dieting that you can relate to as you start to become more accustomed to what to expect from future mono-diets.

You can be assured that, with practice, it will become clear to you how to best incorporate mono-dieting into your life-style. Those whose lives are very orderly and regimented and who like the preciseness of knowing exactly when they are doing what, will schedule their mono-diets the same way they schedule other important events in their lives. Those who are more spontaneous will wake up one morning and declare, "I'm doing fruit and juice for three days." One is not better than the other.

To give you an understanding of precisely what a mono-diet of a day or a week would be like in terms of what foods are taken, the following **examples** are provided. These are only examples, not dictums. Although you could follow these examples and they would work extremely well for you, know that you can modify them in any way you wish in order to personalize them to your likes and dislikes.

181

1) One day on juice.

2) Three days on juice, smoothies and fruit.

3) A week on only uncooked food.

One Day On Juice - For one day, intermittently throughout the day your only intake of food is juice, either fruit or vegetable or both. I have found that fruit juices for the first part of the day and vegetable juice for the second part, with more fruit juice in the evening works best for me. But any way you want to do it is fine. You can have only fruit juice, only vegetable juice or switch off, fruit, then vegetable, up and back throughout the day and evening. As long as it's only juice, it doesn't matter which you have or when. Also, when having only juice, it's best to have approximately ten to fourteen ounces about every two hours. Here again, that is only a very loose guideline that can be altered to fit your particular needs and desires.

What is important is that only fresh juice is consumed for twenty-four hours. There are many books on the market these days on juicing that supply an amazingly wide array of different juice mixes, both fruit and vegetable. Experiment. They're fun and they're delicious. One of my very favorite juice mixtures is apple-celery juice. If you've never had it, you may be thinking, "Ugh, apple-celery?" You're in for a big surprise because apple-celery juice is one of the most refreshing and delicious combinations I've ever had. There's something about that mixture that works. Believe me on this one and just try it. You'll be hooked like so many other people I have turned on to it.

If you have read *FIT FOR LIFE*, you might be saying, "Hold on there, I thought it was a huge no-no to mix fruit with any other food." That is true, but like everything in life, there are exceptions to the rule. Celery, being very high in water content, and having no complex starches, proteins or fats, causes **no** problem when eaten with fruit. Celery juice is very potent so when mixing it with apple juice, the mixture should be approximately three-quarters apple juice, one-quarter celery juice.

Three Days, Juice, Whole Fruit and "Smoothies" - In addition to having fresh juices, fruit and/or vegetables throughout the day, you also eat pieces of fresh fruit and have fruit smoothies. When doing this type of mono-diet **any** fruit is O.K. as long as it is fresh. This includes dates, raisins and other dry foods so long as they are dried naturally and do not contain sulfur dioxide. Dried fruit is very concentrated, so go light when having them. Smoothies are extremely easy to make. Put either apple or orange juice (fresh, of course) in a blender, add a frozen banana and **any** other fruit you like and presto, a fabulous smoothie. When making these drinks, you can add frozen blueberries, strawberries, peaches or other fruits to the juice and frozen banana. Have fun with these. There are an infinite variety, and they taste incredible. To freeze bananas, peel them first and put them in the freezer in an air tight tupperware-type container.

A Week On Only Uncooked Food - For a week's time you eat nothing but raw, uncooked food—all fruits and vegetables, their juices and salads. Have as much juice and whole fruit and vegetables as you like and have a good sized mixed salad late in the day. A salad dressing of olive oil (which has been associated with a significant reduced risk of breast cancer[288A]), lemon juice and whatever herbs and spices you like is best, but you can have other types of dressing, preferably with a minimum of chemical additives. After having a salad, refrain from having fruit or fruit juice for three hours.

Once again, I'm going to say that these are only examples. You could do any of these three for any length of time. Number one can be done for several days or a week, as could number two. Or number three could be done for one day or three. Or you could do number one for a day, number two for a day and number three for a day.

Anything goes when mono-dieting in terms of length or food eaten as long as what you have is uncooked.

TIPS AND TIDBITS
FOR PERIODIC MONO-DIETING

1) For the results of mono-dieting to be most effective it is imperative that the juices you drink be fresh, not pasteurized, canned or made from concentrate. Drinking other than fresh, unheated juice almost entirely defeats the very purpose of mono-dieting. These days, thanks to people like "The Juice Man," home juicers are readily available and are very reasonably priced. When measured against the benefits you will reap, the cost of a home juicer is insignificant. Owning your own juicer is a smart move. I'll bet you have at least one television in your house. A juicer is a whole lot less expensive and has the added enticement of **helping you prevent breast cancer**. Will your television do that for you? Even if you don't own a juicer, you can certainly buy fresh squeezed juice and that will do fine.

2) When drinking juice, it is best not to gulp it down. Sip it instead. Drink it slowly so it does not all wind up in your stomach at once which is hard on the body, can cause stomach aches and is counterproductive. You should swallow one mouthful at a time after it has had a chance to mix with your saliva.

3) Fruit has a very interesting nature. Unlike other foods, fruit does not require a lot of time in the stomach for digestion. Most all foods stay in the stomach about three hours. Fruit leaves the stomach in about twenty minutes to half an hour. Fruit juice leaves the stomach in less time than that. Therefore, whether you are mono-dieting or not, you should not have fruit or fruit juice for about three hours after eating anything else.

4) Those who have never eaten highly cleansing food exclusively for a few days, **may** experience a side effect that is uncomfortable but quite valuable: diarrhea.

Understand that a certain amount of waste will accumulate in the digestive track over time. When all of a sudden nothing but juice and fruit, which are over 90% water, goes through for a few days, it is as though the digestive tract is being flushed and scrubbed. This will **rarely** last over forty-eight hours, and usually will last only twenty-four hours. It is not something to be alarmed about. Remember, every action of the body is the result of a cause. Diarrhea after consuming only high water, cleansing foods is not at all surprising. Of course, anyone experiencing diarrhea for longer than forty-eight hours, for any reason, should check with his or her health care practitioner right away. But to experience it because of eating cleansing food is not at all a problem.

5)   Some people think that because their intake of food is so restricted while mono-dieting that they may not have enough energy to go to work or to do other things they need to do. Interestingly, the exact opposite is true. Energy levels **soar** when mono-dieting. Remember that digestion requires huge amounts of energy. Since, when you are mono-dieting, you are only eating uncooked food, you are eating the foods that require the least amount of energy to digest but supply a great deal of energy. The one thing more people comment on when they mono-diet is the enormous increase in energy.

6)   People who are prone to hypoglycemia (low blood sugar) start to get a little nervous when you talk about eating only fruit or eating very lightly. First of all, let's look at what low blood sugar is. The brain constantly monitors the blood stream to make sure there is sufficient sugar and nutrients in the blood. If not, it sets off an alarm in the form of edginess, discomfort and sluggishness. Fruit, whose sugar component of fructose turns to glucose, gets into the blood stream faster than anything else. So if you have low blood sugar and you eat fruit, it will stop the symptoms very quickly. There's nothing better for low blood sugar

than fruit. But others with hypoglycemia have to eat quite frequently to stem the symptoms. No problem. When mono-dieting, if you have hypoglycemia tendencies you can eat as frequently as you feel you need to.

7) When mono-dieting on all raw, uncooked food, many people like to eat nuts. It's O.K. to eat raw nuts when mono-dieting; however, one has to take great care. Nuts are an **extremely** concentrated food that is exceedingly easy to overeat. They should be eaten very sparingly, and not more than one time per day. Ten or twelve almonds, for example, is plenty. More than that is overeating and causing too much work for the digestive process, exactly what you want to avoid. If you can't eat only ten or twelve, leave them alone.

Also, whenever I eat nuts, and I am partial to raw almonds and raw cashews, I **always** have either cucumber slices or celery with them. Not only does it taste great, but the high water content of the cucumbers or celery seems to assist in moving the nuts through the stomach more easily. You may question the suggestion of eating nuts at all because of their fat content. You should know that **some** fat in the diet is absolutely essential. Without some fat, you would die. In fact, vitamins A, D, E and K cannot even be broken down and utilized unless in the presence of fat. The issue is where is the fat in your diet coming from. The fat in animal products is the culprit, not the fat from raw nuts and seeds, or avocados.

8) If you are mono-dieting for a week or longer on all uncooked foods, meaning you are having salads, in addition to juices, fruit, smoothies and vegetables, you may start to crave something cooked, but still want to continue your mono-diet. There is a way to do that, which is a slight exception to the rule of only uncooked food, that allows you to continue to cleanse but also eat a little heavier. Add steamed vegetables to your salad. Whatever vegetables you like, broccoli, cauliflower, zucchini, whatever, steam up

one, two or three, put them in your salad, add the dressing and that is an incredibly tasty and satisfying meal.

What I suggest is that you don't do that on short mono-diets of only three or four days. But if you're going for a week, ten days or two weeks, you can do it for the last part of the mono-diet. In other words, on a one week mono-diet, add steamed vegetables the last two days. On a ten day, add them the last three or four days. Also, make sure there is more salad than steamed vegetables, not the other way around. Remember, it is the regular eating of uncooked food that is the goal.

9)   A beautiful side effect of periodic mono-dieting is that your overall diet tends to improve. After eating clean, healthy food for a while, you're not so anxious to put just any ol' thing in your body. Sometimes it's obvious and sometimes it's more subtle, but as time goes by and you are free of pain, you've lost weight, your mammograms are all negative and you're feeling very good about yourself, your tendency is to want to keep it that way. You'll find yourself making healthier choices in restaurants and less frequently eating those death burgers and the like at the thousands of fast food stands all over the country that contribute so greatly to the level of ill health suffered by so many.

10)   After a mono-diet of five days or more, you have to be particularly careful of what you eat the first one or two days after the mono-diet. Jumping right into a lot of very heavy foods too quickly can make you feel horrible. Your body accustoms itself to light, clean, uncooked food and you can catch it off guard by too quickly eating too heavily.

I'll give you a couple of examples so you know what I'm talking about. Let's say you do a one week mono-diet of juices, fruit and salads. On the eighth day if you have a big lunch of, say, pizza or fried chicken or a burger and fries, and a dinner of steak and potatoes, bread, and apple pie, you're going to feel miserable the next day. It would be better to eat very lightly in the morning, only fruit and/or juice. Have a salad for lunch with a baked potato or piece of toast if you need more than just a salad, and perhaps a pasta with vegetable dish and a salad for dinner. This way you gradually reintroduce the cooked food without jumping straight into the heaviest foods possible. I would wait until the second or third day after a mono-diet before having meat, chicken or fish, and I would eat them sparingly (more on that in the next principle).

11) This tip is of such importance that I considered making it the fourth principle. It has to do with what foods you eat in the morning hours. I know that we have been raised in this country to believe that a "big hearty breakfast" is the best way to start the day, but it ain't necessarily so.

To date, the *FIT FOR LIFE* books (*FIT FOR LIFE* and *FIT FOR LIFE II*) have sold somewhere in the neighborhood of ten million copies worldwide. Nearly half a million people have written to share their thoughts, ask questions and make comments on the books and the principles they impart. Without question, the number one comment made far and away more frequently than any other had to do with what foods were eaten in the early part of the day to insure the greatest level of success. I want to very briefly summarize that for you.

What we are trying to accomplish here is a cleansing of your body, the elimination of waste, so that the lymph system will not be so overburdened that it has to store those toxic wastes in the lymph nodes opening the door for breast cancer. Every physiological function of your body operates under cycles that are called circadian rhythms. The eight-hour period that the body's internal eliminative processes are most heightened is from 4 A.M. until

12 Noon. That is when the lymph system is most active in picking up waste from the cells and taking them to the eliminative organs.

As we know, digestion takes enormous amounts of energy, so if you eat a heavy meal in the morning hours, some of the energy being used to cleanse and eliminate is diverted to the stomach for digestion. My suggestion to you, to get the absolute **most** out of the three principles, is to eat as lightly as possible in the hours from the time you awaken in the morning until noon. If you can eat exclusively fruit and juice until noon, as much as you like, that is certainly the very best routine possible, because fruit and its juices require practically **no** energy at all to be digested. That way, the elimination cycle can operate at its fullest efficiency.

If you don't feel you can eat only fruit and juice until noon, let me make two suggestions.

• Eat only fruit and its juices until noon as often as you can. If that's only two days a week, so be it. If it's every other day, that's fantastic.

• At least make fruit and juice the first thing you put into your body, even if a half hour later you're having cereal or toast or whatever.

The goal should be to go as close to noon as you can on only fruit and juice. You will have to try fruit until noon for only one week to see the phenomenal difference it makes in your energy level and feeling of well being. Millions have already learned of it, have made it a permanent part of their lives and are enjoying the many benefits of doing so. You will be astounded at the results this simple practice brings about. **In terms of preventing breast cancer, this is very important for your overall success, please do not minimize it.***

---

* An in-depth explanation of the circadian rhythms and the value of fruit until noon and the reasoning behind them can be found in *Fit For Life*.

12) A question you are sure to have is, "How often should I mono-diet and for what duration?" This is a very difficult question to answer because of the many possible variables that can come into play, and what your goals and motivations are. But there are **loose** guidelines I can give you. Most generally speaking, if you have never mono-dieted or fasted, or taken any other measures to cleanse or detoxify your system, and you are fairly certain your inner body could use a good cleansing, the more frequent and the longer, the better. In other words, at **first** you should diligently mono-diet at regular intervals, more frequently than later on when you know your body is pretty clean. Then your mono-diets are more for maintenance, especially if you upgrade your diet so as to minimize those foods which would encumber your lymph system.

The best illustration I can give you would be my own experience with mono-dieting. When I was first introduced to Natural Hygiene and mono-dieting, I was highly motivated. I was sick, fat, tired, in pain and living in fear because of the death of my father. The person who taught me the fundamentals of what I am here attempting to impart to you **assured** me that a series of mono-diets and simultaneous improvement in my dietary habits would quickly bring me to a level of health I had not enjoyed for a very long time.

Let me tell you, he sounded totally sure of himself and I **sorely** wanted to believe. But for as long as I had been dealing with excruciating stomach aches, for as many diets as I had been on to lose weight, for as frustrated as I was over my continually declining health, I have to admit that I was more than a little skeptical that it would all be wiped away by what on the surface seemed to be hardly any effort. But there was something else. I was willing!

He told me that the first thing I needed to do, since I was eating anything I desired at any time, was have only fruit and vegetable juices and fresh fruit for five days. To me, at that particular stage of my life, the idea of having only fruit and fruit juice for five days was like suggesting that I wet my finger and stick it in a light socket. But I did it because I desperately needed **something** to happen in my life to turn things around for me. The first day was the hardest. The first day is **always** the hardest. But on the **sixth** day, when I was to start eating other foods, the most amazing, most unexpected thing happened; I felt so darned good, so energetic, so positive, so light and **clean**, that I decided to go for another five days! **Me!** The guy that would rather fall down a flight of cement stairs than miss a meal.

I was riding my bicycle every day and reading books by Herbert M. Shelton, the acknowledged father of Natural Hygiene. At the end of ten days, my life was forever changed. I simply could not believe how good I felt. My stomach, which had hurt me **every day** for over twenty years did not bother me at all, I had lost about ten or twelve pounds, my energy level was through the roof and I felt like I owned the world.

My mentor, who had a rather quirky sense of humor, said to me, in a totally professional, serious tone, "Well, you have a decision to make now, you can either alter your dietetic life-style a bit and continue to cleanse your system, lose more weight, and feel euphoric, or you can go back to the way you were eating before your ten days and have your health go back to what it was. What's it going to be?" I didn't say anything, I just looked at him in a way that left no doubt what my decision was.

He told me that for the best results, the **quickest** results, I should cut out all meat at least at first. Then after I felt really good, I could reintroduce the meat back into my diet, but not the way I was eating it before which was not only every day, but every meal.

I decided to eliminate all meat, chicken and fish from my diet at least until I lost the fifty pounds. I basically ate whatever I wanted other than that, being sure to not over-eat. Although I ate breads, cheese, pasta and the like, fruits and vegetables dominated my diet. I mono-dieted two days a week, one day on only juices (fruit and vegetable) and another day (three days later) on juice and whole fruit, as much as I liked.

Astonishingly, I lost my fifty pounds in one month. Not only was my body ready to heal itself, but I also helped it along by improving my diet, riding my bike every day and flooding my consciousness with positive thoughts about how well I was doing and how successful I was going to be.

I made a commitment to do a ten day mono-diet at **least** four times a year, one every three months. For the next two years, I did exactly that, every three months I did either ten days on juices and fruit or ten days on juice, fruit and salads. In between, I ate **very few** animal products, exercised regularly and did shorter mono-diets of one or two days in a row every week. After the first two years, with my weight loss maintained, no pain and an exuberance for life that I thought I'd never achieve, I knew I had found a life-style that would serve me forever. Now I do ten day mono-diets two or sometimes three times a year, and I mono-diet every other day.

I tried different kinds of mono-dieting routines. Once I ate only uncooked foods (fruit, vegetables, juice and salads) every other day for three months. In between, I ate what I wanted. It was great! I felt absolutely incredible. When I was preparing for my first television tour for *FIT FOR LIFE*, I ate only fruit and juices for two weeks and only uncooked food for a month. Touring is unbelievably grueling, but I sailed through three weeks of nonstop work with interviews from morning until night and a plane ride every day, with an abundance of energy and positiveness.

Over and over, television talk show hosts would comment on how, "up and energetic I was for being in the middle of a tour."

My advice to you is to start with a three or five day mono-diet of fruit and vegetable juices and whole fruit just to see what it feels like. Mono-diet one or two days a week with longer ones (a week or ten days) every two to three months, depending on how much you feel you need to cleanse your body and how motivated you are to get your lymph system cleaned out so no lymph nodes will fill up. I think as you can see from what I have written that it can be done in a very non-structured way in terms of how long and how frequently you mono-diet.

Having said that, I know there are those of you who want a more definitive program to follow—something that takes the guesswork out of it and tells you precisely how frequently and how long you should mono-diet. Allow me once again to use a quick analogy to set the stage here.

If you were in a canoe or a rowboat that had a lot of water in it because of a leak, you would have to aggressively bail water out to lower the level and prevent capsizing. Once you got the level of water way down you could relax and only periodically bail water to keep the level low. So it is with your body. To start, you should mono-diet more frequently and for longer durations, to lower the level of toxins in your body. Then you can mono-diet more infrequently as a means to keep it low.

For the first year I suggest that you mono-diet for at least 10 days every three months. That's four 10-day mono-diets for the year. Two should be only juice (both fruit and vegetable) and fruit, and two should be all raw foods (fruits, vegetables, their juices and salads). In between the 10-day mono-diets, you should mono-diet at least two days a week, either two days in a row or twice within the week.

After the first year it would, of course, be ideal to do the same every year for the rest of your life to be absolutely certain that your toxic level never gets out of control and your lymph nodes never become swollen, but as a maintenance program you can cut it in half. That would be two 10-day mono-diets a year and at least one day a week.

Understand this: **You cannot mono-diet too much!** The more you do it, the healthier you'll be and the less likelihood there will be of you ever developing breast cancer. You can, however, mono-diet too little. Therefore, you have to find out what your personal comfort level is and how motivated you are. As time goes by, you will know exactly what's right for you and how much you need to mono-diet for your particular life-style, especially when you experience the well-being that is the automatic result of periodic mono-dieting with any kind of regularity.

When you are mono-dieting, you are allowing your body to be cleansed. You are cleaning and rejuvenating your lymph system. **You are preventing breast cancer.** Please, **please** do not make the mistake of taking periodic mono-dieting lightly or minimizing the extent to which it can achieve that much desired goal of helping you live your life without the fear of becoming a breast cancer statistic. Considering the havoc breast cancer has caused in so many people's lives and its apparent complicated and puzzling characteristics, I can understand an initial reaction being something to the effect of, "Yeah, right. Eating nothing but fruit and vegetables every so often is going to prevent something as pervasive and bewildering as breast cancer." Is there a problem with the solution being more simple and straightforward than you have been led to believe? If it were far more complicated, expensive and difficult to do, would you have more confidence in it?

In Chapter One I told you of the woman who called me from the hospital because she had a walnut-sized lump in her breast. **She got rid of the lump by mono-dieting!** As far as she was concerned, mono-dieting saved her life.

For most of you, periodic mono-dieting is an aspect of your life that you have yet to experience. If for no other reason than curiosity, you should want to try it just to see what, if anything, you've missed. Having done so, you will certainly know your body better. When you buy a car or a VCR or a camera, don't you read the owner's manual to learn all about their features so you can use them to your best advantage? It would be great if our bodies came with an owner's manual, but that isn't the case. Still, don't you want to learn all about **its** features so that you can use it to its fullest and not miss out? Here is something that holds such great promise and, until now, the knowledge of it has somehow escaped you. Now is your chance to discover a part of **you** that you haven't known before.

If you own a fax machine or a computer, you probably at some point have marveled at the way such machines have revolutionized our lives. Have you ever heard people say such things as, "I don't know how in the world my business ran before fax machines?" Or, "How on earth would I ever get by without my computer?"

These are common expressions of those who have learned to depend heavily on these modern technological wonders. Imagine how people who are so aware of the time saving benefits of these machines would feel if all of a sudden they had to give them up and not use them again. They would feel sorely deprived. It would be one thing if they had never experienced them and were not aware of the ways in which they could dramatically improve their lives, but to have them and use them and then lose them would be unbearable. And that is exactly what periodic mono-dieting is like. If you don't know what you're missing, then you don't know, and that's it. You're always looking for that certain something that is simple, not requiring a complicated treatment or restructuring of your life, but is still enormously effective.

However, once you discover firsthand how periodic mono-dieting can transform your health and, therefore, your life, it's not something you would ever want to give up and do without. You mustn't allow the fact that mono-dieting is simple, inexpensive and totally in your control, to discourage you from trying it. Breast cancer will only be prevented if you live a life-style that does not cause it. Making periodic mono-dieting a **permanent** part of your life-style is that certain "something" people have been looking for to finally win the battle over breast cancer. Mono-dieting is a gift, a blessing, and once experienced, you'll thank the day it became a part of your life.

Chapter Twelve

THE SECOND PRINCIPLE:

THE GRADUAL REDUCTION OF ANIMAL PRODUCTS

There are numerous benefits to cleansing the inner body with periodic mono-dieting in addition to that of preventing breast cancer, which you will start to find out as you become more familiar and more comfortable with it. One of the more subtle side effects of this inner cleansing is the body's natural inclination to consume less of those foods which clog it with the most toxic waste and result in the greatest amount of energy being required for processing.

As you might guess from what you've already read in this book, the food category that fits this description most accurately is **animal products**. Considering the fat, cholesterol, hormones, pesticides, antibiotics and other chemical pharmaceutical contaminants, uric acid and bacterial putrefaction and contamination they contain, it's hard to come up with a food more responsible for toxifying the body with harmful wastes than animal products. And animal products are also structurally the most complex and difficult foods to break down in the body, thereby requiring more energy than any other. Add to this the fact that animal products are devoid of fiber and are associated with every major disease that afflicts the population, and you have **more** than ample reason to actively seek out ways of cutting down on them in your diet. But although people generally know that animal products are no longer the "celebrity"

197

foods they used to be, and we now do have authorities the world over recommending diets that de-emphasize animal products, there is perhaps still that nagging feeling in the back of your mind that protein is an important food and protein means meat and other animal products.

So before presenting you with a simple, comfortable, doable strategy for reducing the amount of animal products in your diet, I think it's important to give you at least a brief bit of background on why it is that you hold these not-so-healthy foods in such high regard in the first place.

The health statistics in this country today are the result of a deliberate campaign waged by the industries that would profit from our ignorance. For decades we were pummeled with an avalanche of one-sided information pushing an animal-based point of view called the "four food groups," half of which just **happen** to be animal products. This was done for profit, not health.

Interestingly, the idea that animals supply us with the finest source of protein can be traced back to studies on rodents that showed rats grew better on a diet including animal products than on a diet of plant foods.[290] From these studies on **rats** researchers jumped to the conclusion that animal protein was superior to plant proteins—for **humans!** Now, that is a jump that can only be compared to leaping across the Grand Canyon in a single bound in a heavy thunderstorm with both legs in a cast, because physiologically and anatomically we are **very** different from rats.

The animal product industries, however, ran with the rat research and promoted it to the outer reaches of the universe. These studies were later shown to be **inapplicable to humans**, in fact, **ludicrous**, because rats require a much more concentrated source of protein, such as meat, and their amino acid needs are different. It was too late. The myth had been born and the industries were hardly going to let it die.

In 1923, the United States Department of Agriculture (USDA) came up with "the Twelve Food Groups." Oddly, the Basic Twelve revolved around four diet plans that incorporated choices from each group and were structured to apply to different income brackets,[291] so protein could be obtained from the legumes (beans, lentils, split peas) and nuts category for lower income individuals, or from the meat category for those who could afford higher priced protein sources. Prestige was attached to animal products, portraying them as preferred foods for the higher class. They were now "elitist foods." Long forgotten, and what is of extreme importance to bear in mind, is that it was never stated that animal protein was **superior** to plant protein, only **more expensive!**

The Basic Twelve hung on until 1941, when the Food and Nutrition Board of the National Research Council, feeling that twelve were too cumbersome and difficult to remember, reduced the number to the "Seven Food Groups." Legumes and nuts were listed in the same category as meat, poultry, fish and eggs. All during the time from the 1940's on, the National Egg Board, the Dairy Council, and the National Livestock and Meat Board were running heavy campaigns praising the "ideal" protein in animal products.

By 1960, the now famous (or infamous) "Four Food Groups" became the dominant dietary model in the country. Fruits and vegetables, which could rightly have been two groups, were lumped together and animal products, which could rightly have been one group, were separated. Legumes and nuts were pushed out altogether as a **named** protein source! Animal products were now king of the mountain, representing **50%** of our daily recommended dietary intake, being emphasized to appear as important as everything else **combined**. The animal products industries, for reasons that hardly need explanation, were in Nirvana.

Ironically, at this same time, research funded by the National Dairy Council uncovered the link between increased blood cholesterol and dairy fat. Subsequent studies confirmed this link and verified the increased risk of heart disease when cholesterol levels were increased. At the same time that dairy products were being pushed by the industries, it was beginning to be known that they were not the boon they were touted to be.

During the 1950's, from a most unexpected source, more conclusive evidence that linked heart disease to the consumption of animal products came to light. During the Korean War, both American and Korean soldiers killed were autopsied. In the Americans, with their high animal product intake, **77% already** had narrowed blood vessels due to atherosclerotic deposits. No such damage appeared in the arteries of the equally young Koreans whose national diet included far fewer animal products with a higher vegetable and grain intake.[292]

At the same time, studies on Japanese individuals who had a long line of healthy hearts showed that those Japanese who moved to the United States and adopted the western diet dominated by animal products, had **enormously** higher rates of heart disease than their counterparts who stayed behind and consumed diets low in fat and cholesterol. By the early 1960's it was becoming apparent that there were some significant problems with the basic "four food group" approach to diet.

As research increasingly began to prove conclusively that animal products were harmful, the meat and dairy industries **increased** their efforts to encourage meat and dairy consumption. As the 70's rolled around, it became more and more difficult to pull this off because the evidence started to rapidly build. The Senate Select Committee on Nutrition and Human Needs brought together many of the nation's most respected researchers and their resulting recommendations reflected the growing obvious relationship between the American diet and disease. Their "alternative diet" **de-emphasized** animal products, and encouraged more selections from the plant kingdom. This was the first **official** statement that openly suggested a move away from a meat-based diet and made it clear that the result would be an improvement in health!

In 1977 a follow-up to the panel's findings was released in a report entitled "Dietary Goals for the United States," which supported the need for a new national diet and once again de-emphasized animal products. The meat, dairy and egg industries unleashed the pressure of the incredibly powerful cholesterol lobby and the original phrase in the report, "eat **less** meat" was changed to read, "eat **lean** meat."[293] **The original text actually advised Americans to eat less meat in the mid 1970's, but the animal products industries were successful in pressuring your legislators to keep that from you!** How lovely.

The 1980's looked to be as progressive in terms of improving the American diet as the 70's with further official recommendations instructing the public on the importance of minimizing foods high in saturated fat and cholesterol (animal products). But right when everything was going along swimmingly well, catastrophe struck. There was a political shift that very nearly sounded the death knell for nutritional reform.

The superpowerful food industries won out with the presidential election of 1984, after which efforts to continue educating the public were severely thwarted. In the words of Michael Jacobson, head of the Center for Science in the Public Interest, "When Ronald Reagan was elected President, the Department of Agriculture, the lead agency for nutritional education, was basically given over to the meat industry."[294]

Reagan's Secretary of Agriculture was a hog farmer. His Deputy Secretary had been president of the American Meat Institute for eight years. One of the assistant secretaries had been head of the National Cattlemen's Association and the head of the Bureau of Land Management, the organization that decides how much public land would be given over to animal agriculture, was a Colorado cattleman. Not a moment was wasted in undoing advances that had been made in the effort to increase our knowledge concerning diet and health. Dissenting nutritionists were either silenced or fired.

Although the 1980's were not kind to nutritional education, they did end on a high note with the release of the *Surgeon General's Report on Nutrition and Health*, the report from the National Academy of Sciences, the Heart and Cancer Associations' positions and urgings from other health-related organizations. All were imploring the American people to reduce their consumption of foods high in fat and cholesterol, specifically animal products.

So, here we are in the 1990's, all primed to step into the 21st century. The year 2000 is but a cosmic breath away. Where do we stand with the "four food groups?" To what extent is the government involved, either in terms of helping us or capitulating to industry? These days there's hardly anyone who walks upright who is not aware of the dangers of meat. When was the last time **you** read an obituary column full of the names of people who died due to an insufficient amount of fat and cholesterol in their arteries?

This brings us to the most provocative story of the "four food group" controversy to date. Thirty-five years of haggling and maneuvering to replace the four food groups "wheel" with something more in line with our actual needs finally came to a resolution in 1991. "The Eating Right Pyramid" was unveiled by the Department of Agriculture to replace the four food group wheel. In this pyramid, although the actual recommended servings of each group were not changed, the difference is in the visual effects of how they are presented. The foods we are being encouraged to emphasize in our diets occupy the biggest space.

Those which are harmful are no longer represented in 50% of the diagram. You see, the **average** number of servings of animal products recommended is five per day, the average number of servings recommended of fruits, vegetables, and grains is fifteen a day, **three times as many**. So you can see that the wheel, which gave the **visual** impression that animal products were to be consumed in equal amounts to everything else combined, was totally misleading. The pyramid ingeniously rectified this glaring inconsistency.

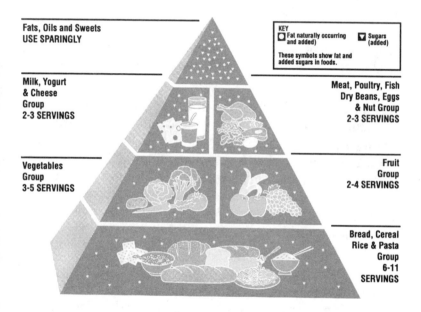

Those foods which we should eat the most, grains and legumes, are on the broad bottom. Then, in ascending order by number of recommended servings, are fruits and vegetables, then animal foods, then fats, which are represented by the tip of the pyramid, along with the admonition to use sparingly. Brilliant!

But only days before its release date, like a bolt of lightening out of the blue, Agriculture Secretary, Edward R. Madigan, nixed it, withdrew it. "But **why**?" you must be asking. Just prior to the release of the pyramid, Mr. Madigan had a private meeting with board members of the National Cattlemen's Association.

A few days later, he received a letter from the American Meat Institute, and then the National Milk Producers Federation complained that dairy products were too close to fat in the pyramid. The next thing we knew, the pyramid was out the window.[295-296] The Center for Science in the Public Interest released a statement that said, "The Department of Agriculture is just what the name says, The Department of Agriculture. It consistently puts the interests of the meat, egg, and dairy industries ahead of the public's health."[297]

In what can only come under the category of rubbing hot sauce into an already open wound, Mr. Madigan's highly suspect reason for withdrawing the pyramid was "because it had not been tested on children."[298] This didn't come to him until only moments before the release date and after **three years of testing?** He would have had fewer eyes rolling skyward if he were to have said extraterrestrials came into his bedroom and warned that the earth would be destroyed if the pyramid were released!

But, fortunately, in a rare but welcome instance of victory for the beleaguered consumer, under tremendous pressure from an outraged health and nutrition community, the Pyramid was reinstituted in 1992 and scheduled to supplant the antiquated food group wheel. The director of nutrition at the Center for Science and Public Interest summed it up best when she said that the decision, "shows that, at least sometimes, the public wins."[299] It's a funny thing with the truth, it doesn't go away. It can be stomped on, abused, distorted, corrupted or buried, but like a balloon full of air that is pushed underwater, it keeps popping back up. And the truth here is indisputable and undeniable. Notwithstanding the self-serving, greed-motivated propaganda from the industries, we **must** start to reduce our consumption of animal products, for many reasons in addition to that of preventing breast cancer.

Undoubtedly, there are many people who **know** that they should and genuinely **want** to eat less of these foods but are at a loss as to **how** to do it in a way that allows them to enjoy the eating experience without creating turmoil in their lives. This Principle is **how**. It provides you with an intelligent approach to gradually change your "eating style," a workable formula that shows you a specific plan of action rather than just saying "cut back." It shows you **how** to cut back day by day, systematically, and in a way that will allow you to feel comfortable and not deprived.

The mistake most people make when confronted with the need to change behavioral patterns—in this case, an excessive consumption of foods that are killing them—is the all or nothing approach. We say, O.K., I'm not going to eat these things anymore and then, when our habits are too strong to be abruptly broken, we feel frustration, weakness or failure. In this principle you are going to learn the key to successful detoxification through a **gradual** reduction of the animal products you are accustomed to eating. You will be able to eat reasonable amounts of the animal products you desire, in the healthiest way, offsetting their harmful effects through new behaviors you will be using, and at the same time you will be realizing your goal to CARE for your body by cleansing and rejuvenating it energetically.

Once again, please keep in mind that these new techniques you will be learning are **guidelines**, **not** edicts. The only reason I keep repeating this over and over whenever giving recommendations, is because of the seemingly ingrained tendency people have to view as failure any digression from the guidelines given which only serves to add undue pressure to the goal at hand. Plus, I would rather over stress it than under stress it. It simply is not realistic for me to try and address every possible variable, life circumstance and personal choice of everyone in one book. So the guidelines serve as a pool of suggestions that can be drawn upon to satisfy each person's individual needs.

In the figure below, you will see that the area marked with an "A" is the largest, with "B" and "C" equal to each other but very much smaller. This is a way to illustrate the extent to which people practice certain habits. For example, if it were to show how often people exercise, the area marked "A" would represent the number of people who exercise at least sometimes. The area marked "B" would represent people who exercise **every day**, and the area marked "C" would represent those who **never** exercise.

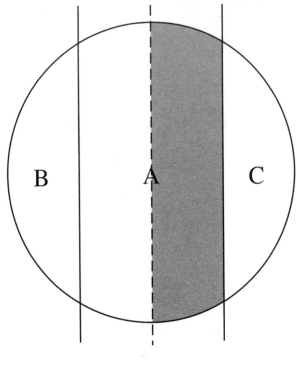

Here it is used to illustrate to what extent people eat animal products. The large area "A" is the percentage of people who eat some form of animal product daily. Area "B" is the percentage of people who eat some animal products at **every** meal, and area "C" is the percentage of those who **never** eat animal products.

Areas "B" and "C" have no varying degrees. You either eat animal products at every meal or you don't eat them at all. Area "A," however, can have a wide and varying range of amounts of animal products eaten. Now, in terms of reducing animal products sufficiently to promote cleanliness of the inner body, keep your lymph nodes from swelling, keep energy levels high and to optimize health, while preventing breast cancer, you want your level of consumption of animal products to be in the shaded part of area "A" divided by the dotted line that is closer to area "C." Somewhere in there should be your goal. Obviously, the closer to area "C" the less you are eating. The closer to the dotted line, the more you're eating.

To achieve the goal of being in the shaded area next to area "C," there are three simple, **general** guidelines to strive for. I emphasis again that they are **general guidelines**. For the purposes of clarification, I will refer to flesh foods when talking about meat, chicken, fish and eggs, and dairy products to indicate **any** dairy product from milk to cheese to yogurt.

1) Try to avoid flesh foods and/or dairy products for breakfast.

2) Try to have flesh foods no more than once a day. Try to have dairy products no more than once a day. (On occasion, you will have both more than once a day, but again, I am talking about direction. The direction you're going in is to **strive** for no more than once a day.)

3) On some kind of regular basis, there should be some days where neither flesh foods nor dairy products are eaten at all.

This is exceedingly important. The body needs a break from having to expend its energies to process animal products. I know people who only eat animal products every other day. They do not feel deprived in any way and they experience phenomenal good health. One small exception for non-animal product days is the use of a little butter on potatoes or vegetables or in cooking something. This small digression will not hurt anything. And by all means, use butter not margarine, which is nothing but plastic fat and has been associated with a significant increase in the risk of breast cancer.[299A] At least butter is real.

It is obvious that the more closely you adhere to and use these three tips, the more successful you will be in reducing your animal product consumption. One of the ways you can be more successful in implementing these tips is to understand as much as you can about **why** they are relevant. I have already given you ample reasons to cut back on animal products as you begin to CARE for your body. This is just one more understanding you will be able to incorporate into your life-style and use to your benefit for the rest of your life.

These three tips may appear to be too simplistic to have any major impact on supporting the lymph system and preventing breast cancer, but just the opposite is true. If you will practice them diligently and incorporate them into your life-style, you will be contributing **greatly** to your goal of prevention.

We have already seen that elimination in the body is an integral part of cleansing. It is the actual removal of waste matter through the bowels, the bladder, the lungs and the skin, and because it cannot proceed without energy from the body, your dietary choices and your life-style will **dramatically** affect it.

If most of the foods you eat are highly processed, full of chemicals, heavy, concentrated, high in fat and cholesterol, denatured, preserved or irradiated, you can expect that elimination in your body will not be smooth. Too much energy will be required by the body merely to break these foods down and neutralize their negative elements, and unless you are like the lion who sleeps twenty hours a day, your body simply **will not** be able to **thoroughly** eliminate the waste products and toxins from the foods you are eating. Yes, it **will** eliminate **somewhat**, but not completely, and complete elimination is the key to a clean lymph system and the prevention of breast cancer.

The idea in upgrading your diet is to **gradually** remove from your diet those foods which have proven to be harmful. All I can tell you is that the fresher the food, the closer to nature, the better. You want to minimize highly-processed, chemicalized, packaged foods, coffee, sodas, refined sugar, etc. **You know** the stuff that's not good for you. It's what we're always being told to "have in moderation." Do the best you can in minimizing them. That's all. With periodic mono-dieting and reducing animal products, you are way ahead of the game. You can get away with periodic indiscretions with no problem because your **overall** approach is so healthy.

The world-renowned biochemist and researcher, Dr. Paul Stitt, has said: "The cure for cancer will not be found under the microscope, it's on the dinner plate."[299B] The more foods that come from the plant kingdom, and the less that come from the animal kingdom, the less likely it is that cancer will ever be a part of your experience.

If you have decided that periodic mono-dieting and the gradual reduction of animal products make sense to you, and you are willing to try these CARE Principles in your life, you are now going to begin to make the health supporting dietary choices so many others are making (and that you have perhaps been secretly **yearning** to know how to make) in a rational, systematic and **very enjoyable** way. CARE gives you a game plan for life to prevent breast cancer, rather than just a haphazard, hit or miss approach. You don't have to **hope** you will get results. From the moment you start, you will **know** you are getting them.

These Principles will change forever the attitude you have toward your body, as you experience **firsthand** your own power to revitalize your physical body. You will be witnessing your ability to eliminate, by your own actions and behavior, the underlying causes of breast cancer that you thought were beyond your control. The result will be a higher level of health and energy than perhaps you ever thought possible! And most importantly, you will live with the knowledge and confidence that you **can** prevent breast cancer.

Chapter Thirteen

THE THIRD PRINCIPLE:

THE MIND MATTERS

"If we are to be well and happy, not only the body, but the mind also must be peaceful and harmonious."

Ernest Holmes
The Science of Mind

"It is well documented that in a climate of negativity, the ability to heal is greatly reduced—depressed people not only lower their immune response, for example, but even weaken their DNA's ability to repair itself."

Deepak Chopra, M.D.
Quantum Healing

"Many of (the mind's) effects are achieved directly on the body's tissues without any awareness on our part. The body responds to the mind's messages whether conscious or unconscious."

Bernie S. Siegel, M.D.
Love, Medicine and Miracles

"Your thoughts create your experience of your health, wealth and every detail of your world."

Wayne Dyer, M.D.
Real Magic

"If you would perfect your body, guard your mind."

James Allen
As A Man Thinketh

"What things soever you desire, when you pray, believe that you receive them, and you shall have them."

Jesus

"All that we are is the result of what we have thought."

Buddha

The temptation was to continue the list of quotes above and let seventy or eighty of them be the extent of this chapter, so great is the amount of material that has been written over the years on the inextricable relationship between the mind and the body. There are two parts of the mind that can be discussed; that part of the mind which we know something about, and that part of which nothing is known. Studying the mind is like studying the cosmos itself.

What is actually **known** about the mind can be likened to a single grain of sand on a vast stretch of beach. Nevertheless, the tiny bit that we **do** know about is extraordinary and supercharged with power. **And it is a power we can use!** It is what Norman Cousins was referring to when he said, "The growth of the human mind is still high adventure, in many ways the highest adventure on earth."[300]

Have you ever heard statements such as "attitude is everything," or "you are what you think you are," or "your mind can make a heaven of hell or a hell of heaven?" Haven't you heard athletes in all areas of sports, when talking about a win or a loss, referring to their "mental game" and the role it played in the outcome?

One of the most renowned tennis instructors in the world told me that the game of tennis is 10% talent, 90% mental. In fact, you'll hear tennis players frequently say before a match, "If my mental game is there, I'll win." And after a loss, "My mental game just wasn't there."

You know the story of the little red engine going up a steep hill, don't you? "I think I can, I think I can." And, of course, the Master Teacher, Jesus, tried to teach us all this lesson when he said, over and over again in many different ways, "It is done unto you as you believe." What other possible message could this statement mean but that the power of the mind, through right thinking, can bring into our experience absolutely anything we desire.

Volumes have been written on the power of the mind and its ability to strengthen us or weaken us, to uplift us or bring us down, to heal us or make us sick. And yet, although there is more than ample evidence that the mind, properly channeled, can be a most potent tool in the health and healing of the body, no other area of health care has been more minimized and neglected. It seems that when we cross over from the seen to the unseen, all manner of biases come into play.

As long as it is the physical world that we can hear, see or touch that we're dealing with, we're comfortable. But as soon as we're moving from the seen to the unseen, the part of our existence that has no physical presence that we can relate to with our senses, the terra firma gets mighty shaky. There's an air of hocus-pocus, or cultism, or some other such nonsense attributed to references to the power of the mind to heal that result in skepticism.

All one would have to do is read any of the books by Dr. Deepak Chopra, Dr. Wayne Dyer, Louise Hay, Dr. Bernie Siegel or Ernest Holmes to learn of the many remarkable instances of people using their minds to send positive messages of love and healing to their bodies to overcome even catastrophic cases of cancer to see that this is an area well worth one's consideration.

In the physical world, it is well understood that there are natural laws that are simple and undeviating. If one plants the seed for a peach tree, a peach tree will grow. On the other hand, if the seed for a thistle bush is planted, there will be no peaches, only thistles. This is so utterly simple and obvious that some may say, "Gee, you don't say." But few understand that in the mental world, the law still holds true and is just as unyielding.

Your thoughts are like seeds. Good thoughts produce good things and negative thoughts produce negative things. Good thoughts will never produce negative results, and negative thoughts will never produce good results.

Although far too many medical scientists are quick to discount the role the mind plays in healing, favoring drugs instead, there is a wealth of scientific evidence proving the astounding power of the mind to heal. In the area of psychiatry and psychology, there has been an explosion in mind-body research over the last decade. Dr. Martin Seligman, a professor at the University of Pennsylvania and author of *Learned Optimism,* has done research showing that pessimistic people have weaker "immune systems," are more prone to colds and flu, and have more major health problems after age fifty. Their bodies are less likely to fight off killer diseases such as cancer.[301]

A colleague of Dr. Seligman, Dr. Gregory Buchanon, also a researcher at the University of Pennsylvania, conducted tests on a group of subjects to determine if they were essentially pessimists or optimists. According to Dr. Buchanon, more of those who were identified as pessimists died within ten years. Those who ranked within the top 25% as the most negative had the highest death rate: twenty-six of thirty-one died. By contrast, only ten of the thirty-one who ranked as the most optimistic had died.[302]

Some of the most impressive and convincing evidence of the power of the mind to heal the body comes from what is referred to as the "placebo effect."

In studies to determine the effectiveness of a drug, a group afflicted with a certain malady is divided into two groups. One group receives the drug to be tested, the other group receives a dummy pill or placebo, usually a coated sugar pill. Neither group knows which it is receiving, the real drug or the placebo. If the group receiving the real drug shows a marked improvement over the placebo group, the drug is deemed effective. But what has happened over and over again is that in many instances, the placebo turned out to be as effective as the drug. Not everyone responds this way, but generally 30-60% will report relief of pain, even stabbing pain, from the placebo, thus the placebo effect.[303]

Stated differently, being convinced of the potential effectiveness of a particular medicine or surgical procedure actually assists in making one well and improves chances of recovery. Conversely, feelings of skepticism and doubt in the same situation will bring about the exact opposite, less of a chance of recovery.[304] This phenomenon has been noted for **centuries!**[305] William Osler, M.D., at the beginning of this century enjoyed enormous notoriety as a foremost physician and healer. He regularly taught his students that the healings of disease he facilitated were frequently due to his patients' **faith** in the treatment they received, **not** the treatment itself.[306]

One of the most celebrated cases in history of the mind as healer of the body was early in the 1800's and involved Dr. Isaac Jennings. After twenty years of practicing medicine, Dr. Jennings became so disillusioned with drugging and bleeding his patients that he discontinued those treatments. To meet the demands of his patients for "medicines," he gave them an assortment of bread pills, a variety of powders made of wheat flour variously scented and colored, and vials of pure water of various hues. Much to his surprise, his patients made recoveries far in excess of what he saw when he administered drugs.

It was not long before his fame spread far and wide and his practice extended over a large territory, putting drugging doctors out of business. He continued substituting his innocent placebos for between fifteen and twenty years before he revealed to his medical colleagues and to the community what he had been doing. Some of his colleagues were intrigued. Others were angry at him. Some of his patients said they didn't care what he gave them, it healed them. Some were angry and called him an imposter and refused to continue seeing him.

The fact that the length of their illnesses were greatly shortened did not weigh in Dr. Jennings' favor. They paid for drugs and they wanted drugs. In spite of the puzzling, mixed reactions of his patients, Yale University conferred an honorary degree upon Dr. Jennings in recognition of his unheard of success.[307]

The reason placebos work is because the people taking them are **convinced** that they will help. In their minds, they think the treatment will make them well, so it does! Placebos support the fact that positive beliefs enhance healing. In spite of skepticism among certain present-day "authorities" who doubt the scientific validity of the ability of the mind to heal the body, that opinion ignores a large body of scientific studies that lend credence to the argument. There are examples galore, all documented, of people healing themselves of sometimes very serious problems, all with their minds, their thoughts. They so strongly believed they were going to get well that they did! A most fascinating and informative book on the subject of the power of prayer to heal was recently published by a medical doctor named Larry Dossey. The name of the book is *Healing Words*. Very interesting stuff.

This awesome power resides in **you** right now. Nothing prevents you from using it on your own behalf other than your own thoughts. Whatever you want to call it, be it a positive mental attitude or the power of prayer, that power **will** respond to your thoughts, words and beliefs. If you wish to make the determination with absolute certainty that you have tremendous influence over your health and well-being and **know** that it is so, you **can!** You can just as easily think you are in charge as not.

Before giving you a few tools on how you can start to redirect your mind to think in a more positive light about your power over your health, let's look at just a few of the more impressive examples of the placebo effect. Placebos have provided relief in cases of angina, arthritis, pain, hay fever, headaches, coughs, ulcers, hypertension, cancer and heart disease.[308-312] Numerous studies of certain religious practices have shown a direct correlation between deeply held beliefs and the lessening of health problems.[313-314]

In one ten-year study on elderly people, evidence showed that those who actually thought of themselves and labeled themselves as old or elderly had significantly higher death rates over the course of the study than those who thought of themselves as middle aged.[315]

The number of specific examples of documented cases proving the power of the mind to heal the body would easily fill this entire book. I will share two particularly striking examples, one each pertaining to the two biggest killers in this country—heart disease and cancer.

In the late 1950's and early 1960's, a new operation for the relief of angina became quite successful and popular. Angina is the medical term for pain and it causes sudden and severe discomfort of the lower chest accompanied by a feeling of suffocation. It is more often than not a precursor of a more serious heart condition if not dealt with, because it is a warning that blood is being restricted from the heart.

Anyone who has experienced this excruciating pain does not cherish the idea of a repeat performance.

The operation, which has been largely replaced by what is referred to as a coronary bypass, involved opening the chest and ligating or tying off a certain artery in order to force more blood through other branches that were being obstructed. The operation brought a marked relief of pain in 70% of the patients who received the operation. In a controlled study on randomly selected patients who were to receive this operation, they were anesthetized and an incision in their chest was made in the appropriate area, and that was all that was done. There was no tying off of arteries or anything else. The incision was closed back up and the patients were told it was a successful operation. These individuals, **believing** they had the operation, experienced a 70% improvement in relief of their pain. **Precisely the same degree of relief as those who actually had their arteries tied off!**[316]

The example relating to cancer is as startling as anything I have ever come across. It pertains to a profoundly sick gentleman who, amongst other attendant problems, had large cancerous tumors all over his body. All standard treatment had been tried and abandoned and he was close to the end with a prognosis that he would not survive another month. At the time, there was a widely touted cancer "cure" called Krebiozen. The man heard about it and felt it would help him and begged for it to be administered to him. His condition was so bad that the thought must have been, what would be the harm, he was already so close to death?

Two days after the first injection, the tumors had shrunk to one-half their original size. He was given injections three times a week and was discharged from the hospital in ten days. He enjoyed two months of practically perfect health, but as fate would have it, he received some conflicting reports on Krebiozen. He immediately relapsed to his pre-terminal state. The tumors returned. His physicians told him he could disregard what he read because they were talking about Krebiozen that had deteriorated from standing too long and they were going to give him a new "double strength, super refined batch." He perked up with a very strong anticipation of cure, but this time he was injected with **distilled water**. Nevertheless, the tumors once again melted and he was again symptom-free for two more months! He then had occasion to read the final American Medical Association report that Krebiozen had been shown to be worthless. He died two days later.[317]

So powerful is the mind in creating whatever reality it is convinced of that up to 50% of subjects in some studies actually exhibit **side effects** from the placebos![318-320] In one astonishing case involving the testing of an antihistamine, the subjects receiving the placebos had more side effects than those who received the medication![321] The results of recent studies show the placebo effect to be **twice** as powerful as previously thought,[322] and is most powerful when a trusted physician enthusiastically offers a patient a new therapy.[323]

Knowing that there are those who accept suggestion from authority figures so strongly that they view the suggestion as reality and actually cause the expected result to occur, it should be a crime punishable by law for **anyone** in an authority position to tell a patient that he or she is going to die or has but a short time left before dying. Even if the chance is minuscule at best that a person would survive if not told death was inevitable, it is ignorance and arrogance of the highest order for anyone to tell another person when he or she is going to die. That's God's decision. And only God knows how many people have been ushered to an early grave because they had the idea planted in their minds that their time was up.

I wonder if there is anyone who hasn't at least **heard** of an instance of someone living far beyond the time they were told they would die. Medical doctors have notoriously discounted the idea that the mind can heal the body. The American Medical Association queried its members in 1990 and found that only 10% believed in the mind-body connection.[324] Nevertheless, wouldn't the decent thing be to tell a patient of those instances where other patients conquered the disease and survived or beat the odds? I cannot think of even one woman who I know that had a mastectomy that was not told it was either a mastectomy or death. It's just not right. The death sentence approach in our health care system is one that sorely needs to be changed.

After what you've read, you could easily be thinking that the mind could be the most powerful tool of all in your quest to prevent breast cancer. And who's to say you would not be right? The task for many of us, however, is to figure out how to retrain ourselves to think in such a way as to take full advantage of the potential that resides in the mind, the same way a mighty oak tree resides in a single acorn. Under the right circumstances, that acorn will become the oak tree. And under the right circumstances, the extraordinary and dynamic source of power that is the mind will unleash its gifts. It waits patiently for your direction.

If your commitment is such that you will be periodically mono-dieting and gradually reducing your consumption of animal products, the addition of your knowing, **really knowing**, that your efforts **will** prevent you from ever developing breast cancer, then you have a winning combination that vastly improves your chances of success. But trying to turn around a lifetime of negative thinking, or thinking not supportive to your goals can be a challenge. Like other habits that have become fixed or routine, the way to change them is to crowd them out with other more favorable ones.

There is no question that this can be accomplished. **You** are in charge of how you think and at any moment you have the choice to change your thoughts in any direction you wish. The mind is enormously receptive to your directives. It doesn't matter how long you have been thinking negatively. You can instantly turn it around by positive thoughts which will override negative ones right away. It's like turning on a light in a dark room. No matter how long the room has been dark, the moment you switch on the light, the darkness is removed.

There are in all likelihood hundreds of tools or guidelines you could use to assist you in training the mind to think about your daily life in a more positive way. Following are three that I and many thousands of others have used with enormous success, and that you can use specifically to help in your quest to prevent breast cancer:

1) Ask better questions.

2) State your best case to the universe.

3) Acknowledge and accept your many "I's."

Ask Better Questions

This is a tool that can bring about remarkable, almost miraculous results, is as easy as anything could ever be, and is interesting and fun to use. I first learned about the power of questions from Anthony Robbins, author of the best-sellers, *Unlimited Power* and *Awaken The Giant Within.*

You may not even be aware of it, but you are constantly asking yourself questions either silently or out loud, and your brain is constantly supplying answers. "Ask and you shall receive." Most everyone has heard this phrase from the Bible. When you ask for something from the brain, it snaps right to and answers. It's just like a computer that has thousands or millions of pieces of information in it.

221

You punch in a question and up pops the answer on the screen. Whatever you ask of yourself, **good or bad**, receives an answer. So if you ask "Why can't I ever lose weight?" your brain tells you why you can't. "Well, you eat too much, you don't try hard enough, you're not real serious, you don't exercise enough, you were born that way." Your brain **will** come up with an answer. So questions have the power to create positiveness or negativeness in your life. But what if you asked instead, "How can I lose weight and enjoy myself while I'm doing it?" Wouldn't you rather have an answer to **that** question?

Have you ever heard some of these?

"Why can't I ever get ahead?"

"Why does this always happen to me?"

"Why does so and so always treat me so badly?"

"Why am I so fat?"

"Why am I always suffering from one thing or another?"

If you ask why you can't do something, your brain will tell you why and you compound your unwanted situation. The secret of turning this around is to **ask better questions!** You can make a **major** positive change in your life starting **right now** with the right questions. It has a lot to do with on what you choose to focus. You see, whatever you focus on, **you get!** And the decision is **yours**, and no one else's. You can focus on what's good in your life or what's not. It's totally up to you.

If you watch the news on television and hear a story about some heinous crime committed, and later hear a story about a group that takes children with balloons to a retirement home to visit with the old folks there just to bring some joy and light into their lives, on which would you focus? You can see people walking around decrying all the pain and suffering in the world, and there are those who choose to see the beauty and goodness that exists in the world as well. You always have a choice to focus on either the positive or the negative in your life.

If you focus on how things just don't seem to work out, **they won't!** But, hey, guess what? The opposite is also true. Focus on how things **will** work out and they **will**. Remember, "It is done unto you as you believe."

The only difference between you and people you admire greatly for what they have achieved and the positive feelings they always seem to project, is what you have chosen to focus on and what questions you ask of yourself. You can be sure that the people you admire are not asking themselves negative, disempowering questions. They're the ones asking questions like, "How can I turn this around and benefit from it?" Instead of, "Why does this always happen to me?" They are asking the kind of questions that constantly spur them on to more and more achievements.

If you want things to work out in terms of the health goals you have, you must decide on what you're going to focus and what questions you're going to ask yourself. The right questions can change your focus and that can change your life. Ever hear the story of the man who constantly lamented his situation of not having any shoes until he met another man without any feet? His focus changed in a hurry.

This all may sound **so** simple, even silly, but it makes such a **massive** difference it would be a tragedy to have this powerful tool right in front of you and not take advantage of it.

As you pursue your goal to prevent breast cancer, always be asking yourself positive, uplifting questions:

"How can I support myself today to be healthier?"

"What can I do to specifically assist my lymph system's effort to remove toxins and waste from my body?"

223

"What can I do to make exercise more interesting and
enjoyable?"

"What will I do with all of the new found energy I'm
going to have?"

"What did I do to be so blessed to find this
information?"

Ask questions on a regular basis that the only possible
result of answering will be to create a positive atmosphere
around you, and good things are going to happen. And
before you ask a question like, "Gee, do you think this can
really work?" ask instead, "How can I **make** this work?"

Here's something you can start doing **tomorrow
morning** that will progressively make you stronger and
stronger, and more positive-feeling about CAREing for
your body. Just take a few moments in the morning every
day to start the day off with a burst of positive energy.

Have you ever awakened in the morning with the
question on your lips, "Why do I have to go to work today?"
or some other negative-based question? Not a very good
way to start the day.

What if you woke up and said, "What can I do today
to make it an even healthier day?"

Further, if you will think of a general group of
positive questions to ask yourself every morning, you will
energize your entire life. Here's a sampling, but you can
think of your own also:

"What am I happiest about in my life?"

"What are the things I have to be grateful for?"

"Who are my friends?"

"Who loves me?"

"What have I accomplished that I am deeply proud of?"

Before leaping out of bed and tackling the tasks of the
day and becoming all involved in everything you have to

do, lie there and ask yourself positive questions and briefly answer them to yourself. It will take three to five minutes to ask and answer these questions.

What if you started every day like that? You might begin to buzz with positive energy! If this were to become a habit in your life every morning, just like brushing your teeth, over time, merely waking up would automatically put you into a positive state. This is **how** the mind can be retrained to think in a way that is more supportive of the life-style you desire. One last question to ponder: "Isn't it great that you are so open to making these positive changes to improve your life, and these tools are now available to help you?"

State Your Best Case to the Universe

Have you ever been in someone's home or office and seen either on the wall, desk or table a plaque with some kind of inspirational or uplifting quote or saying by someone or another? Why do you think they have them in prominent places like that? Do you have them around your home or office? If so, why? The answer couldn't be more obvious. They are reminders designed to inspire the reader, to remind the reader of all the good and positive things that can exist. When you read a message on love or happiness or success or some other positive aspect of life, for these few moments while you are reading it, don't you feel good? If it's particularly appropriate for something you happen to be able to relate to right at that time, don't you kind of purse your lips a little, nod in recognition and think to yourself, "of course, of course." It's as though it was written just for you.

The written word can be and is enormously powerful. "The pen is mightier than the sword" is a wise saying that illustrates the point. Words written on a page can make you weep or make you laugh, make you sad or make you

you weep or make you laugh, make you sad or make you happy, make you feel anger or make you feel compassion. When you read something, it is imprinted in your mind's eye. Have you ever heard the name of a person or place or object of some kind and not been able to pronounce it properly until you saw it written?

The power inherent in writing something down is the very reason so many people write affirmations on a regular basis. Say, for example, someone is trying desperately to change jobs for something more rewarding both financially and professionally. He or she may write the affirmation, "I know that the position I am looking for that is perfect for me will present itself soon." It may be written one time, ten times, fifty times or a hundred times **every day**. It becomes a permanent part of the person's consciousness, a way of thinking that leaves no room for anything but what is desired. It is also felt that by writing it down it is actually created and is just a matter of time before it appears.

That is why so many people believe in writing goals down on paper. Seminars are held all over the country on goal setting to show people exactly how to use it to attract that which they desire. Invariably these seminars involve the writing down on paper what you wish to have to memorialize it.

Other people will write a word on a piece of paper every morning with the idea of concentrating on that one word all day. Words such as health, love, peace, compassion, forgiveness, success, joy, concentration or any number of different possibilities. The next day, another word is written and it is the focus of attention for the day.

There are many tools such as these that people devise to use the written word to not only attract what they want, but also to train their minds to focus in a positive rather than negative way. I have one I have used for years that I would like to suggest. It works well with the first tool of asking better questions by **stating something as fact rather than asking about it**. This can be done with one, two, three, four or however many statements you wish. You write neatly on a piece of paper statements of fact as you **wish for them to be**. For example:

• My body is becoming cleaner, stronger and healthier every day.

• My lymph system is working at optimum efficiency, preventing breast cancer from ever developing.

• My lymph nodes are clean and they are going to stay that way.

• I am open and receptive to all of the vast number of possibilities available to me.

• I enjoy the work I have chosen to perform and it is important.

• Outer circumstances cannot disturb my sense of well-being. I am in charge of my happiness.

• My life is supercharged with all the energy I need to be happy and well.

I have many of these statements all around my home. I would like to share with you one that I saw many years ago and I have been reading to myself every day sometimes several times a day, ever since. It sits on my desk where I write and I always read it before writing.

I go forth as an empowered and am empowering person. I come from strength, and I bring strength into all that I do. I call upon inner wisdom and love to guide me in the right use of my time and talents, all to bring a greater good to life.

Remember, there can be as many or as few as you like on any subject whatsoever. You then put the piece of paper with the most empowering statements you can think of in some **conspicuous** place where you will be sure to see it during the day. On your desk, on the refrigerator on the dashboard of your car, anywhere. You then make a commitment to read them at least once a day. This can be at any time during the day that you feel is most convenient, upon awakening in the morning, before going to sleep at night, at lunch time. I'm not talking about a huge expenditure of time here. It's less time than it takes to see what's on television tonight. When you read the statements, don't just read them mechanically, **say** them to yourself with feeling and conviction. **Mean it!**

Now, you may be asking if it's being suggested to read them just one time a day, why does it have to be in a **conspicuous** place? If you **are** asking that question, then you are really paying attention here, so thank you. This is why **I** keep them conspicuously placed: Being a writer, I spend considerable time at my desk. My statements are within easy grasp. As it happens, as I pause to ponder something or another pertaining to my work, I can see the statements sitting there.

This has two benefits. First, it's so easy to read one or two of the statements which immediately refocuses my thoughts and gives a real charge, an energy boost, making sure my thoughts remain positive and high-minded. Second, after you have made the daily reading of your statements a habit and you have been doing it for several weeks or months, just **seeing** the piece of paper with the statements on it instantly has the same effect as reading one or more of them.

You **know** what's on the list. So every time you look at it, you are in effect keeping your mind on track. The positive track. You can add or delete statements at any time and to be sure, feel free to read them as many times a day as you wish. The minimum is one time, but you **can't** read them too often. Please don't minimize this. It is a powerful tool as you will quickly find out.

Acknowledge and Accept Your Many "I's"

Have you ever made comments similar to these:

"I don't know what came over me. That's just not like me at all."

Or,

"I had a real battle with myself."

Or,

"I can't make up my mind. I keep going up and back."

Or,

"If I did that, I'd never forgive myself."

Or,

"One moment I want to do one thing, the next moment I want to do the opposite."

Do these sound at all familiar? It is probably a safe bet to say that at one time or another we have all had thoughts like these. It's as though there is more than one person living in our bodies, all with their own likes and dislikes, wants and needs, and all vying to be heard and be in charge. The idea may sound a bit odd to you, but it is a point of view held by quite a few people around the world and one which was written extensively about by one of the most intriguing philosophers to ever live, George Gurdjieff. His writings and works, and writings about him, have been the object of study and discussion by huge numbers of people all around the world.

One of the central themes of Gurdjieff's philosophy was that we all have many "I's" but that we don't realize it. Because we have one body and one name, we think we are one. But we are many. We may have dozens, perhaps hundreds of lesser "I's" all wanting to be heard.

What exactly do I mean when I say "I's?" The "I's" refer to the different parts of you that want different things

229

at different times. For example, "I want to buckle down and get on a good diet and lose some weight." Now when these words are spoken, they're **meant!** But at another time of day, that particular "I's" resolve is weakened and a different "I" says, "I want to enjoy myself and eat whatever I like." These two "I's" are each trying to get an upper hand over the other. "That does it. I'm going to start exercising a half hour a day at least four times a week. I'm going to get in shape."

You say it with absolute conviction. Then,

"I have so much to think about, I'm going to start exercising first thing next month."

"I want to clean out the garage."

"I want to kick back, read a novel and have some chocolate."

"I'm going to put in some extra hours at work and really solidify my position there."

"I can't wait to get home and just forget about work."

"I want to read a good book."

"I want to go to the movies."

"I'm going to have a really healthy lunch today."

"I want a burger and fries."

"I want to do more with the children on the weekend."

"I just want to take it easy and do nothing this weekend."

"I want to go out tonight."

"I want to stay home."

And on and on and on for practically every situation in life. The fact is, each and every one of these statements is **real!** When they are spoken, the "I" that is in charge is speaking for the whole, even though many other "I's" may disagree but do not have the floor at that moment. Think of fictional Jane Doe going through a day. Each of her separate "I's" is able to call itself Jane, is able to act in her name, agree or disagree in her name, make decisions or promises in her name for which another "I" in Jane will have to deal. This explains why people so often make decisions that are frequently not carried out. One "I" makes the decision, another "I" ignores it. It's as though someone writes a check in your name and then you have to make good on it.

Understanding this aspect of your life can be very freeing. You can start to recognize certain "I's" and become familiar with them. Once you know which ones are there and how they operate, you can start to bring them in line with the "I's" that are more aligned with your quest for health. You **know** that there are "I's" in you that absolutely want to eat properly and exercise regularly. And there are other "I's" in you that **don't**. Just having that understanding is a breakthrough.

Each "I," whether a strong, positive one or a weak, negative one wants to have its way whenever it can. It wants to do what it is accustomed to doing and does not want to change or allow any other "I" to take precedence.

This creates a lot of turmoil in people who are not aware of the many "I's" and don't know what's causing them so much indecision and anguish. But when you know what's going on, you can observe the different "I's" and even say out loud to the ones you know don't care about your optimum well-being, "So, you're back. Here to try and influence me to disregard my health, are you?"

Of course, this is done in private. If you do it in front of people, they may start to chase you with a big butterfly net. Standing around waving your finger at yourself, admonishing yourself to go away and leave you alone could attract the wrong kind of attention. But observing the different "I's" that come up in a day and confronting them can be very interesting. And only when you recognize that they're there can you begin to take charge of them and have some order.

Knowing this theory of the many "I's," the next time you say something like, "I can't believe I ate those donuts. I don't know what I was thinking. I'm trying to cleanse and rejuvenate my body!" you will know that there are two different "I's" at work. One wanting to CARE for itself, the other hell bent on self-destruction. The more you observe this phenomenon, the more familiar you will become with your own diverse makeup, and the more likely you will be able to give dominance to the "I's" that support your health goals and maintain a positive direction in your life.

You can also stop browbeating yourself or feeling guilty about something or another you did or wish you didn't do, or didn't do and wish you did. Just know that at some time different "I's" are stronger than other times and forgive yourself your human frailty. Better to work at strengthening your positive "I's" than bemoaning the action of your negative ones.

This whole idea of many "I's," all vying for control, can be likened to a house being built by a group of workers with no foreman in charge. The workers have not been instructed as to their specific duties so each, feeling he knows best what to do, takes a hand at being in charge. But others feel they could better handle the situation and disagreements erupt.

The building of the house is not progressing in an orderly fashion. Instead, there is chaos and disorder. The only chance is for the foreman to show up and organize everyone and assign the right job to the right person so the entire crew is working as a team. When it comes to your many "I's," the "foreman" in this case would be your strong, positive, health-seeking "I." The one that is committed to keeping you on track and seeking out the most supportive conditions in your life. The only way to make this "I" stronger and more capable of governing the other "I's" is to habitually perform certain practices that will strengthen it and give it power and confidence. There **is** an "I" in you that wants to believe, that **does** believe, that you have the information, the tools and the ability to prevent breast cancer.

There is also that "I" that doesn't believe, so anything you can do to strengthen the positive "I" and silence the negative "I" is going to weigh heavily in your success. By recognizing that you have these different "I's," and consciously asking better questions so your strong "I's" will answer, and stating your intentions to the universe, you are taking a huge step in strengthening the strong, positive, health seeking "I" that **knows** you will never develop breast cancer, so that it is the one that predominates in your life.

The stronger you become, the more you will want to utilize the three Principles I have laid out. The frequency with which you use them is wholly dependent on your level of motivation. How quickly do you want to start to cleanse and strengthen your lymph system which in turn protects you against developing breast cancer? How truly committed are you to experiencing a long life predominated by high spirits, vitality and health, rather than aches, pains and illness?

These are the kind of questions we are **all** grappling with. At night when you lie your head on your pillow and you are alone with your thoughts in the dark, these are issues that can loom large. By using these three Principles, with an attitude of **knowing** that they will work and that breast cancer will never be a part of your life, you will be able to live out your life in health, confident that **you** are the one in charge and in control of your destiny.

233

*   *   *   *   *   *

There is one last issue I must address as regards breast cancer—either preventing it or beating it. Although this is an area of immense importance, it somehow has received only scant, if any, attention. As indicated earlier, there are many variables that contribute to the development of cancer. I have focused primarily on the effects of diet both because I am certain that it is **the** main risk factor, and because diet happens to be my area of expertise.

Scholars and researchers have shown that repressed, unvented anger, coupled with a lack of self-love, has been a major contributor in many cases of cancer, be it of the breast or otherwise. Although this is not my area of expertise, I would be remiss if I did not bring it to your attention and encourage you to take a close, hard look at this area of your life. To help you do so, I would like to introduce you to the work of a most remarkable woman.

Louise L. Hay is an internationally respected author and lecturer. I have the very good fortune of having a personal relationship with Ms. Hay and I can tell you without hesitation that she is one of the most genuinely loving, compassionate and concerned people I have ever met. Merely being in the same room with her lifts your spirits and fills you with good feelings.

Ms. Hay was diagnosed as having incurable, terminal cancer. Even if she were to submit to incredibly extensive surgery, her chance of survival, as she was told at the time, was nil. She rejected the medical approach entirely and instead decided to focus on why she had such negative feelings about herself. She scrutinized the abuses she had endured both as a child and as an adult and realized the full extent to which these unresolved issues in her life had been fermenting within her, culminating in cancer. She simultaneously detoxified her body with a cleansing diet.

In one of the most remarkable instances of self-healing I have ever heard of, she **totally healed herself!** Only six months after her diagnosis, her medical doctors told her there was not even a trace of cancer. This was many years ago and she is still cancer-free.

Ms. Hay has many books and tapes available and I want to suggest that you take a look at *YOU CAN HEAL YOUR LIFE*, which made the *New York Times* Best-seller list and has been read by millions of women worldwide. I know people whose lives have been changed merely by **reading** this book.

Chapter Fourteen

CONCLUSION

In an article in the *New York Times*, Dr. Yitzhak Koch states that, "The breast is a unique gland, an under estimated gland. Its activity is much more complex than people had thought."[325] And I would like to add to that, that your breasts are exactly where they belong. They do not have to be removed and they do not have to be mutilated. You **can** prevent breast cancer, there is no doubt whatsoever about that. It is a daunting challenge, I know, especially in light of the "experts" who are supposed to know how, declaring that they don't.

What I have offered in this book is one way to prevent breast cancer. There may be other ways, to be sure, and if there are, I am hopeful that they will be discovered and presented to women everywhere so that the suffering can end. Preventing breast cancer is not something that is accomplished by taking a onetime action that achieves the goal. It certainly would be lovely if there were a pill or a shot, or some other "magic bullet" that would do the job and remove the need for ongoing diligence, but there isn't, and that's that.

If you have a doorway in your home that is too low and you smash your forehead into it every time you go through it, all you have to do to prevent that from happening is to have the doorway raised and that's the end of the problem. You don't have to think about it anymore.

When it comes to the prevention of breast cancer it's not that simple. It's not one action that you perform. **It's the way you choose to live your life!** You can either live in a manner that opens the way for cancer to develop or you can live in a manner that significantly reduces your risk of it ever occurring. To prevent breast cancer, to really, truly prevent it, an ongoing effort is called for.

I may be accused of being naive in thinking that by cleansing the lymph system, cutting back on animal products and maintaining a positive attitude, something as **seemingly** complex and baffling as breast cancer can be prevented when medicine's greatest minds have not yet been able to get a handle on it. But my questions to you are: What if I'm right? What if it will do the job? If it works, does it matter one way or the other that I'm not a medical doctor and that the approach is straightforward, uncomplicated and not dependent upon expensive diagnostic procedures and treatment?

I'm not saying that this book will end breast cancer, but I can tell you it will definitely prevent it for a lot of women and perhaps you are one of them. The thing is, what do you have to lose by trying what I'm suggesting? Even if I'm wrong, what possible harm could there be in you cleansing your inner body so it operates more efficiently, reducing your intake of the foods that every health professional recommends you should eat less of, exercising regularly and keeping a positive mental attitude? You sure as the dickens will never see any of those things on a death certificate.

What else are you being offered? Remember, the experts "don't know" how to prevent breast cancer and only 5% of research money goes toward prevention. If you sit around and wait for some magic bullet to come along, you might find yourself under the knife. That **must** be avoided. To do that, you **must** think prevention, prevention, prevention. If someone offers you something to prevent breast cancer that makes more sense to you than what you have read here, then **do it!** By all means. But don't do **nothing!**

You wait for early detection like it is being suggested to you and you **have** the disease. I guarantee you, if you were to hear the words, "I'm sorry, you have cancer," you would try **anything** to avoid losing a breast and undergoing chemotherapy. **DON'T WAIT!** The time is now and prevention is the key.

Devra Lee Davis is a specialist in public health policy and a scholar in residence at the National Research Council of the National Academy of Sciences, a prestigious position she has held since 1989. She has compiled one of the few systematic comparisons of current changes in deaths from cancer. With one out of three people a cancer victim in this country, we are all pained by the abysmal failure of the highly publicized and costly "war on cancer." Ms. Davis is fully aware of this situation as well, and when it comes to demanding change, she's **not** shy!

She rightly points out that the National Cancer Institute's 1982 goal of reducing cancer deaths by fifty percent by the end of the century looks ludicrous today. The mortality rate is actually **higher** than it was when the "war on cancer" began over twenty years ago. Referring to the need to investigate further life-style changes such as diet and exercise and environmental causes, she states that, "The United States is not putting enough money into research on cancer prevention!"[326] She offers a plausible reason why, too. "When you treat cancer, profits are made through drugs and surgery. But when cancer is prevented, nobody makes any money."[327]

As you might well imagine, her public position has not exactly endeared her to the "old boy" network of the cancer establishment. Fortunately, standing outside the "old boy" network are progressive and enlightened physicians like Dr. Edmund Sonnenblick, Chairman of Cardiology at the Albert Einstein College of Medicine in New York. In Dr. Sonnenblick's words: "The public wants drama, but prevention is more important. The major thrust has to be prevention."[328]

At the end of an article on Ms. Davis in the *New York Times*, she ponders where the constituency for prevention is. The article ends with, "Perhaps Davis knows better than anyone how hard building that constituency will be." It may be idealistic of me, or perhaps it's just positive thinking with a dash of wishful thinking thrown in, but in my opinion it's **you** who are that constituency. In taking this step to eliminate the **causes** of breast cancer by CAREing for your body, you thereby distance yourself from the disease establishment and those who "don't know." You become a vital part of the **real** "health care" system. That network of health conscious people who have taken charge of their lives and their health and are living the vibrant and vital life that our creator intended us to live.

On her nationally televised show, Oprah Winfrey made these comments on a show dedicated to the subject of breast cancer:

"I have always felt very passionately about women's health and the crisis behind breast cancer....a disease that is really needlessly killing millions of women....they're our mothers, our sisters, our daughters, they're dying from this every day, and we can't allow this to go on. We really can't anymore."

Armed with the information in this book, it can and **will** be stopped.

Congratulations, and may God bless your every breath and step.

PRODUCTS FROM
THE 21ST CENTURY

O ver the years, especially since the success of *FIT FOR LIFE*, I have been introduced to numerous products. On occasion, some are so intriguing, so innovative and so ahead of their time, that the immensity of their potential benefit simply cannot be ignored. It gives me a great deal of pleasure to be able to introduce two such products to you. They are: GREENS+® and **Prime 1**™

Now, due to my obvious enthusiasm for these products, perhaps your first impulse may be to think I have a vested interest in them or that I am in some way going to benefit financially from their sale. No such arrangement exists. I am in no way financially involved with these products. My one and only interest is an obligation I feel I have to let as many people as possible know that they are available.

The first is a relatively new product on the market that I learned about in late 1993 and have been using every day since. I am 100% convinced that it is the finest product of its kind available anywhere. I have met the people who manufacture and distribute the product and if there were more people like them in the world, it would be a much nicer place to live. You know, sometimes you read about people who set themselves up selling a product that is purported to be the best there is and the whole thing is a scam to make as much money as quickly as possible.

At the other end of the spectrum are those people who are impeccably honest and of the highest integrity, whose greatest desire is to do something of inestimable value for humankind. The people who have brought this product to the marketplace are the epitome of this type of person. Their commitment to excellence and the health of all people everywhere is truly inspiring. The product is called GREENS+® and the brainchild behind it is Mr. Sam Graci, a chemist and psychologist by profession and a joy of a person to know.

I am not a chemist, so rather than try to explain the product to you, Mr. Graci, who can do a far better job, has graciously agreed to describe it to you.

THE STORY OF GREENS+®

In the 1970's, I had the privilege of working with a group of Down's Syndrome teens. My main objective was to help them develop better social interaction skills and determine why they missed so much school due to the flu, constant colds and low energy. While working closely with Dr. Zoltan Rona, M.D., an orthomolecular physician in Toronto, we discovered that each of the teens had severe vitamin, mineral and enzyme deficiencies. Then I consulted with Dr. Abram Hoffer, a Ph.D./M.D., in Canada, who was just discovering that many of his patients experienced vitamin and mineral imbalances. Remember, this was in the 1970's. Clearly, we noticed that the standard American diet was based on overly cooked or processed foods. As a result, these foods were low in fiber, enzymes, vitamins, organic minerals and quality water, but high in fat.

Next, we adjusted these teenagers' diets to the "mono-diet" consisting of fresh, organically grown foods and eight to ten glasses of quality water a day. We included proper exercise and sufficient rest to their daily program. After six months, we documented the dramatic increase in their health, energy and outlook on life. At that time, we all realized that foods, every day foods, can either put us in a coffin and nail it shut or stimulate and sustain us with vibrant good health and well-being. The choice was clear.

242

I continued my research and was most fortunate to be tutored in various degrees by Dr. Erwin Stone (vitamin C pioneer), Dr. Linus Pauling, Dr. E. Shute (vitamin E pioneer) and many other humanitarian nutritional researchers. These physicians and Dr. Rona encouraged me to develop high quality vitamin and mineral formulas for professional use. This I did. In early 1988, I realized that vitamins and minerals, selectively taken from foods and put into capsules or tablets, were actually missing many of the other complex nutrients found in the original foods. Simply, it is better to eat the whole food, raw if possible and organically grown preferably, for superior good health. Later in 1988, I began researching the most nutritious, easily digested foods we have on earth. I stopped producing vitamins and minerals.

By 1992, my research was complete and the outcome was the development of a synergistic blend, nutrient rich, enzyme live, alkaline-forming whole food we call GREENS+.® It is a combination of **every nutrient required by the human body**. Four years of conscientious and intense research showed my research group how to properly combine twenty-eight organic foods derived from the ocean and those grown in naturally fertilized soils, in very select places around the world.

For example, we have chosen to use a blue-green algae called Spirulina, grown on the pristine Kona Coast of Hawaii (Spirulina is 65% biologically complete protein, nature's richest source of vitamin B-12, and the most easily absorbed form of iron for red blood cell development); organically grown wheat grass and beets grown on the chemical-free plains of Kansas (both rich in chlorophyll which helps to purify the liver, lungs and colon, and are a potent source of all necessary vitamins and minerals); acerola berries grown without herbicides in Brazil (these berries are the richest natural source of vitamin C and bioflavinoids, which enhance immunity and protect us from infection and cancer); echinacea grown without chemicals

243

and wildcrafted in western Canada (this herb, as a food, strengthens the immune system and helps detoxify and pull waste residues out of the lymph glands); organically, as well as hydroponically grown soy sprouts (these sprouts contain no allergy causing gluten and are nature's richest source of antioxidant enzymes that prevent cancer cell growth, caused by free radicals that form in all of us as a byproduct of oxygen. Antioxidants prevent the oxidation, or cell damage, caused by these oxygen-free radicals).

GREENS+® was designed and is today an alkaline whole food, concentrated as a powder that you simply mix with quality water, or fresh vegetables or fruit juice. It tastes remarkably good! It is ideal for a mono-diet or to support superior well-being in any diet. GREENS+® is economical, convenient and naturally good tasting without the added use of any sugars, salt, dairy products, animal products, fats, gluten, preservatives, MSG, yeast or eggs. It is a powder you mix with four to eight ounces of liquid and sip.

It is best to drink it on an empty stomach so it is thoroughly absorbed and digested. It will be emptied from your stomach in fifteen minutes, then you may consume other food. For optimum results, first drink a glass of room temperature water upon rising. Then drink your GREENS+® fifteen minutes later. Enjoy eating your breakfast, preferably consisting of fruit, throughout the morning. On days of extra stress and demands, take your GREENS+® a second time. This will give you added energy, mental acuity and a continued sense of well-being.

You cannot overuse GREENS+® as it is a food. Because I travel so frequently and have many demands placed upon myself, I use it three to four times a day with great results. Sip it rather than gulp it down and GREENS+® will begin to be digested and absorbed immediately while in your mouth. The live enzymes will help you digest and absorb it easily.

The USDA's new food pyramid recommends we consume at least five servings of fresh vegetables daily and two to four servings of fresh fruit. Sounds easy, right? But only 9% of the population consumes five servings of fresh vegetables daily. When one does consume five servings of fresh vegetables, the incidence of cancer is reduced by 50%.[289] In today's busy world, it is sometimes difficult to find the time and opportunity to prepare and eat all of the needed vegetables. GREENS+® is a convenient way to increase one's daily intake of organic vegetables. Each daily three teaspoon serving (a one day serving) is equal to six full servings of organic raw vegetables. You may be surprised to learn that children really enjoy taking GREENS+.® Children should take one teaspoon a day up to the age of six, two teaspoons up to the age of eight and three teaspoons daily through adulthood.

Our commitment to premium quality created two challenges. Where would I make the product—in a big urban area setting where almost all manufacturers are located? The solution became obvious. We chose to make it in the pristine Rocky Mountains. There we have a pure air and water environment. The second challenge I faced was how to make a lot of nutritious vegetables in their original form and reduce them to a blendable powder without altering the delicate enzymatically alive nutrients of each whole food.

We discovered a patented process which reduced vegetables to a fine powder without the application of heat, thereby maintaining their molecular makeup and retaining their living enzymes. It works perfectly. After gently washing and juicing these vegetables, they are spray dried with absolutely no heat to preserve each delicate nutrient. Spray drying is like putting your garden hose on an extremely fine mist. The small mist-sized particles dry immediately with no heat. To keep these foods alive and fresh inside the bottles, we nitrogen flush each one pushing out all the oxygen. We also put both an oxygen and moisture absorber in each bottle, and it is shipped in 100% recycled cardboard boxes.

What Will GREENS+® Do For You

1) Gently sweep your intestines clean with its 17.2% soluble and insoluble fibers.

2) Expel toxins and poisons from the body. As an alkaline food, it neutralizes acidity.

3) Set the right PH in your intestines.

4) Replenish "friendly bacteria" in your intestines so you can digest foods better without eating dairy products such as yogurt. There are 2.5 billion per serving.

5) Support the "immune," adrenal and lymphatic systems.

6) Assist with menopause and PMS.

7) Increase your mental acuity and support good brain functioning.

8) Support hair and nail growth and give the nutrients necessary for skin tone.

9) Allow you more extended energy throughout the day without any stimulants.

10) Give you eighteen various food pigments, i.e., orange, yellow, red, green, blue, etc., full of phytochemicals that are proven to prevent cancer at one or more stages of cancer growth.

Did you know that the National Cancer Institute has just initiated a five-year, six million dollar research program into the disease preventing (i.e., cancer) "secret ingredients" in vegetables? These "secret ingredients" in vegetables are phytochemicals. GREENS+® is a synergistic blend of such vegetables. It was especially designed to give us maximum health protection and assist in fighting cancer through these whole, live, nutrient rich foods. Let's look at a few examples of some of these vegetables and their ingredients, and hence the anticancer activity of GREENS+.®

*Glycytizin—found in licorice root, protects the digestive tract, and reinforces cellular and antioxidant protection.

*Catechin Polyphenols—found in Japanese green tea, a strong health defender. An anticancer component called EGCG reduced the number of lung tumors by 38% caused by nitrosamines and tobacco.

The potent antioxidants protect blood cholesterol from oxidative damage, thereby protecting artery walls. They act as anti-carcinogens in the stomach.

*Alpha and beta-carotene from spirulina, chlorella and barley juice normalize pre-cancerous cells.

*Fiber from apples and brown rice absorbs bile and cancer-causing substances.

*"Friendly" bacteria, dairy free and grown on brown rice, enhances immunity and decreases levels of carcinogens in the intestines.

*Triterpenoids from licorice root and genistein from soy slow down rapidly dividing cancer cells and block estrogen that usually attaches itself to cells in the breast. This helps prevent breast cancer.

*Vitamin E in brown rice inhibits tumor development and HDL from oxidizing.

*Polysaccharides and Glycosides in Echinacea are antiviral, antifungal and antitumor.

*Silymarin, from milk thistle, is a powerful liver detoxifier. Good liver function is crucial for a healthy defense system.

GREENS+® is a powerful food that is easily digested, readily absorbed and contributes every nutrient needed for superior good health. My one hope is that GREENS+® will encourage you to renew your commitment to supporting the healing power of your body, give you vigor and zest to live your life fully and allow you to contribute to the development of all humanity.

Wishing you abundant good health,

Sam Graci

What I can tell you about my experience with GREENS+® is that since I have been using it, my appetite is kept more in check, I don't need to eat as frequently or as much as I used to, I am more alert, I sleep more soundly, my energy level is high and constant and I feel great all the time. I personally like to have it with apple juice because the combination of the juice and greens is so delicious I can hardly believe it's legal. It is a perfect food to consume while mono-dieting or not. I have found that it makes mono-dieting very much more easy and effective. In fact, because it contains all the nutrients required by the body, you feel satisfied and do not crave food as much when mono-dieting. It is as though this product was **made** for mono-dieting. It helps make it such a breeze. For further information about GREENS+®, you can call 1-800-643-1210 (U.S.) or 1-800-258-0444 (Canada).

THE STORY OF PRIME 1™

Another 21st century product that I must share with you is a most remarkable herbal complex developed by Russian scientists to develop performance superiority for their cosmonauts, their military, and their Olympic athletes. **Prime 1™** is an amazing anti-stress product that consists of seven carefully selected "adaptogenic" herbs extracted from virgin Eastern Siberian forests, and formulated as a liquid elixir to be taken two tablespoonfuls daily. So you ask, "Okay, which herbs, what do they do, and who discovered them? What are 'adaptogens'? and what do they have to do with our health and preventing cancer?"

From Dr. Ben Tabachnik, Vice-President of Research and Development for PrimeQuest International, I obtained a pile of reports and abstracts and want to tell you about their amazing product. Dr. Tabachnik was head of track and field sports research for the Soviet National Research Institute of Sports in Moscow, 1977-1990. He has published more than 150 articles and books on enhancing sport performance, and is a world authority on athletic performance.

Let me first tell you about the man behind **Prime 1**™ and why his discoveries are so remarkable. Israel Itskovich Brekhman was born in Russia, the son of a tailor. After Soviet middle school, he won a coveted place at the USSR Naval Medical Academy in Leningrad specializing in pharmacology. He graduated as a medical doctor in 1945 and was assigned to the Far East of Russia called the Primorye—a region of age-old forests, jungles and mountains. Plants were in such abundance there and of such variety that Brekhman has called the Primorye "the greatest laboratory on earth"—reflecting his great interest in plant substances.

Being an M.D. as well as a research scientist, he developed a special interest in the relation of nutrition to health. In early writings he expressed that *"nutrition necessitates the closest and most permanent contact between man and nature; chemical elements in food are the threads that bind the human being and his environment together."*[329] Brekhman became part of top-secret Soviet efforts to develop substances that would provide superiority for Soviet cosmonauts, for the Soviet Military and for Soviet Olympic athletes. As a young scientist with the Russian Academy of Sciences in Vladavostok, his research was a key factor in the early success of the Soviet space program. His research focused on complex plant substances with special benefits to humans. Initial work in the late 1940's was with a traditional Chinese medicine, Panax Ginseng. Brekhman then made the breakthrough discovery which started to bring him fame among Soviet researchers. Brekhman discovered another root herb, Eleuterococcus senticosus which had human-energizing and bio-modulating qualities which were even more remarkable than those of the legendary Panax Ginseng.

Dietary formulas developed by Dr. Brekhman from these plant extracts were found to protect cosmonauts from the stresses of motion, vertigo, weightlessness and "g" forces. So dramatic were the results, that all cosmonauts were put on Dr. Brekhman's program, as well as were elite Russian Olympic athletes.

In the sports arena, Brekhman's work was an athlete's dream. Stamina and endurance were extended to new levels, and Soviet athletes began winning gold medals in unprecedented numbers.

Over the years, Brekhman's program achieved wonders for other Soviet elite. Military special-forces adopted it. It brought controlled energy, concentration and focus to master chess players and star ballet performers in the Bolshoi. Great Russian pianists and violinists used Brekhman's supplement, as did high-ranking government officials. In honor of his scientific achievements, Dr. Brekhman was presented the Order of Lenin in 1981, the Soviet's most prestigious award. Dr. Brekhman holds nearly 40 patents, including 21 international patents. He has published hundreds of scientific articles, monographs, and books.

The story now takes a couple of interesting twists. In the late 1980's, the Soviet Union was slowly unraveling. The Socialist Republics were collapsing economically and Soviet state secrets were starting to slip through KGB disarray. Dr. Ben Tabachnik had emigrated to the USA in early 1990 and written a book *Soviet Training and Recovery Methods,* which had caught the eye of a famous American entrepreneur family—the Feathers (of Eileen Feather Fitness Studio fame, The Cambridge Diet fame, etc.). They immediately recognized the importance of the Soviet program for athletes and of Brekhman's botanical discoveries.

The Feathers contacted Dr. Tabachnik and met several times for discussions. Subsequently, a meeting was arranged between the Feathers and Dr. Israel Brekhman. Dr. Brekhman invited the Feathers to Russia, showed them through Soviet space trainers and shared his botanical-nutritional discoveries with them.

Just a few years before, the Feathers had launched the first scientifically-formulated high-nutrition meal replacement (*The Cambridge Diet,* which had been developed at Cambridge University). The point here is that the Feathers were ideally positioned in the health-food, natural-products arena to fully appreciate the potential of Brekhman's work. The Feathers contracted with Brekhman to develop his formulations to a form that could benefit the health of all people who took it, and provide it at a price all could afford. They formed a company in 1992— **PrimeQuest International**, whose mission statement is *"To search the world and to share the discoveries in science and nature that can make the greatest contribution to the health and well-being of humankind."*

The final patented formulation created by Dr. Brekhman consists of seven Siberian herbs, the primary one being Eleutherococcus (Siberian Ginseng). This phenomenal herbal blend was subsequently found in clinical trials to have surprising synergistic qualities—so that the blend was significantly more effective than any of the single herbs taken alone. Thousands of published research papers have tested and retested the herbs in this amazing formulation. Having more than **500 million dollars** in Soviet-sponsored research behind it, this product has to be one of the most-researched, scientifically-sound nutritional supplements in the natural products marketplace.

And so, *what are the benefits of taking* **Prime 1**™ and how does it work? Let's start by quoting Dr. Brekhman himself on **Prime 1**™.

"It has always been my dream to create a special formula to prepare people for life to make them healthy, stable, happy and to protect them from stress. All my life I have worked toward this goal--and now, finally, I have achieved a breakthrough. It is a complicated preparation of natural plant materials which are the best and most effective ingredients I have studied in all my years of research...ingredients that work together in a combination that derives additional power from the mixture itself."

So what are these seven herbs and what do they do?

The herbs in **Prime 1**™ are Acantho Root (Eleutherococcus senticosus), Chinese Magnolia (Schizandra Chinensis), Maral Root (Raponticum carthamoides), Golden Root (Rhodiola Rosea), Manchurian Thorn Tree (Aralia mandshurica), Ural Licorice Root (Glycyrrhiza uralensis), and Cinnamon Rose (Rosa majalis). These herbs, in carefully worked out proportions, are blended in a patented natural plant base of bio-activating substances.

Herbs have been around for centuries and have been acclaimed "nature's wonders," but it was Israel Brekhman who, for the first time, did scientific studies to demonstrate that adaptogenic herbs could protect the human being from all types of unfavorable toxic influences. His criteria for any herb finding its way into formulations were that:

1) it must be totally safe and non-toxic, even with prolonged use,

2) it must provide resistance to a wide range of external and internal stresses, and

3) it must provide a restorative, normalizing action on metabolic processes of the body.[330]

Dr. Brekhman's legacy to the world and humankind is this product, **Prime 1™**. Years of testing this group of herbs on humans and animals revealed that they have general bio-modulating and bio-stimulating effects included in the term "adaptogens," as well as important specific health-protecting actions. The word "adaptogens" is new to most Americans, but means simply natural substances that help people *adapt* to a wide variety of stresses. Modern civilization has produced an unusually stressful environment to humans, with high demands on our physical and mental abilities.

Within a hundred years we have brought unique new stresses to the human species; physical, intellectual, emotional and spiritual stresses brought on by invention of the automobile, TV, airplanes, computers and by water pollution, air pollution, cigarettes, thousands of man-made drugs and chemicals added to our food, our drink, our skin and swallowed for any form of illness. The modern assault on the body and mind is horrific.

From morning until night we consume foods that have been "manufactured," de-vitaminized, denatured, and bleached (e.g. white flour, white sugar), then chemically "preserved," and all too-often toxic. Whether it is mercury-silver (both extremely toxic to living systems) fillings in our teeth, "preserved" sandwich meats or sausages in our lunch bags, or 6 hours daily of rapid-fire violence on television—the assault is real—and deadly to body, mind, and spirit. Alvin & Heidi Toffler describe it in *Future Shock*, and tens of thousands of bestselling books try to help us cope, adjust or tune out.

Yes, mind-and-body-destroying STRESS surrounds us, and in turn produces widespread physical and emotional breakdown in America. Psychologists agree that our most widespread emotion is not joy, but rather *depression*. Energy and excitement have been replaced by chronic fatigue, anxiety and insomnia.

Our most widespread physical state is not slender, athletic bodies, but rather *obesity* and obesity not just for the over-fifty sedentary types. Obesity is now widespread even among our school children.

Sociologists point out that the most common emotion among our school children isn't the excitement of learning, but rather fear of violence from their own classmates. While politicians and sociologists argue about what went wrong, we the living, remain victims.

But the paramount question for each of us concerned about health is whether WE can find a way to reduce, undo, ameliorate and buffer the damaging effects of this stress upon our beings. That's precisely what Adaptogens are all about. Israel Brekhman and his colleagues tested these plant extracts on large groups of people under physical and mental stress (truck drivers, Russian cosmonauts, computer encoders) and found dramatic improvements in performance (fewer errors, less illness, less accidents and calmer functioning).[330-331-333]

Thousands of research papers from laboratories around the world revealed that Eleutherococcus had a wide range of *body-strengthening, emotion-modulating, mind-clarifying and immune-enhancing properties*. Other studies show Eleutherococcus to have *antidepressant, cardio protective, CNS-stimulant, and antifatigue properties*. But most important to the prevention-of-cancer theme of this book, scientific studies with Eleutherococcus and with the other agents in **Prime 1**™ showed impressive evidence that these particular herbs act to protect animals from a variety of cancers. Studies were too numerous and too detailed to outline here.[332-334-335] But in breast cancer, uterine cervix cancer, leukemia, endocrine cancer, sarcoma, lung cancer and many others—regular use of these adaptogens markedly reduced initial cancer formation. Stressors—like toxins, pollutants, oxidants, chemicals in processed foods, radiation, depression, and fatigue—are now thought the cause of DNA mutations that produce cancer. Adaptogens are the missing nutrients from nature that protect us from such stressors.[333]

Of particular interest was the work of Dementyena and Ogrek[336] from the Thomsky Institute who studied the cancer prevention properties of Rhodiola rosea—one of the adaptogens in **Prime 1**™— in a high cancer risk strain of mice as regards breast cancer. The frequency of cancer was 3.3 times lower in the animals taking the adaptogen than in controls not given the adaptogen. Of similar interest, Gramichaa and coworkers reported that the combination of Eleutherococcus extract plus chemotherapy was more effective than chemotherapy alone, in long term treatment of women with breast cancer.[336]

Other studies with adaptogens have shown immune system enhancement with increases in T-helper lymphocytes and increased cytotoxic T-cell activity against cancer cells. Adaptogens have also demonstrated anti-mutagenic activity and DNA repair capabilities, both essential to preventing breast cancer.[330-332-334-335]

And remember, this substantial list of cancer-preventing, health-maintaining properties occurs **with no known toxic effects or side effects**—in stark contrast to the large roster of synthetic drugs developed by pharmaceutical manufacturers. It is important to know that PrimeQuest sells this all-natural plant product only as a food supplement and makes no claims that it can heal or treat any disease. But it has health-enhancing benefits that

Brekhman and dozens of other scientists have described in over **2,000 scientific studies**.

So in summary, **Prime 1**™ is an all-natural mixture of highly-tested plant adaptogens that enhance human resistance to a broad variety of physical, emotional, metabolic and environmental stresses. The natural plant extracts of **Prime 1**™ also contain trace minerals, coenzymes, metabolites, antioxidants and vitamins that give it a balance not likely in processed vitamin-mineral tablets.

Prime 1™ is certainly a 21st Century Elixir par excellence and represents the crowning accomplishment of one of the 20th Century's great scientists. In contrast to most 19th and 20th century scientists whose energies defined the nature and treatment of human disease, Israel Brekhman remains a visionary whose dream to enhance human health and to **prevent** disease—talks to a new generation.

His was a journey away from disease, toward a vigorous health that will **prevent** disease. Israel I. Brekhman is the "Father of Adaptogens" and the importance of his discoveries will grow as rapid change and increasing stress accelerate in this next century. His forty-five years of living among the primitive forests of Eastern Russia, gave him a reverence for the natural sanctity of life, and for the quiet abundance provided us from nature's riches.

Prime 1™ stands as a monument to his memory—a source of health for all. (Dr. Israel Brekhman died quietly at his home in Vlodivostok in July 1994.) For more information on **Prime 1**™ you can call 1-800-697-7463.

FOR YOUR INFORMATION

American Natural Hygiene Society
P.O. Box 30630
Tampa, FL 33630
813/855-6608

Life Science Institute, Inc.
2929 W. Anderson Lane
Austin, TX 78757
800/889-9989

National Institute of Fitness
202 N. Snow Canyon Road
Box #380938
Ivins, UT 84738
801/673-4905

GREENS+®
Orange Peel Enterprises, Inc.
2183 Ponce de Leon Circle
Vero Beach, FL 32960
800/643-1210 (U.S.) / 800/258-0444 (Canada)

PrimeQuest
2354 Garden Road
Monterey, CA 93940
800/697-7463

I would dearly love to hear of your experiences with the CARE principles. If you are so inclined to share them, please write to me.

Harvey Diamond
5221 Ocean Blvd.
Suite #271
Sarasota, FL 34242

Please share this book with your relatives and friends. And those wishing to have their own copies may obtain them by calling 1-(800) 231-1776.

BIBLIOGRAPHY

1. CNN Health Week, March 14, 1992.
2. "No Breasts, No Cancer," the Maury Povich Show, June 18, 1992.
3. "Preventive Mastectomy, Part I & Part II," Health talk, March 10 & 11, 1993.
4. "Siblings Opt for Preventive Mastectomies," All Things Considered (National Public Radio), Aug. 8, 1993.
5. Angier, Natalie, "Vexing Pursuit of Breast Cancer Gene," N.Y. Times, July 12, 1994.
6. "Surviving Breast Cancer," Health Works, CNN News, March 12, 1994.
7. Raloff, Janet, "EcoCancers," Science News, Vol. 144 #1, July 3, 1993.
8. "The Breast Care Test," PBS-TV, Oct. 18, 1993.
9. Ibid.
10. Quillin, Patrick, Dr., Beating Cancer With Nutrition, NTP Press, Tulsa, Ok., 1994.
11. Ellerbee, Linda, "The Other Epidemic—What Every Woman Needs to Know About Breast Cancer," ABC-TV, Sep. 14, 1993.
12. Stephen, Beverly, "Her Most Serious Medical Problem," Los Angeles Times, Dec. 5, 1982.
13. Ibid.
14. Op. cit. note #11.
15. Op. cit. note #11. "Fighting Cancer—Are We Doing Enough?" CNN-Newsmaker Sunday, July 7, 1991.
16. "Conflicting Advice in Breast Cancer," ABC-NIGHTLINE, March 19, 1993.
17. New England Journal of Medicine, Oct. 24, 1985.
18. "Funds Urged for Breast Cancer Study," The Associated Press (Sarasota Herald-Tribune), Oct. 28, 1993.
19. Op. cit. note #11.
20. "Breast Cancer - Speaking Out," PBS, Oct. 13, 1993.
21. Op. cit. note #8.
22. Kolata, Gina, "Weighing Spending On Breast Cancer Research," New York Times, Oct. 20, 1993.
23. Op. cit. note #16.
24. Op. cit. note #7.
25. Op. cit. note #16.

26. Op. cit. note #8.

27. Kolata, Gina, "Mammograms Before 50? A Hung Jury," New York Times, Nov. 24, 1993.

28. Op. cit. note #15 - CNN Newsmaker.

29. Kolata, Gina, "Avoiding Mammogram Guidelines," New York Times, Dec. 5, 1993.

29A. NBC Nightly News, Oct. 3, 1994.

29B. Ibid.

30. Op. cit. note #8.

31. "It Could Happen to You," ABC News— 20/20, Aug. 27, 1993.

32. Op. cit. note #5.

32A. Angier, Natalie, "Move Abroad Can Change Breast Cancer Risk," N.Y. Times, Aug. 2, 1995.

33. McDougall, John, M.D., McDougall's Medicine: A Challenging Second Opinion, New Century, Piscataway, N.J., 1985.

34. Angier, Natalie, "Chemists Learn Why Vegetables Are Good For You," New York Times, April 13, 1993.

34.1 Elizabeth Berg, Author of Talk Before Sleep, on the Oprah Winfrey Show, Aug. 1, 1994.

35. Op. cit. note #15, CNN Newsmaker.

36. "Breast Cancer Defenses Sought," The Associated Press (Sarasota Herald-Tribune), Dec. 15, 1993.

37. Op. cit. note #16.

38. Op. cit. note #8.

39. Op. cit. note #27.

40. Op. cit. note #29.

41. Op. cit. note #27.

42. Kolata, Gina, "Value of Mammograms Before 50 Debated Anew," New York Times, Dec. 16, 1992.

43. Ibid.

44. Ibid.

45. Ibid.

46. "Ten Facts About Breast Cancer That May Surprise You," The Breast Cancer Fund, San Francisco, Ca.

47. "Mammography: Investigation," ABC News Primetime Live, Feb. 27, 1992.

48. "Medical Malpractice Law," Good Morning America, Aug. 29, 1991.

49. "Woman Wins $2.7 Million for Mistaken Mastectomy," The Associated Press (Sarasota Herald-Tribune), April 20, 1994.

50. Op. cit. note #47.

51. Op. cit. note #33.

52. Ibid.

52A. "Mammogram Interpretations are Questioned in a Report," New York Times, Dec. 2, 1994.

53. Taylor, Paul, "Mammogram Study Sparks Controversy," The Toronto Globe and Mail, Nov. 14, 1992.

54. Op. cit. note #33.

55. McDougall, John, M.D., & McDougall, Mary, The McDougall Plan, New Century, Piscataway, N.J., 1983.

55A. Kolata, Gina, "New Ability to Find Earliest Cancers: A Mixed Blessing?" New York Times, Nov. 8, 1994.

55.1 The Oprah Winfrey Show, Aug. 1, 1994.

56. Op. cit. note #22.

57. Darnton, John, "Church of England Ordains 32 Women to Join Priesthood," New York Times, March 13, 1994.

58. Ibid.

59. Gonzalez, David, "Endorsing Growing Practice, Vatican Approves Altar Girls," New York Times, April 15, 1994.

60. Goldfarb, Herbert A., The No-Hysterectomy Option, John Wiley & Sons, Inc., New York, 1990.

61. O'Neill, Molly, "A Surgeon's War On Breast Cancer," New York Times, June 29, 1994.

62. West, Stanley, M.D., The Hysterectomy Hoax, Doubleday, New York, 1994.

63. Op. cit. note #60.

64. Ibid.

65. Op. cit. note #62.

66. Ibid.

67. Ibid.

68. Ibid.

69. Dolnick, Edward, "Super Women," In Health, July/Aug., 1991.

70. United States Department of Commerce, Bureau of Census, Statistical Abstract of the U.S., 1982-1983.

71. National Institute On Drug Abuse, Publ. #(ADM) 89-1636,1989.

72. Ibid.

73. Ibid.

74. United States Department of Agriculture Nutritionist, Dolly Castro, personal conversation, July, 1991.

75. Ibid.

76. Wall Street Journal, July 9, 1991.

77. Op. cit. note #74.

78. Ibid.

79. Op. cit. note #70.

80. Ibid, 1990.

81. Ibid.

82. Ibid.

83. Ibid.

84. Ibid.

85. Ibid.

86. Montagu, Ashley, The Natural Superiority of Women, MacMillan, New York, 1992.

87. Op. cit. note #62.

88. Op. cit. note #86.

89. Ibid.

90. Ibid.

91. Ibid.

92. Op. cit. note #70, 1990.

93. Op. cit. note #8.

93A. Brody, Jane, "Personal Health," New York Times, May 17, 1995.

94. Op. cit. note #16.

95. Op. cit. note #31.

96. Passwater, Richard A., Ph.D., Cancer Prevention and Nutritional Therapies, Keats, New Canaan, Ct., 1993.

97. American Cancer Society, Cancer Facts and Figures.

98 Ibid.

99. Ibid.

100. Bailor, John, et. al., "Cancer: Are We Losing the War?" New England Journal of Medicine, #314, May 8, 1986.

101. Op. cit. note #15 - CNN Newsmaker.

101A. "Cancer War Has Stalled," New York Times, Oct. 30, 1994.

102. Seely, Rod R., Ph.D., Stephens, Trent D., Ph.D., Tate,Philip, D.A., Anatomy & Physiology, Mosby, St. Louis, 1992.

103. "Breast Cancer - Speaking Out," PBS-TV, Oct. 13, 1993.

104. Walker, N.W., Dr., Become Younger, Norwalk Press, Phoenix,1979.

104.1 Guyton, A.C., M.D., Medical Physiology, W.B. Saunders, New York, 1962.

105. Op. cit. note #102.

106. Ibid.

107. "Tonsils Bargain," The London Observer, Feb. 21, 1988.

108. Op. cit. note #8.

109. Op. cit. note #102.

109.1 Janofsky, Michael, "Results of Biopsy Show Simpson to be Cancer-Free, Doctor Says," New York Times, Aug. 16, 1994.

110. "Workers Told of Risks In Handling Cancer Drugs," Los Angeles Times, Sep. 13, 1983.

111. Friend, Tim, "Lymphoma's Progression Was Swift," USA Today, May 20, 1994.

112. Altman, Lawrence K., "Doctors Told Mrs. Onassis There Was Nothing More They Could Do," New York Times, May 20, 1994.

113. Ibid.

114. Ibid.

115. Ibid.

116. Ibid.

117. Altman, Lawrence K., M.D., "Lymphomas Are On the Rise In U.S., and No One Knows Why," New York Times, May 24,1994.

118. The Surgeon General's "Report On Nutrition and Health," U.S. Department of Health and Human Services, 1988.

119. Welch, C., "Cinocoronary Arteriography in Young Men," Circulation, #42, 1970.

120. Page, I., "Prediction of Coronary Heart Disease Based On Clinical Suspicion, Age, Total Cholesterol and Triglycerides," Circulation, #42, 1970.

121. Zampogna, A., "Relationship Between Lipids and Occlusive Coronary Artery Disease," Archives of Internal Medicine, #140, 1980.

122. Cohn, P., "Serum Lipid Levels In Angiographically Defined Coronary Disease," Annals of Internal Medicine, #84, 1976.

123. Jenkins, P., "Severity of Coronary Atherosclerosis Related to Lipoprotein Concentration," British Medical Journal, #2, 1978.

124. Pocock, S., "Concentrations of High-Density Lipoprotein Cholesterol, Triglycerides and Total Cholesterol In Ischemic Heart Disease," British Medical Journal, #298, 1989.

125. Rosengren, A., "Impact of Cardiovascular Risk Factors On Coronary Heart Disease and Mortality Among Middle-Aged Diabetic Men, A General Population Study," BritishMedical Journal, #299, 1989.

126. Pekkanen, J., "Risk Factors and 25-year Risk Of Coronary Heart Disease: The Finnish Cohorts of the Seven Country Study," British Medical Journal, #299, 1989.

127. Benfante, R., "Is Elevated Serum Cholesterol Level A Risk Factor for Coronary Heart Disease In the Elderly?," Journal of the American Medical Association, #269, 1990.

128. Castelli, W., "Epidemiology of Coronary Heart Disease: The Framingham Study," American Journal of Medicine, #76, 1984.

129. Kannel, W., "Cholesterol In the Prediction of Atherosclerotic Disease: New Perspectives Basedon the Framingham Study," Annals of Internal Medicine, #90, 1979.

130. Stamler, J., "Is the Relationship Between Serum Cholesterol and Risk of Premature Death From Coronary Heart Disease Continuous and Graded?" Journal of the American Medical Association, #256, 1986.

131. Connor, W., "The Key Role of Nutritional Factors In the Prevention of Coronary Heart Disease," Preventive Medicine, #1, 1972.

132. Pritikin, N., The Pritikin Program For Diet and Exercise, Grosset & Dunlap, New York, 1979.

133. McDougall, J., McDougall's Medicine, A Challenging Second Opinion, New Century, New Jersey, 1985.

134. Ornish, D., Dr. Dean Ornish's Program For Reversing Heart Disease, Random House, New York, 1990.

135. Whitiker, J., Reversing Heart Disease, Warner, New York, 1985.

136. Connor, W., "Serum Lipids In Men Receiving High Cholesterol and Cholesterol-Free Diets," Journal of Clinical Investigation, #40, 1961.

137. Imai, H., "Angiotoxicity of Oxygenated Sterols and Possible Precursors," Science, #207, 1980.

138. Keys, A., "Lessons from Serum Cholesterol Studies In Japan, Hawaii and Los Angeles," Annals of Internal Medicine, #48, 1958.

139. Levy, R.I., "Declining Mortality In Coronary Heart Disease," Arteriosclerosis, #1, Sep./Oct., 1981.

140. Shekelle, R.B., "Diet, Serum Cholesterol and Death from Coronary Heart Disease," New England Journal of Medicine, #304, 1981.

141. Wissler, R.W., "Studies of Progression of Advanced Atherosclerosis In Experimental Animals and Man,"Annals of New York Academy of Science, #275, 1976.

142. Samuel, P., "Further Validation of the Plasma Isotope Ratio Method for Measurement of Cholesterol Absorption In Man," Journal of Lipid Research, #23, 1982.

143. Insull, W., "Cholesterol, Triglyceride and Phospholipid Content of Intima, Media and Atherosclerotic Fatty Streaks In Human Thoracic Aorta," Journal of Clinical Investigation, #45, 1966.

144. Katz, S., "Physical Chemistry of the Lipids of Human Atherosclerotic Lesions: Demonstration of A Lesion Intermediate Between Fatty Streaks and Advanced Plaques," Journal of Clinical Investigation, #58, 1976.

145. Proudfit, W., "Selective Cine Coronary Arteriography: Correlation With Clinical Findings In 1,000 Patients," Circulation, #33, 1966.

146. Blankenhorn, D.H., et. al., "Dietary Fat Influences Human Coronary Lesion Formation," Circulation, #78 (SuppII), 1988.

147. . Brown, E.G., et. al., "Arteriographic Assessment of Coronary Atherosclerosis. Review of Current Methods, Their Limitations, and Clinical Applications," Arteriosclerosis, #2, 1982.

148. Gould, K.L., et. al., "Improvement of Stenosis Geometry by Quantitative Coronary Arteriography After Adequate Cholesterol Lowering In Man," Circulation, #80, 1989.

149. Leaf, A., "Management of Hypercholesterolemia," New England Journal of Medicine, #321, 1989.

150. Shekelle, R.B., "Dietary Cholesterol and Ischemic Heart Disease," Lancet, #1(8648), 1989.

151. Sorenson, Marc, Mega-Health, Sorenson, Utah, 1993.

152. Whitiker, J., Reversing Health Risks, G.P. Putnam's & Sons, New York, 1988.

153. Glick, D., "New Age Meets Hippocrates," Newsweek, July 13, 1992.

154. "Second Opinions For Bypass Surgery," Health & Healing, Vol. 2, #1, Jan. 1992.

155. Op. cit. note #151.

156. Cragg, Juli, "No Fault Of Their Own," Sarasota Herald-Tribune, Dec. 5, 1993.

157. "Smokers Have A Higher Breast Cancer Death Risk," New York Times, May 25, 1994.

158. Willit, W.C., et. al., "Relation of Meat, Fat and Fiber Intake to the Risk of Colon Cancer In A Prospective Study Among Women," New England Journal of Medicine, #323, 1990.

Whittemore, A.S., et. al., "Diet, Physical Activity and Colorectal Cancer Among Chinese In North America and China," Journal of the National Cancer Institute, #82, 1990.

159. Kolata, G., "Animal Fat Is Tied To Colon Cancer," New York Times, Dec. 13, 1990.

160. Katsuoyanni, K., "Diet and Breast Cancer: A Case-Control Study In Greece," International Journal of Cancer, #38, 1986.

161. "Council Urges Major Changes For U.S. Diet," Los Angeles Times, March 2, 1989.

162. McMurray, M., "The Absorption of Cholesterol and the Sterol Balance In the Tarahumara Indians of Mexico Fed Cholesterol-Free and High Cholesterol Diets," American Journal of Clinical Nutrition, #41, 1985.

Wells, V., "Egg Yolk and Serum Cholesterol Levels: The Importance of Dietary Cholesterol Intake," British Medical Journal, #1, 1963.

163. Connor, W., "The Interrelated Effects of Dietary Cholesterol and Fat Upon Human Serum Lipid Levels," Journal of Clinical Investigation, #43, 1964.

164. Op. cit. note #33.

165. Ibid.

166. Lea, A., "Dietary Factors Associated With Death Rates from Certain Neoplasms In Man," Lancet, #2, 1966.

167. Caroll, K., "Experimental Evidence of Dietary Factors and Hormone-Dependent Cancers," Cancer Research, #35,1975.

168. Drasar, B., "Environmental Factors and Cancer of the Colon and Breast," British Journal of Cancer, #27, 1973.

169. Armstrong, B., "Environmental Factors and Cancer Incidence and Mortality in Different Countries With Special Reference to Dietary Practices," International Journal of Cancer, #15, 1975.

170. Knox, E., "Foods and Diseases," British Journal Coc. Preventive Medicine," #31, 1977.

171. Hiryama, T., "Epidemiology of Breast Cancer With Special Reference to the Role of Diet," Preventive Medicine, #7, 1978.

172. Gray, G., "Breast Cancer Incidence and Mortality Rates in Different Countries in Relation to Known Factors and Dietary Practices," British Journal of Cancer, #39, 1979.

173. Hems, G., "The Contributions of Diet and Childbearing to Breast Cancer, "British Journal of Cancer." #37, 1978.

174. Howe G., "A Cohort Study of Fat Intake and Risk of Breast Cancer," Journal of the National Cancer Institute, #83, 1991.

175. Henderson, M., "Cancer Incidence in Seattle Women's Health Trial Participants by Group and Time Since Randomization," Journal of the National Cancer Institute, #83, 1991.

176. Yu, S., "A Case-Controlled Study of Dietary and Non-Dietary Risk Factors for Breast Cancer in Shanghai," Cancer Research, #50, 1990.

177. Van't Veer, P., "Dietary Fat and the Risk of Breast Cancer," International Journal of Epidemiology, #19, 1990.

178. Willett, W., "The Search for the Causes of Breast and Colon Cancer," Nature, #338, 1989.

179. Berrino, F., "Mediterranean Diet and Cancer," European Journal of Clinical Nutrition, #43 (Supp. 2), 1989.

180. Howe, G., "Dietary Factors and Risk of Breast Cancer: Combined Analysis of 12 Case-Controlled Studies," Journal of the National Cancer Institute, #82, 1990.

181. Brisson, J., "Diet, Mammographic Features of Breast Tissue, and Breast Cancer Risk," American Journal of Epidemiology, #130, 1989.

182. Toniolo, P., "Calorie-Providing Nutrients and Risk of Breast Cancer," Journal of the National Cancer Institute, #81, 1989.

183. Op. cit. note #7.

184. Goldin, B., "The Relationship Between Estrogen Levels and Diets of Caucasian-American and Oriental-Immigrant Women," American Journal of Clinical Nutrition, #44, 1986.

185. Schultz, T., "Nutrient Intake and Hormonal Status of Premenopausal Vegetarian Seventh-day Adventist and Premenopausal Non-Vegetarians," Nutrition and Cancer, #4, 1983.

186. Bennet, F., "Diet and Sex-Hormone Concentrations: An Intervention Study for the Type of Fat Consumed," American Journal of Clinical Nutrition, #52, 1990.

187. Woods, M., "Low-Fat, High-Fiber Diet and Serum Estrone Sulfate in Premenopausal Women," American Journal of Clinical Nutrition, #49, 1989.

188. Rose, D., "Effect of a Low-Fat Diet on Hormone Levels in Women With Cystic Breast Disease," Journal of the National Cancer Institute, #78, 1987.

189. Rose, D., "Effect of a Low-Fat Diet on Hormone Levels in Women With Cystic Breast Disease, II. Serum Radioimmunoassayable Prolactin and Growth Hormone and Bioactive Lactogenic Hormones," Journal of the National Cancer Institute, #78, 1987.

190. Gorbach, S., "Estrogens, Breast Cancer and Intestinal Flora," Review of Infectious Diseases, #6 (Supp. 1), 1984.

191. Op. cit. note #7.

192. Frommer, D., "Changing Age of Menopause," British Medical Journal, #2, 1964.

193. Trichopoulos, D., "Menopause and Breast Cancer Risk," Journal of the National Cancer Institute, #48, 1972.

194. Armstrong, B., "Diet and Reproductive Hormones, A Study of Vegetarian and Non-Vegetarian Postmenopausal Women," Journal of the National Cancer Institute, #67, 1981.

195. Hill, P., "Environmental Factors of Breast and Prostatic Cancer," Cancer Research, #41, 1981.

196. "Breast Cancer—Complacency Is the Enemy of Cure," FDA Consumer, July/Aug., 1991.

197. Kagawa, Y., "Impact of Westernization On the Nutrition of the Japanese: Changes in Physique, Cancer, Longevity and Centenarians," Preventive Medicine, #7, 1978.

198. Op. cit. note #171.

199. Haenzel, W., "Studies of Japanese Migrants, I. Mortality From Cancer and Other Diseases Among Japanese in the U.S.," Journal of the National Cancer Institute, #40, 1968.

200. Kolonel, L., "Nutrient Intakes in Relation to Cancer Incidence in Hawaii," British Journal of Cancer, #44, 1981.

201. Buell, P., "Changing Incidence of Breast Cancer in Japanese-American Women," Journal of the National Cancer Institute, #51, 1973.

202. Wynder, E., "Strategies Toward the Primary Prevention of Cancer," Archives of Surgery, #125, 1990.

203. Powell, Bill, & Myers, Patrick S., "Death By Fried Chicken," Newsweek, Sep. 24, 1990.

204. "Fat Poses Dual Threat of Breast Cancer," Science News,Vol. 138, #19, Nov. 10, 1990.

205. Ibid.

206. Op. cit. note #34.

207. Ibid.

208. Recer, Paul, "Broccoli Extract Shown to Block Breast Cancer," The Associated Press, (Sarasota Herald-Tribune), April 12, 1994.

209. Block, Gladys, Ph.D., "Epidemiologic Evidence Regarding Vitamin C and Cancer," American Journal of Clinical Nutrition, #54, 1991.

209A. Carper, Jean, Food—Your Miracle Medicine, Harper-Collins, N.Y., 1993.

209B. Ibid.

210. Kritchevsky, David, Ph.D., "Nutrition and Breast Cancer," Cancer, #66(6), Sep. 15, 1990.

211. Howe, Geoffrey, R., Ph.D., et. al., "Dietary Factors and the Risk of Breast Cancer: Combined Analysis of 12 Case-Controlled Studies," Journal of the National Cancer Institute, #82, 1990.

212. McKeown, L.A., "Diet High in Fruits and Vegetables Linked to Lower Breast Cancer Risk," Medical Tribune, July 9, 1992.

212.1 "Strong Views on Origins of Cancer," New York Times, July 5, 1994.

212.2 Ibid.

212.3 Ibid.

212.4 "Low-fat Diet Slows A Cancer in Mice, Study Says," New York Times, October 4, 1995.

213. Power, Lawrence, M.D., "Lowering the Risk of Breast Cancer," Los Angeles Times, Dec. 4, 1984.

214. "Personal Health," New York Times, Feb. 16, 1994.

215. Op. cit. note #16.

216. Op. cit. note #15 - CNN Newsmaker.

217. Holland, Jimmie, M.D., "Cancer Do's–Cancer Don'ts," Health Confidential, Vol. 7, #12, Dec., 1993.

217.1 "New Risks For Meat Eaters," Science News, Vol. 146, #3, July 16, 1994.

218. Op. cit. note #16.

219. Dowling, Claudia G., "Fighting Back," LIFE, May, 1994.

220. Campbell, T. Colin, M.D., et. al., "Cornell-Oxford-China Project on Nutrition, Health and Environment, Diet Life-style and Mortality In China: A Study of the Characteristics of 65 Counties," Oxford University Press, The China People's Medical Publishing House, 1990.

221. "Huge Study of Diet Indicts Fat and Meat," New York Times, May 8, 1990.

222. Mead, Nathaniel, "The Champion Diet," East-West Journal, Vol. 20, #9, Sep., 1990.

223. Ibid.

224. Regan, Tom, "But For the Sake of Some Little Mouthful of Flesh," The Animals Agenda, Vol. 2, #1, Feb., 1989.

225. U.S. Dept. of Agriculture, Agricultural Statistics, 1988.

226. Hellmich, Nanci, "In Healthful Living, East Beats West," USA Today, June 6, 1990.

227. Sherman, H., "Calcium Requirements Of Maintenance In Man," Journal of Biological Chemistry, #44, 1920.

228. Breslau, N., "Relationships of Animal Protein-Rich Diet to Kidney Stone Formation and Calcium Metabolism," Journal of Clinical Endocrinology and Metabolism, #66, 1988.

229. Zemel, M., "Calcium Utilization: Effect of Varying Leveland Source of Dietary Protein," American Journal of Clinical Nutrition, #48, 1988.

230. Lewinnek, G.E., "The Significance and a Comparative Analysis of the Epidemiology of Hip Fractures," Clinical Orthopedics and Related Research, Vol. 152, Oct., 1980.

231. Solomon, L., "Osteoporosis and Fracture of the Femoral Neck in the South African Bantu," Journal of Bone and Joint Surgery, Vol. 50B, Feb., 1968.

232. United Nations Food and Agriculture Organization. FAO Production Yearbook, Vol. 37, 1984 and Food Balance Sheets, 1979-1981 Average.

233. Walker, A., "The Human Requirement of Calcium: Should Low Intakes Be Supplemented?," American Journal of Clinical Nutrition, Vol. 25, May, 1972.

234. Walker, A., "Osteoporosis and Calcium Deficiency," American Journal of Clinical Nutrition, Vol.16, March, 1965.

235. "Consensus Conference: Osteoporosis," Journal of the American Medical Association, #252, 1984.

236. Op. cit. note #220 & 222.

237. Op. cit. note #220 & 221.

238. Abdulla, M., "Nutrient Intake and Health Status of Vegans.Chemical Analysis of Diets Using the Duplicate Portion Sampling Technique," American Journal of Clinical Nutrition, #34, 1981.

239. Ellis, F., "Veganism, Clinical Findings and Investigations," American Journal of ClinicalNutrition, #23, 1970.

240. Sanders, T., "Hematological Studies On Vegans," British Medical Journal, #40, 1978.

241. Anderson, B., "The Iron and Zinc Status of Long-Term Vegetarian Women," American Journal of Clinical Nutrition, #34, 1981.

242. Op. cit. note #151.

243. Op. cit. note #220 & 221.

244. Ibid.

245. Op. cit. note #220 & 222.

245A. Chalmers, Irena, The Great Food Almanac - A Feast of Facts From A to Z, Collins, San Francisco, 1994.

246. Op. cit. note #226.

247. Ibid.

248. Op. cit. note #222.

249. Op. cit. note #219.

250. "Position Paper of the American Dietetic Association: Vegetarian Diets— Technical Support Paper," Journal of the American Dietetic Association, Vol. 88, #3, March, 1988.

251. As cited in Vegetarian Times, Feb., 1991.

252. Op. cit. note #102.

253. Blair, S.N., et. al., "Physical Fitness and All Cause Mortality. A Prospective Study of Healthy Men and Women," Journal of the American Medical Association, Vol. 262, #17, Nov. 3, 1989.

254. Op. cit. note #102.

255. Op. cit. note #253.

256. Koplan, J.P., et. al., "Physical Activity, Physical Fitness, and Health: Time to Act," Journal of the American Medical Association, Vol. 262, #17, Nov. 3, 1989.

257. Conversation With Dan Kaser of National Sporting Goods Association, Nov. 12, 1991.

258. Rippe, J.M., Dr. James M. Rippe's Complete Book of Fitness Walking, Prentise Hall Press, New York, 1989.

259. Ibid.

260. Ibid.

261. Ibid.

262. "Progress Toward Achieving the 1990 National Objectives for Physical Fitness and Exercise," Centers for Disease Control, MMWR #38, 1989.

263. Leon, "Leisure-Time Physical Activity Levels and Risk of Coronary Heart Disease and Death," Journal of the American Medical Association, #258, 1987.

264. Ibid.

265. Wiley, C., "Walk This Way," Vegetarian Times, Jan., 1992.

266. Ibid.

267. Op. cit. note #256.

268. Gavin, J., The Exercise Habit, Human Kinetics Publ., Illinois, 1992, as quoted in Bottom Lines, Vol. 13, #14, July, 30, 1992.

268A. "Study Links Exercise to Drop in Breast Cancer," New York Times, Sep. 21, 1994.

268B. Bazell, Robert, NBC Network News, Sep. 20, 1994.

269. "A.M. Exercisers Stay With It," Aviation Medical Bulletin, Dec., 1990.

270. Op. cit. note #258.

271. Ibid.

272. Ibid.

273. Ibid.

274. Ibid.

275. Ibid.

276. Ibid.

277. Hottinger, B., "Walking Your Way To Fitness," VegetarianVoice, Vol. 18, #4.

278. Study Conducted at the Veteran's Affairs Medical Center, Salt Lake City, reported in Bottom Line, Vol. 12,#19, Oct. 15, 1991.

279. Study by David Nieman, Exercise Physiologist, reported in Bottom Line, Vol. 12, #21, Nov. 15, 1991.

280. The Wellness Encyclopedia, University of California Berkeley Wellness Letter, Houghton Miflin, Boston, 1991.

281. Op. cit. note #265.

282. Study headed by James R. White, Ph.D., Director of the Exercise Physiology and Human Performance Lab at the University of California, San Diego, reported in Bottom Line, Vol. 12, #12, Jun. 30, 1991.

283. Data from Betty Kamen, Ph.D., writing in "Let's Live," reported in Bottom Line, Vol. 13, #1, Jan. 15, 1992.

284. Op. cit. note #258, 265 & 277.

285. Op. cit. note #265.

286. Ibid.

287. Carter, Albert E., "The Miracles of Rebound Exercise," Nat'l. Inst. of Reboundology & Health, Edmonds, Wa., 1979.

288. Leahy, M., "Can This Man Help You Live To 140?" Los Angeles Magazine, April, 1983.

288A. Trichopoulou, Antonia, "Consumption of Olive Oil and Specific Food Groups In Relation to Breast Cancer Risk In Greece," Journal of the National Cancer Institute, #87(2), Jan. 18, 1995.

289. Op. cit. note #209.

290. Osborn, T., "Amino Acids in Nutrition and Growth," Journal of Biological Chemistry, #17, 1914.

291. Clinton, S., "The Vegetarian Perspective - An Examination of Nutrition Education and the American Diet," <u>Vegetarian Journal</u>, Vol. 9, #3, May/June, 1990.

292. Ibid.

293. Ibid.

294. Ibid.

295. "U.S.D.A. Cancels Nutrition Chart: Who's Being Served?" <u>New York Times</u>, May 8, 1991.

296. "U.S.D.A. Wilts Under Pressure, Kills New Food Group Pyramid," <u>Washington Post</u>, April 27, 1991.

297. Ibid.

298. Op. cit. note #295.

299. Nesmith, J., "Pyramid's Something to Chew On," <u>Cox News Service</u> (Sarasota Herald-Tribune), April 29, 1992.

299A. Op. cit. note #288A.

299B. "Fear of Fat," CBS-TV, 48-Hours, Oct. 9, 1994.

300. Cousins, N., <u>Anatomy of An Illness</u>, Norton, New York, 1979.

301. Talan, J., "Good Thoughts-Good Health," <u>Sarasota Herald-Tribune</u>, June 12, 1991.

302. Ibid.

303. Chopra, D., <u>Quantum Healing</u>, Bantam, New York, 1989.

304. Frank, J.O., <u>Persuasion and Healing: A Comparative Study of Psychotherapy</u>, Johns Hopkins University Press, Baltimore, 1973.

305. Op. cit. note #303.

306. Cushing, H., <u>The Life of Sir William Osler</u>, Oxford University Press, New York, 1940.

307. Shelton, Herbert M., <u>Natural Hygiene: Man's PristineWay of Life</u>, Dr. Shelton's Health School, Texas, 1968.

308. Benson, H., "The Placebo Effect," <u>Journal of the American Medical Association</u>, #232(12), June 23, 1975.

309. Booth, G., "Psychobiological Aspects of Spontaneous Regressions of Cancer," <u>Journal of the American Academy of Psychoanalysis</u>, #1(3), 1973.

310. Everson, T.C., et. al., <u>Spontaneous Regression of Cancer</u>, Philadelphia, 1966.

311. Simonton, O.C., <u>Getting Well Again</u>, Tarcher, New York, 1978.

312. Anderson, R.A., <u>Dr. Robert A. Anderson's Comprehensive Guide To Wellness Medicine</u>, Keats, Connecticut, 1987.

313. Vaux, K., "Religion and Health, <u>Preventive Medicine</u>, #5(4), Dec. 1976.

314. Seventh-day Adventist Mortality Study, 1958-1965, School of Health, Loma Linda University, California.

315. Oberleder, M., Avoid The Aging Trap, Acropolis, Washington, D.C., 1982.

316. Beecher, H.K., "Surgery As Placebo," Journal of the American Medical Association, #176(13), July 1, 1961.

317. Klopfer, B., "Psychological Variables In Human Cancer," Journal of Projective Techniques, #21(4), Dec., 1957.

318. Beecher, H.K., "The Powerful Placebo," Journal of the American Medical Association, #159(17), Dec. 29, 1955.

319. Wolf, S., "The Pharmacology of Placebos," Pharmacology Review, #11(4), Dec., 1959.

320. Pogge, R., "The Toxic Placebo: Side and Toxic Effects Reported During Administration of Placebo Medicine," Medical Times, #91, August, 1963.

321. Brown, S., "Side Reactions to Pyribenzamine Medication," Proc. Soc. Exp. Bio. Med., #67(3), March, 1948.

322. Goleman, Daniel, "Placebo Effect Is Shown To Be Twice As Powerful As Expected," New York Times, Aug. 17, 1993.

323. Ibid.

324. Chopra, D., Unconditional Life, Bantam, New York, 1991.

325. Op. cit. note #117.

326. Wright, K., "Going By the Numbers," The New York Times Magazine, Dec. 15, 1991.

327. Ibid.

328. Becnel, T., "Looking To The Future," Sarasota Herald-Tribune, Dec. 18, 1991.

329. Brekhman, I.I., Man and Biologically Active Substances. Oxford: Pergamon Press Ltd., 1980.

330. Brekhman, I.I., Eleutherocossuc. Leningrad: Nauka (Science), 1968.

331. Williams, Moira. "Eleutherococcus Senticosus: Bridging the Gap Between Alternative and Orthodox." J. Altern. and Compl. Med., April 1992.

332. Yaremenko, K.V., Adaptogens as Means of Prophylactic Medicine. Tomsll: Tomsk Univercsit et., 1990.

333. Fulder, Stephen, The Tao of Medicine. 1990, Healing Arts Press.

334. Wagner, H., Hiroshi Hikiko and Norman R. Farnsworth. Economic and Medicinal Plant Research. London: Academic Press, Volt, 1985.

335. Wikman, G., The use of Russian Root in Preventive Medicine in Industry. Gothenburg: Swedish Herbal Institute, 1981.

336. Quoted from: Yaremenko, K.V., Adaptogens as Means of Prophylactic Medicine, Tomsll: Tomsil Univeresit et, 1990. (In Russian)

273